WINNING WAYS

Dermot Reeve

with

Patrick Murphy

B🍃XTREE

To my Mum with thanks

First published in the UK in 1996 by Boxtree
an imprint of Macmillan Publishers Ltd
25 Eccleston Place, London SW1W 9NF and Basingstoke
Associated companies throughout the world

ISBN: 0 7522 0229 4

10 9 8 7 6 5 4 3 2 1

Typeset by SX Composing DTP, Rayleigh, Essex.
Printed and bound in Great Britain by The Bath Press, Bath.

A CIP catalogue entry for this book is available
from the British Library

Contents

1

The Lara Factor

'Brian, don't!'
 'F*** off! Go on f*** off!'
 'Brian, don't tell me to f*** off.'
 'I'm telling you to f*** off – now f*** off!'
 And with that, the world's greatest batsman turned away from his captain, and in front of his team-mates, repeated his terse message twice more. The rest of the side melted away in embarrassment, leaving the captain to deal with a superstar out of control. I was that captain, the incident was at Northampton in late June 1994, the year of Brian Lara's supreme batting for the West Indies and my county, Warwickshire. It was also a summer when Lara's cavalier attitude to playing county cricket put me under severe pressure and made me think seriously about giving up the captaincy at a time when we were in the process of making championship history, with the prospect of a clean sweep of four domestic trophies.

That flashpoint out in the middle at Northampton was the worst example of player indiscipline I have experienced in my career. I had never heard a team-mate speak like that to another, never mind a captain being on the receiving end. It led to the worst week of my cricketing life, as Warwickshire handled Brian Lara with kid gloves and made me realise I lacked support at the club. In the end, I had to swallow my pride, think about my own future and bite the bullet while the club kept a superstar happy. It cast a shadow over the rest of that historic season for me, and I was close to drifting out of the game because of Lara.

Brian's antics in midsummer were a far cry from the atmosphere of sweetness and light in April 1994, when he arrived at Edgbaston, off the back of his 375 against England in the Antigua Test a couple of weeks earlier. Even though he was now the world's highest scorer in Test history, he said all the right, modest things and seemed to have an ideal temperament for the inevitable trappings of mega-stardom that were bound to come his way. Brian had acquired an agent – Jonathan Barnett, who handled the business affairs of Waqar Younis and Wasim Akram – and there seemed no reason why the association with Warwickshire shouldn't be of huge mutual benefit. At the club, we were clapping our hands with glee, having signed Brian just before he scored that amazing 375. The phones jangled off the hook at Edgbaston after that, membership went through the roof, the sponsors loved all the exposure and the players and myself were thrilled to have such a player in our dressing-room. We were sorry to have lost our old mate, Allan Donald, to the South African side that was touring England, and I was intrigued to see how the side would fare with a world-class batsman replacing a top bowler.

I didn't realise what a phenomenal player Brian was until I saw him from the other end and, despite our serious differences, he remains the best batsman I have ever seen. The man is a genius, a truly great player. I have never seen someone able to find the gaps like Brian: he waits for the ball that little bit later than anyone, and just keeps piercing the field. Brian has so much control of the blade, despite the speed of his downswing from such a high backlift. It was a privilege to watch him bat and none of us in the Warwickshire dressing-room could believe his talent until we saw it in the flesh. Brian started off the season with a string of glorious hundreds, including the best innings I have ever seen in county cricket. In the second innings against Leicestershire at Edgbaston, we faced defeat on a fast wicket, with cracks developing all over the place. The odd ball was keeping low, others were taking off. Every other batsman was either getting rapped on the knuckles or jabbing down late on a shooter, but at the other end, Brian made it look a doddle. He adjusted so late that the shooters would be kept out easily and, if the ball took off, he'd either play it over the slips' heads or leave it alone. The bad delivery would just be dismissed to the boundary with no fuss. Brian farmed the bowling and got us what proved to be a valuable draw. At the end of that season, Leicestershire finished second to us in the championship and who knows how it all might have ended if they'd beaten us that day in May? We ended up 206/7, with Lara 120 not out, with the next top score just twenty. Brian just seemed from another planet as a batsman and we couldn't believe our good luck.

A few weeks later, he made history again, scoring 501 not out against Durham at Edgbaston. It was the highest first-class score in history, beating Hanif Mohammad's 499, and we just sat in awe. It was an amazing feat physically, because he had to concentrate for such a long time. At lunchtime on the final day, he was 285 not out, capitalising on a very flat pitch, a Durham side lacking David Graveney's spin bowling because of injury and the game going nowhere. I was disappointed that I hadn't been able to do a deal with Durham, so that they could set us a fourth innings target. We had lost the third day because of rain, and Durham decided just to play for bonus points. So when Lara said to me that lunchtime, 'You're not going to declare are you?' I was curious to know why. He told me about the record of 499, that he fancied it and I thought, 'This guy's a confident character – he's still got to get another 200-odd before the close.' Well he did, and despite so much being weighted in his favour, it was a phenomenal performance. We just watched open-mouthed as he kept hitting boundaries. I was even more impressed by his innings the next day in a Benson and Hedges Cup semi-final. I can only imagine the sense of anti-climax and release of adrenalin Brian felt as he came off the field that evening at Edgbaston with the world record in his pocket – and then he had to go through all the media razzamatazz for an hour.

After all that, he had to drive down to London to check into a hotel for the big game next day against Surrey at the Oval. The way he raised his game to score seventy in a tight finish was remarkable. Brian had to come in at number six, down the order, because he had felt dizzy in the field after his exploits, and had to go off and lie down. That was understandable, but by the time he came in, the match was in the balance. Somehow he found the reserves of energy and concentration and brought us to victory. It was his best one-day innings that season for us and I was hugely impressed.

So, after six weeks of the '94 season, everything seemed perfect for Warwickshire. We were into a Lord's final, we had the world record holder at Test and first-class level batting like a dream for us, and the crowds were flocking in. Our profile with the media was getting higher and higher and Brian was impressing outsiders as a mature, level-headed guy who had settled very quickly into our dressing-room and was proving a supportive team-mate to players who rightly revered him. The reality is that, even then, I was looking for the Elastoplast to hold things together. It was all too easy for Brian, and early on I realised that he didn't have a great deal of respect for county cricket. He started to look for ways to get out of fielding and made it clear he really only wanted to bat. That 501 not out seemed to convince him that the standard of county bowling was far inferior to that in the Caribbean, and soon he was in need of motivation when he turned up at the ground to play. With the inevitable commercial deals raining down on him, he soon lost his edge.

Brian might have kept up his commitment longer if he'd been captained by someone other than me. Right from the start, the chemistry wasn't right between us. From day one, we never had a beer together and he went out of his way to avoid me socially. Early on, I invited him round to my flat to share a bottle of champagne, to get to know each other, but he declined. I could live with that – a captain doesn't need to be liked, just respected – but it soon got back to me that he was making sniping comments about me on the field. Because of this daft rule about bowling a minimum of 18½ overs an hour in county cricket, the over rate is always a worry to captains, and the rest of the side would understand when I chivvied them along to move around quickly in the field. But Brian would saunter from slip to square leg when I moved him and I'd clap my hands and shout, 'Come on Brian – over rate!' He didn't like that, confiding to some of the lads that not even the West Indies captain, Richie Richardson, talked to him like that. He also questioned my tactics on the field to some of the other guys and inevitably it got back to me. So I thought I'd have a quiet word early on with our new chief executive, Dennis Amiss. His response was disappointing: 'Keep him sweet, Dermot, he's special, he's the best player in the world.' Fateful words that would eventually ruin my relationship with Lara and affect my captaincy and standing in the club. I turned to our coach, Bob Woolmer, a supportive friend. Yet Bob was in awe of Brian's remarkable talent, and his advice was equally disturbing: 'Handle him with kid gloves. It's only for this season. He's different.' To me that was just storing up trouble after just a few weeks of a season that was scheduled to run for four and a half months. I was proved right in the long run, and at a cost to my self-esteem.

We had our first spat in the third championship match down at Taunton and it stemmed from a harmless bit of fun that you experience in every county dressing-room. I'd been in the England squad for a one-day international so I turned up to watch the closing stages of our match against Somerset. It had been agreed that Warwickshire would feed some runs to Somerset for a few overs, then we'd embark on a run chase. That morning, Brian had just received a new mobile phone – appropriately the number was 375375 – and he took it onto the field with him to see if it would work. Now that's not exactly the done thing in English first-class cricket, but the atmosphere was going to be light-hearted for the first few overs as we gave them cheap runs. Just for a laugh I agreed with some of the other lads that I'd phone Brian as he went to his place at slip. Before a ball was bowled, as the batsmen were sorting themselves out, Brian answered his phone and heard me say, 'Brian, I think you're standing a bit close to Keith.' He looked up at the balcony, saw me and some of the other lads waving and promptly put the phone away. We had a chuckle and thought no more about it. A year later, I read in Brian's autobiography that I'd got him in trouble with the umpires for calling him on the mobile phone in the day's *second* over. That was nonsense: if he'd had a call then, it wasn't from me, I only called him before a ball was delivered. After the game (incidentally won by us with yet another wonderful hundred from Brian), the umpires told me to have a word with him, that you can't take calls during a first-class match. Brian was very sniffy with me about it and in his book he said I was having a joke at his expense. He didn't seem to realise that it was just a gentle bit of leg-pulling. After all, he kept saying that he was loving the dressing-room atmosphere, that he was just one of the boys – and a sense of humour has always been part of the Edgbaston atmosphere in my experience. I realised though that Brian would laugh at himself if the joke or quip was from others in the team, rather than me.

So, after a few weeks, there were various sub-plots swirling around Brian and me, with wounds already festering. Another one opened in the next championship match at Lord's against Middlesex. At one stage, on the final day, Keith Brown and Paul Weekes were blocking out for a draw and I decided to dangle the carrot, get Middlesex interested again in a run chase as I felt this would bring us a greater chance of victory. So I brought on Brian to bowl his leg-breaks. Now he's not the worst bowler and I thought he would either get a wicket or help boost the Middlesex run rate; either way, I wanted an attacking field and I had to put my foot down and insist. He was a little unlucky with a couple of deliveries, but he went for 31 in his two overs. I didn't mind that, because it perked up Middlesex and they went for the runs again. They finished 24 short with the last man, Angus Fraser, blocking the last three balls to deny us the match. Fair enough, a good effort from both sides and I would've been delighted if we had pulled it off. But Brian wasn't happy. As soon as he had finished his second over, he pointed to his knee, signalled to the umpire and walked off the field.In the dressing-room afterwards he had a go at me, saying he couldn't understand what I was playing at, putting him on without a run-saving field. I tried to explain to him that with 20 overs left I felt we needed to keep Middlesex interested in the target by feeding them some runs, but he wouldn't see it initially. After Brian left the dressing-room, Bob Woolmer told me that he also had tried to explain the tactics to him during those closing overs. Bob confided in me that Brian was unimpressed by my tactics but felt by the end of the game he could see what I was getting at. Bob said I wouldn't have been all that enamoured by Brian's remarks on entering the dressing-room, so it was clear to me then that he didn't value my captaincy all that highly.

By now, I was having to work at getting Brian on to the field on Sundays. He clearly didn't fancy the helter-skelter style of the Sunday League, he wasn't making runs in these games and he was trying hard to get a day off. 'I don't like Sunday cricket,' he would tell me, complaining about his sore knee. I would compromise by saying that I'd put him in certain positions that wouldn't tax his knee – yet when he really had to, Brian fielded like a gazelle and he still put in some tremendous sprints between the wickets when he was pushed. So I was taking all his protestations with a pinch of salt, trying to keep the lid on the whole situation for the good of the team, trying to ignore the fact that the star player didn't like or rate his captain. I called a meeting of our senior players to ask their advice. I was worried that team spirit might get eroded when they saw the amount of leeway Brian was getting, arriving late almost every morning when everyone else knew the time to be on parade. I told the players about Dennis Amiss' preference for the softly-softly approach and Gladstone Small said he'd have a word with Brian. We agreed the important thing was to get him on the field, and to make sure our own personal standards didn't drop. Obviously the cricket management couldn't come down on another player if he was late or unshaven – one of Amiss' new rules on becoming the boss. So when Paul Smith turned up half an hour late one morning and Bob Woolmer wanted to tackle him, I had to say, 'Let it go, Bob, you can't be hard on the others because Brian gets away with it. Let it go just for this year.'

But I was worried about this preferential treatment. The goalposts had moved from the previous season, and I wondered how much indiscipline might creep in as the club tried to accommodate Brian. When Brian asked to miss a Nat West Cup game, I was really put on the spot. We were at home to Bedfordshire, a minor county, as we defended our trophy – on paper a doddle but I hate games like these, where the county side is on a hiding to nothing. Brian informed me he didn't want to play because his girlfriend was arriving that day from Trinidad. 'Listen, it's only a minor county, you'll beat them,' he said. I wasn't happy at all about the situation, but tried to find a compromise – after all it was what Dennis Amiss would have expected me to do. Brian said he was picking her up at Heathrow at 9 in the morning, and that he'd be back at the ground by the start at 10.30. I didn't believe that would happen for a minute, especially as there was a train strike on at the time and more traffic on the roads as a result. I told him to get back as soon as possible. He arrived 90 minutes late. Luckily Roger Twose and Dominic Ostler put on a big stand for the first wicket and Brian could bat in his usual number three position, but it was a totally embarrassing situation for the team. By now, the press boys were beginning to ask questions about why Brian was spending so much time off the field and I was having to bend the truth, to keep the peace. Brian was beginning to chance his arm with me and once he said, 'I've got to go and make a phone call to Trinidad', and raced off the field. I couldn't believe it. No one else would've thought about making such a request. Brian was being paid handsomely to play county cricket, yet he clearly didn't have a great deal of respect for it. I just bit my tongue, and let him get away with it. The sponsors and members were happy, we were bang in the public eye and I felt my hands were tied. I was honestly confused.

And so to Northampton, and that astonishing outburst from Brian at me on the second day. The events are absolutely crystal clear in my mind; it was a nightmare caused by allowing a great player to have his own way, with his captain being undermined. Now I've never been a shrinking violet on the field. I give out as much as I get and, in fact, the more the adrenalin flows, the more I like it and the better I seem to play. But Brian's behaviour over a three-day period still leaves me bewildered. He had started off the match with a brilliant 197 and his duel with Curtley Ambrose was fascinating. Ambrose had never got him out in first-class cricket and it was fantastic to watch these two proud West Indians squaring up to each other. Brian seemed fully motivated and, despite a blow on the helmet from Ambrose, batted as only he can. So much for the first day.

When Warwickshire came out to field on the second day, Brian had already been complaining about a headache and he was clearly in a grumpy mood as we set out to make Northants follow on in baking heat and on a flat wicket. We got two early wickets from Tim Munton but after that we were having to work hard for more success. During Tim's second spell, I was standing beside Brian in the slips, and we had the following exchange:

LARA: 'Take Tim off, you bowl him too much.'

REEVE: 'He's only bowled three overs, and if Tim doesn't get to bowl at least eight overs in this spell, he'll be disappointed.'

LARA: 'Why?'

REEVE: 'He needs rhythm – the more he bowls the better he gets. He always wants to bowl, he's a captain's dream.'

LARA: 'He's a bad captain's dream.'

I spotted the warning signals from that conversation and I realised I had to get out of the slips to concentrate on the game. It wasn't the time to unload a few home truths in Brian's direction, much as I wanted to. Rob Bailey started to bat well for Northants as I fielded at mid-off, hoping Tim Munton would get us another valuable breakthrough. Bailey edged one off Munton and it was taken low down by our wicket-keeper, Keith Piper. From mid-off, it didn't look right to me, but the slips all appealed and Keith claimed the catch. Then the square leg umpire Allan Jones intervened and said firmly, 'I saw the ball bounce – not out.' That should have been the end of it and it was for the rest of us. Except Brian. 'You must have f***ing good eyesight, then,' he shouted at Jones from slip. The umpire's reply was instant: 'There was nothing wrong with my eyesight when I gave you not out first ball yesterday – you concentrate on your batting and I'll do the umpiring.' That didn't please Brian at all and he carried on chuntering at slip, regularly looking over at Allan Jones in a hostile manner. His whole body language was disrespectful and dismissive of Allan Jones and I thought I'd better try to calm him down. So I went into the slips again and we had another frank exchange of views.

REEVE: 'Brian, you've got to be careful about umpires in this country.'

LARA: 'Why? What can he do? All he can do is give me out. So what?'

A few overs later, Bailey edged Graeme Welch to Keith Piper

and he was clearly out. As Bailey walked away and we ran to our bowler, Lara shouted over to Allan Jones, 'Well that one carried by three feet.' Luckily Jonah didn't hear that, otherwise Brian would really have been for the high jump, but he was still bristling with anger as we gathered around celebrating Bailey's dismissal. I simply said, 'Brian – don't', and that led to the torrent of abuse and four-letter words at me, in front of the whole team. I was determined not to swear back at him – something I was very tempted to do – but I instantly realised what an important moment this was. I knew all the boys were listening, as they slowly parted, and that my leadership was on the line, and my credibility in their eyes. After Brian had told me to 'f*** off' seven times, I said firmly, 'Brian, you're turning into a prima donna.' Those were my exact words and said in a clear voice, but not loudly. Some of the guys would have heard it, and certainly Brian, but I knew that I just had to try to douse the situation, appear non-confrontational and hope the club's administrators would back me up when we had the inevitable inquiry.

That incident remains precisely fixed in my memory, despite attempts from other quarters to put a gloss on it. The *Independent* newspaper carried a damaging piece shortly afterwards from its cricket correspondent, Martin Johnson, in which he stated that I had loudly informed Lara that he was 'a f***ing prima donna'. I took great exception to this, because I had deliberately tried to defuse the situation. I met up with Martin Johnson a few months later in Australia, and asked him who his sources were for that false information. He waffled on, saying he couldn't remember if it was a freelance journalist or one of my players. It was a false allegation from a serious newspaper's cricket writer who seemed to spend more time churning out funny asides than writing a match report, but Johnson didn't seem interested in setting the record straight.

But Brian Lara's interpretation of the incident was of more concern to me. At the end of the over, in which he had abused me and the umpire, he pointed to his knee and shouted to Allan Jones, 'Sore knee', and walked off the field. Yet in his book, Brian says he went off because he was feeling dizzy, that the spat was just a minor incident. He said there was no intention to abuse the umpire or dispute the decision to his face, that it was the kind of incident which happens occasionally in cricket, and is forgotten by the time the next interval comes around. That was nonsense.

That night, I tried to keep calm about that flashpoint, telling myself that some good might come of it, that the club's executives would at last realise that the captain had to be supported against the player. I knew the other players were concerned and they were watching me for a lead. I made it quite clear that I wanted serious discussions on the matter, that I expected some form of disciplinary procedure. I was also well aware that the press were sniffing around – can't say I blamed them! I would've loved to mark their cards but I thought it better to keep quiet for a time. In any case, we had an important weekend ahead of us. We'd bowled out Northants cheaply and made them follow on, and there was also a Sunday League game ahead, as we tried to make it six wins out of six.

On the third day of the championship game, it took a monumental effort by our bowlers to take seven Northants wickets after making them follow on. It was a great team effort, one that really pleased me as captain. Brian Lara spent the whole of that day under the dressing-room table resting. At lunch and tea, he roused himself sufficiently to ask the score, only to be told by Roger Twose, 'Why don't you get up and have a look at the scoreboard?' We just had to shut it out of our minds and concentrate on winning the game, which we did on the fourth evening, with a great run chase, with three balls to spare.

Before that, I had another traumatic experience with Brian on the Sunday, one that really disillusioned me. He was late arriving at the ground, after driving down from Birmingham. Brian then announced he wasn't fit to play, that his knee was sore, and that he was still complaining of headaches. Our physiotherapist, Stuart Nottingham, told me there was not much wrong with his knee in his opinion, but Brian insisted he wasn't fit to play, and I didn't see the necessity to coax him after his performance over the last two days. So I went off and told the team that Brian wasn't playing, and then tried to get on with my own preparations for the match. But Bob Woolmer came up to me and said,

'Have another word with Brian about playing.' I replied, 'Bob, he's said he's not fit. Come with me and hear it from him.' We went into the dining area and heard Dennis Amiss saying, 'Do it for me, Brian – please play.' Dennis had said to me earlier, 'Brian's got to play, the TV cameras are here', as if that should make a difference. Clearly Dennis didn't want the press to be alerted to further problems with Brian, and finally he persuaded him to turn out. I was astonished. I had told the eleven the batting order – without Brian – but Dennis was insistent that we must accommodate Brian at the last moment. That left me with the problem of telling Trevor Penney he wasn't playing – 20 minutes before the start, when everyone was waiting for me to go out and toss the coin. I felt desperately sorry for Trevor Penney and furious at the way Brian had been pampered into playing. I then watched him field brilliantly despite his earlier protestations about his sore knee. For once, I was speechless.

That evening, we had a showdown meeting in the physio's room, attended by Dennis Amiss, Bob Woolmer, Tim Munton, Brian and myself. Dennis said, 'We have to keep all this quiet, don't let anyone talk to the press. The official line is that Brian's suffering from the after-effects of a blow to the head. We have to sweep this under the carpet.' There were no apologies and the meeting was over in five minutes.

A day or two later, I had another meeting with the senior players about Brian. The general feeling was that we had to grin and bear it, otherwise he might just disappear on a plane to Trinidad and not come back. One of the guys said he'd happily string him up on a hook in the dressing-room if there was any more nonsense from him, but we all hoped it wouldn't come to that. The senior players agreed that they would handle it if Brian stepped out of line again, but I wasn't optimistic that it would work. On the moral aspect, they were all on my side – you just can't do what Brian did at Northampton and expect to get away with it – but in practical terms, I knew there were one or two players who wouldn't have been too perturbed that I lacked official backing. I wasn't having a great season in the championship with either bat or ball, and if I faded out of the picture it would open up a spot for someone. So I still felt a little isolated, and even more so when Dennis Amiss told me that Brian was demanding an apology from me. I was told that I had called him 'a prima donna' and that he was upset at that, and I should phone him. I was dismayed. Even though Lara's recent behaviour had fully justified the accusation of prima donna behaviour, I had been careful to tell him that he was '*turning into* a prima donna', which is not quite the same thing.

I pointed out to Dennis that Brian had told me to 'f*** off' seven times before I mentioned the word 'prima donna.' He replied, 'Yes we realise that and Brian is sorry for what he said. I've spoken with Brian and if you phone him and apologize, I'm sure he'll do the same.'

'Apologise for what?' I said. 'What are the club going to do about Brian's behaviour?' I was insistent about this, I couldn't believe my ears.

Dennis answered, 'He's having such a good season, we mustn't upset him. He's a great player, Dermot – let him have his way this season.'

At this point I felt so angry that I wanted to deliver this ultimatum: 'Brian apologises or you find a new captain.'

It was an effort to stay composed. My mind was racing with the repercussions of such a statement. I came to the conclusion that I didn't trust the club to stand by what was right or wrong, and support me.

At that point, Brian Lara was bigger than Warwickshire County Cricket Club. I felt that if I refused, I might not be backed up by the cricket committee. With my form below par, Brian was undeniably more productive than me, and they could allow me to fade away, with Tim Munton taking over the captaincy. My place in the side wasn't my concern but hanging over my head was a major consideration in keeping my mouth shut – the benefit system. That's always been one of the ways in which a county keeps a player sweet, as you wait to be granted one, keeping your nose clean. I was due a benefit and I knew that if I refused to play ball over the Lara situation, I might miss out.

I hated doing it, but my pride had to take a back seat, so I picked up the phone and dialled Brian. He was very quiet and non-committal at the start, until I said, 'Brian, I don't like to insinuate that anyone's behaving like a prima donna or turning into one. I'm sorry the incident happened, we have to get a working relationship going for the sake of the team. It doesn't matter if we're not mates.' I had phrased those words deliberately after chewing it over: I was determined not to give him a total apology. He thought it over for a few seconds and said, 'You're right, I'm sorry the incident happened.' That seemed to be a truce, but then he suddenly added, 'But you never wanted me here in the first place.'

I was stunned. It dawned on me that Brian had heard about all the discussions about an overseas player to replace Allan Donald and that he had thought I'd stuck out against signing him. This gave me some insight into why he had no time for me. I tried to explain that the previous August it had been unanimously decided to go for an all-rounder because we were worried about our bowling strength. I told him that top of the list was Phil Simmons, a West Indian opener who could bowl lively medium pace, but he wanted a two-year contract. Our next choice was Manoj Prabhakar, who was an excellent one-day cricketer who could swing the ball. The unanimous decision of the cricket committee was to go for Prabhakar but when he damaged his ankle in the spring of '94, we had to look elsewhere.

I told Brian that I would have preferred an all-rounder because of the balance of the Warwickshire staff and a year ago I didn't realise what a great player he was. I told him enthusiastically and honestly that he was the best batsman that I had ever seen and how lucky we were to have ended up with him. I stated that we must endeavour to make a satisfactory working relationship for the sake of the other players and Brian agreed. End of phone call.

According to Lara's book, this was the worst fortnight of his life. I wonder how he would have felt in my position. I was isolated, out of form as a player, getting no support on a serious disciplinary matter, and having to swallow my pride because I needed a benefit. My daughter Emily was very much in my mind at the time. After my marriage broke up, Emily went back to

Western Australia with her mother, and if I was lucky, I'd get out there to see her for a couple of months a year. If I had a successful benefit, I might be able to fly her over, or just hop on a flight to Perth on a whim. In the end, my love for my daughter helped me overcome the lowering of my self-esteem.

Yet Brian could still surprise me. On the morning of the Benson and Hedges Final, ten days after our phone conversation, he asked for permission to talk to the boys before the start of play. The Lord's dressing-room was hushed as Brian apologised to the team and to the captain for his recent behaviour, that it hadn't been fair on them. He shook hands with everyone and as I stuck out my hand, he embraced me. I was very surprised and moved by that gesture and by what he had said. I looked up and saw Roger Twose wiping away a tear and it was certainly a great way to get the boys together as a unit before going out to beat Worcestershire. What a pity Brian chose to rewrite history in his book, preferring to say that newspaper articles had a lot to do with all the rumours that he had apologised, rather than hard fact. I quote from his book: 'I told the players that I considered myself part of the team, no different from anyone else, and assured them that I was still fully committed to playing with them.' That is pretty close but I'm afraid nowhere in that section does he mention that he in fact apologised to us for his behaviour. Well he did. Perhaps my vocabulary is more limited than Brian's, but I'm under the impression that the word 'sorry' means an apology.

Even after that Benson and Hedges Final, and his apology, Lara still didn't really seem motivated for us during the rest of that season. I felt county cricket was now too easy for him, and that he couldn't get inspired unless it was against a challenge such as Curtley Ambrose at Northampton and Devon Malcolm at Chesterfield, when he made two wonderful hundreds. The one-day game held little appeal for him, especially the Sunday League. A lot of my pre-match preparations on Sundays were spent trying to get him to play, even though we were going for the title and possibly the Grand Slam of all four trophies. I thought he was bluffing me about his sore knee and his fatigue, an impression confirmed when I saw him really motor in the field and whenever he'd disappear to play golf. Brian was bitten straight away by the golf bug when he joined us. After moaning during the day about his sore knee, and feeling tired, Brian would regularly be off out the dressing-room door like a shot to play golf. Towards the end of the season, I was openly asking our physio, 'Is golf good for his knee?' to be told, 'No – that's if the knee is a problem to him.' Try as he could, Stuart Nottingham couldn't find any serious damage to Lara's knee.

For the rest of that season, Brian and I kept a wary distance from each other. We had another flare-up early in August when we lost a Sunday League match in ridiculous fashion to Worcestershire. We only needed 183 in 38 overs and after Dominic Ostler and Neil Smith had put on 105 in just 14 overs for the first wicket, it ought to have been a stroll. But Brian got bogged down, struggling badly with his timing, for once. For some reason, he allowed Richard Illingworth to bowl maiden overs, not using his feet, nor milking him away for singles. In the space of five overs, Illingworth only conceded two runs. It was mystifying cricket from Lara, he just played straight and hit the field. It looked to me that he was having a net for the following Tuesday's Nat West semi-final against Kent at home, on the same wicket. The pressure built up, and I batted poorly when I came in at number seven. Both Brian and I got caught at mid-on and we lost by three runs.

It was a dreadful batting effort and in the dressing-room afterwards I had my first-ever general go at the side, saying we were too complacent after such a great start. I said, 'On that wicket, there's no way a spinner can bowl five overs and just go for two runs.' Lara obviously took that personally, snapping back at me, 'You cost us the game. I was playing well, you scored too slowly and you didn't get me on the strike enough. Can't a guy bowl maidens?' I said, 'No, not on that wicket'. Bob Woolmer asked for calm, telling Brian I wasn't having a go at him personally, but I was close to it. Perhaps I should have handled it differently, saying right away that I'd batted badly, but I was sick at the manner of the defeat and just wanted to talk it out. But Brian didn't appreciate such honest, open discussion, a feature of the Warwickshire dressing-room in recent years.

Even when we created history in September, winning the Sunday League down at Bristol, I got the impression that Brian didn't rate the achievement all that much. As we chased the treble, having won the championship and the Benson and Hedges Cup, Brian had been allowed to skip the championship match at Bristol and was given permission to drive down for the Sunday game. He arrived late and didn't take part in our pre-match practice. Afterwards, in the pumped-up atmosphere in our dressing-room, I looked over at Brian and thought, 'This doesn't mean much to you, mate. We've won three trophies in one season, but it doesn't look like it's been a great day for you, like it is for us.'

I breathed a sigh of relief when the season ended and it dawned on me that I might not have to captain Brian Lara again. With Allan Donald returning for the '95 season, it would be a pleasure to captain a model overseas player, a supreme professional, who takes great delight in Warwickshire victories and in the success of his team-mates.

Within six months of celebrating our triple trophy success, I was dismayed to discover that Brian Lara was due back at Edgbaston for the '96 season, in preference to Allan Donald. I didn't think a decision was needed for at least a year on who would be our overseas player for the '96 season, and Donald would certainly get my vote, despite South Africa's hectic international schedule. But in February '95 I had a phone call in Australia from Dennis Amiss, telling me that Lara was to return, ahead of Donald. I was shattered, especially when I heard that Brian had secured a three-year contract. I was very hurt that the club had not thought to tell me that discussions were imminent, or even ask my opinion. I asked Amiss if Allan Donald had been informed. 'Yes, he's in New Zealand with South Africa,' I was told. 'It's up to you and Bob Woolmer to motivate him now for this season.' So the captain does the motivation, but doesn't get consulted on such a serious cricketing matter. I was worried that Allan Donald might think I had something to do with all this, that I might now have a disillusioned overseas fast bowler on my hands, but I needn't have worried. When I saw Allan in South Africa on our pre-season tour, I told him I hadn't been consulted. He said, 'Skip, you don't have to worry – I'm going to get a hundred wickets and show them.' He was as good as his word and no one gave more to the cause of Warwickshire than Allan Donald, as we won two more trophies in 1995.

Throughout the summer of 1995, there were rumours that Brian Lara wouldn't be coming back the following year as our overseas player. As early as June, several umpires had told me he wasn't coming back, according to their particular grapevine – and that was the word from some West Indies players, as they toured England with Brian. He came to Edgbaston for a chat with club officials and for a private word with Allan Donald, and news seeped through that the club was thinking of alternating with Lara one year and Donald the next. I thought that was grossly unfair to Allan Donald, after all he had done for Warwickshire. He was a casualty of Brian's shilly-shallying as his agent pressed him to commit himself to Warwickshire while the player wanted prolonged rest from the self-induced treadmill of commercialism. In the end, Allan Donald took a lucrative package for '96 that involved league cricket in Lancashire and the post of fitness coach/bowling guru at Edgbaston, but I wish we could have acted more promptly to secure him as a player. He wanted it, the rest of the players wanted it and the South African Cricket Board would just have to realise that Allan preferred to play county cricket, instead of kicking his heels to avoid injuries and fatigue.

So Warwickshire fell between two stools for '96 and we lost both Donald and Lara. I was relieved when I heard that Brian was not returning because I would have resigned as captain. I never wanted to captain him again after the events of '94, even though he sent word back via the club's officials that he would have been perfectly happy to play under me. But what about my desire to captain him? I would still have been worried about his love for the game and passion for Warwickshire cricket, something that would never occur to me when considering Allan Donald. Brian Lara was very hard work for me as club captain and I didn't like the way it seemed as if he wasn't enjoying county cricket after his early dazzling performances. He'd sit in the dressing-room, moaning about fatigue, the demands on his time, the many autographs he had to sign – then if Dennis Amiss asked him to pop next door to do a press conference, he'd put on that angelic smile and tell the media how important it was for him to see his team do well. A genius isn't necessarily a great team man.

Life with Lara complicated my cricketing career at a time when I should have been enjoying the experience of holding up all those trophies to our supporters. It wasn't a scenario I'd envisaged 15 years earlier when I worked the scoreboard at Lord's on the MCC ground staff, just happy to get a game of cricket anywhere.

2

A Restless Lad

If I seem hyperactive now, you should have seen me as a kid. There never seemed enough hours in the day when I grew up in Hong Kong and used to spend all my time zipping around playing football or cricket in between classes, or after school, cramming in my homework whenever I could. One of the early attractions about cricket for me was that it lasted so long – football seemed to be over in a flash and I still had so much energy left. I was the youngest of four boys and one of my earliest memories is running around in the garden, shouting, 'Give it to me!' as my brothers played football, ignoring their little runt of a brother! Since then, I've always wanted to be in the game; it's much more fun being an all-rounder.

My parents were both teachers in Hong Kong, although born in England. Dad was headmaster of King George the Fifth School in Kowloon and Mum taught maths and physical education. We were a sports-mad family, with Mum the most competitive of the lot. She had trialled at netball for Lancashire and was an excellent all-round games player, and her attitude was that you played the game to win, within the rules. My father took the attitude that you played sport for fun – a surprising view from someone born in Yorkshire and an ex-Wimbledon footballer, but he was sincere about it. His favourite saying to me if I'd had a bad day on the sports field was 'Don't worry, it's good for the soul.' Mum would have none of that. She was furious at him one day when he gave me out lbw in a schools game. I blurted out to him that it was a pathetic decision and he agreed:

'I know you weren't out, but it would have looked bad if I'd let you off, because I'm your father.' Mum thought that was nonsense. Whenever we lost, you could see her struggling to cover up her disappointment.

Although my parents separated after 37 years of marriage, they remain totally supportive of all their four sons and my memories of our family life together in Hong Kong are very warm. Mum and Dad were always there for us, driving us around all over the island to play sport, always happy to go into the garden and play with a ball. Mum in particular has been amazingly supportive of my cricket career. Since I made my debut in first-class cricket for Sussex in 1983, she has missed barely ten days of my career in England – and then only because she had gone to see my eldest brother, Mark play cricket. When I made my England debut in New Zealand in 1992, she somehow managed to get out there at short notice. I knew where she was sitting in the stand when I went out to bat for England for the first time, and when I managed to get 50 in my first innings, I remember waving the bat in her direction, feeling very happy for her as well as myself. She even ended up as England's official scorer on the tour to India and Sri Lanka in 1993 when Clem Driver fell ill. I was delighted that she could then join us in the England team hotel, because I'd been a little worried that she'd been staying in a few dodgy places, keeping within her budget. Mum was in her element then, assisting players she had come to see as legends – excluding me of course!

No children could have asked for more from their parents than the Reeve boys, but the family atmosphere was a competitive one. We didn't have a television until I was 13, so we had to make our own entertainment and it was a struggle to get a word in edgeways around the table at night. Perhaps that's why I still talk so quickly, I'm expecting to be interrupted any second. As the youngest, I had to fight to get noticed by the others. Early on, I learned to play board games and cards and tried extra hard to beat my brothers. Mum tells me I could play chess at the age of three, and never gave anyone a moment's peace, always after a game. Because my brothers were that much older than me, I had to fight to get their attention when we played sport in the back garden, but by the time I was six Dad was whacking a ball at me, testing my reflexes and my catching ability.

All four brothers were sports-mad, but we've used that competitive streak to do pretty well in our chosen professions. Mark, the eldest, was a very good hockey player. He did officer training at Sandhurst and now he works in television advertising. Paul was deputy head boy at our school and just passed exams for fun – straight 'A's all the way. An excellent swimmer and rugby player, he became a doctor and practises in New Zealand. Phil, a good sprinter and footballer, studied at the London School of Economics, and works as a freelance photo-journalist for travel magazines when he's not playing in a rock band. We are still a very close family, there for each other at any time. I still see my father whenever I'm in Hong Kong, and we have a round of golf together. It's strange, though – he doesn't mind that much if I beat him. Not like the others in my family!

In Hong Kong, you get roped into all sports if you're co-ordinated and because space on the territory is very tight, you'd play wherever you could. Our cricket pitch was a mat laid down in the middle of a football field/athletics track, with holes in the outfield where the shot putt had landed. The boundaries either side were very short – about 40 yards – and that's where I learned to knock the ball square, one of the most productive areas of my batting when I became a professional in England. I was always hoicking it over square leg as a boy, style meant nothing to me – then and now! I made a point of watching how the best batsmen played and in Hong Kong they all seemed to have good eyes, with no desire to look all that elegant. So I'd also look to smash a ball on the off-stump over mid-wicket, a shot I continued to play, against the better judgment of some coaches when I came to England. At school in Hong Kong, we relied on the teacher's love of the game to find the time to coach us and I was very lucky with our master, David Clinton. David didn't bother too much with technique, but he was very encouraging, helping us to respect the game. He gave up a lot of his free time to help us, and I'll always be grateful to him for making me even more enthusiastic about cricket. The facilities were very rudimentary, so there was no detailed coaching. I found the need to watch and copy older and more successful batsmen. When bowling, I used to run up and try to bowl fast off-cutters, because that was the only way the ball would deviate off the matting. But no one showed me to hold the ball, or the technique needed to make it swing. It was a case of going out there to enjoy it.

At the age of 12, I made my debut in adult cricket for my school. We played Saturday and Sunday for seven months a year and that must have made me even more competitive, playing against men every game. My Mum would drive me all over the island, talking to me about how I should be playing, have a post-mortem on the way back if we'd lost or I'd failed – and I loved it. In club cricket over there, the convention was that you didn't bat and bowl, so I used to miss out on batting, which didn't please me. David Clinton batted me at number nine for a whole season, which didn't appeal to me too much, but after I'd nagged away at him, he put me in as opener the following year and I made some runs. I knew I wasn't a classical player but that didn't bother me – I just looked in the scorebook! I never looked at myself on a cricket video until I'd been at Sussex for a few years – which is just as well because it was then too late to change!

Apart from the support of my parents, the most significant part of my cricket development in Hong Kong came when a certain Geoffrey Boycott came to the territory. He visited our school to do some coaching as part of a deal with Cathay Pacific Airlines and we were in awe of the man. Hardly surprising when you consider his stature in world cricket at the time – and Geoffrey for one wouldn't disagree! At that time, I was only aware of Boycott the great batsman, rather than the quirky Yorkshireman with a fantastic knowledge of the game, who I've come to respect so much. It was an eye-opener when he first came to the school nets at Kowloon. For a start, he batted first – and stayed in the nets for an hour. His justification was typical Boycott: 'You can learn a lot from watching me.' He was right. We saw how high his left elbow was, how side-on he played, the way he respected every ball that was sent down to him. He hardly lofted a shot, he'd defend a straight ball that was doing nothing at all if it was on a good length, and if it was slightly over-pitched, he'd lean into a classical drive. He was so disciplined: if the ball was short, he'd lean back and crack it, but everything else would be played with a straight bat unless it was wide. He was just working on his technique, getting into a groove, and it was unbelievable for schoolboys to watch him at close quarters. I realised then just what a great player looks like. It was the first time I'd been anywhere near a serious, disciplined cricketer and I was dumbstruck with admiration.

After his prolonged masterclass in the nets, he gave us a few minutes of catching practice before making it clear he was done with us. As he was collecting his gear, he said, 'Right, who wants a pair of batting gloves then?' Quick as a flash, I shot up my hand and he said, 'Right, that'll be 90 dollars.' Now that was a lot of money, but I didn't care, nor did I know about Boycott's reputation as a Yorkshireman who was careful with his money. When Mum came to pick me up, I bubbled on about the nets and that Geoffrey Boycott of all people had offered to sell me his batting gloves: how could she refuse? I saw her misgivings, but she handed over a 100 dollar note to Boycott, who said, 'You won't want change, then?' Mum shot back: 'Yes, I do, thanks very much – I'm married to a Yorkshireman.' Geoffrey obviously realised he'd met his match, handed her the change and they got on well after that.

Years later, I had the great thrill of bowling at him in my first season in county cricket. It was at Headingley, and as we walked off the field at lunchtime, I saw him eyeing me. He eventually said, 'Where have I seen you before?' and I answered, 'You coached me in Hong Kong.' It quickly dawned on him and he said, 'Oh aye, the one with the moother. Well done, lad.' He wasn't so pleased later that day, though, when I got him lbw. He was convinced he wasn't out (he has been known to offer that view, hasn't he?) and he didn't speak to me for the rest of the match! I was on cloud nine, though, and Mum was chuffed when I told her the story.

Geoffrey Boycott paid another visit to our school in Hong Kong when I was about 16. He must have had a great deal with Cathay Pacific! This time, he made an even bigger impression on me. By now, I was really getting into cricket, loving its challenges, wondering how I could improve. Boycott showed me his way to improve in no uncertain terms. He took us for a coaching session and started by telling us to play the backward defensive shot. One boy was doing it with his arms and hands away from his body and Boycott walked up to him, jabbed him on the chest and shouted, 'The ball can hit you here – and it hurts.' The boy's eyes were watering from the painful jab, and so we were even more keen on having no gap between body and bat as he walked down the line. Later, one of my pals bowled me a bouncer and I ducked out of the way of it. I smiled, picked up the ball and threw it back. Boycott spotted me grinning as I said, 'You missed' to the bowler. He stopped the net and shouted, 'What are you doing?' My answer ('Batting, Mr Boycott') didn't amuse him and he said in front of everyone, 'You don't coom to my nets to smile and enjoy yourself, you coom here to work. You enjoy it afterwards if you win. You're here now to learn.' That wiped the smile off my face, and although Mum, who was watching, told me to take no notice of him – she is Lancastrian, after all – I could see what he meant. I could see his focus even then, when I knew nothing at all about what was needed to make the grade. He respected the game so much, he knew how technical it was, how difficult it could be. He told us, 'The most important stroke is the forward defensive. Learn to play it, otherwise you'll get out and it's not as enjoyable a game watching others bat. If you can play the forward defensive, you can survive in club cricket.' That advice has stayed with me and I still use it when I coach. It's vital to be able to play it in county cricket if you're trying to save the game and when you first come in to bat. When I first go in, I block it, to get myself attuned to the pace of the pitch. That applies even when we're in a run chase, because I need to get into rhythm and a groove before I can try to play shots. The forward defensive is the key to that for me.

I know Geoffrey Boycott gets up some people's noses in the game, but for me he has been very influential, from my schooldays and when I played for England. He was on television duty when we toured India in 1993 and I was very impressed by the analytical, precise way he talked about batting. He was very quick to praise, as well as point out defects, which will surprise those who think he is too negative and knocking. Boycott is brilliant at getting you in the right focus, at channelling your mind while at the same time getting you relaxed in your body, so that you play the shot properly. All those years previously, he had made me realise what was needed by a cricket-mad kid if he even aspired to play professional cricket. Boycott was determined to have a great net against a bunch of schoolkids, even though he was a world-class player. It was an amazing insight into the mental hardness and self-discipline top sportsmen have to acquire.

I didn't even think about such self-sacrifice for myself at that stage, all I wanted to do was play cricket every day. When I first went to England at the age of 14, I was thrilled to be able to spend a summer playing cricket. One of the many advantages of having parents who are teachers is that they get long holidays, so we would spend long periods of the English summer in the London area, where there was so much cricket available. I joined Mike Gatting's old club, Brondesbury in North London, so I was in my element -cricket all the year round. Up to five games a week, plus evening social games, and I was doing OK. The lads at the club called me 'Yank', because I didn't have an English accent. Must have been all that American stuff on Hong Kong television I'd been watching!

So the pattern was set for me over the next couple of years. I got to play so much cricket in Hong Kong and London that I couldn't help but improve, yet I was still raw, lacking in technical skill, relying on a good eye for batting and aggression when bowling. My parents knew this and when I came back to London at the age of 16, Mum arranged a couple of nets for me at Lord's. I was totally over-awed at the facilities and, after the poor surfaces back home. I couldn't believe the quality of outdoor and indoor nets at Lord's and I wanted to bat and bowl all day, every day. When I had my first indoor net – paid for by my parents – the coach kept telling me to play straight. But it was a perfect surface; the bounce was even and I kept clubbing the slow bowlers and the medium pacers over mid-wicket, like I did in Hong Kong. Eventually the coach, an Australian, came up to me and said, 'You've got the best eye of any young player I've seen.' He said I would have to tighten up my game when I got outside, on wickets that would see the ball jag around, but he encouraged me. That's what young players need above all; he realised you must play to your strengths, instead of applauding politely if you blocked a straight ball that should have disappeared.

Mum could see how much I looked forward to my sessions at Lord's and eventually she wangled regular nets for me, alongside the MCC Young Cricketers. They are deemed to be the elite of the young players in the country, spotted at an early age, earmarked by the various county clubs, some of them destined for international honours, most of them with a very good chance of at least playing first-class cricket. For a raw teenager from Hong Kong with no obvious technical ability, it was a thrill just to be in the same net as them, drinking in the wisdom of the head coach, Don Wilson, a great character who had played for Yorkshire and England. I arrived three months later than the others, but I got on very well with them. They called me 'Hong Kong Phooee', and we had a lot of fun. That year's intake included Norman Cowans, Mark Feltham, Asif Din, Paul Smith and Neil Williams. I knew I wasn't in their class, but I made up for that with enthusiasm. Mum would drive me as far as Kent for the games and, whenever there was nothing on at Lord's, she'd somehow organise a net or a match for me somewhere. She was fantastically supportive, she knew how happy I was playing cricket all the time. What I didn't know at the time was that she was trying to get me taken on as an MCC Young Cricketer for the following year. I didn't think I was any good as a player, especially when I watched the other lads at close quarters, but I was delighted to stay on in September 1980 for an extra month, playing for the Cross Arrows at Lord's. I'd made my way up from the fourth team to the firsts at Brondesbury and that helped my confidence. I'd also won the fielding prize for the club that year, probably because of my enthusiasm but also because I had a strong throwing arm in those days. Times have certainly changed . . .

I went back to Hong Kong with a faint hope that I might be taken on at Lord's next year, but well aware that a lad from Hong Kong with little technical ability couldn't really compare himself with guys of his own age who had looked so impressive in the same side and in the nets. I wasn't surprised when Don Wilson rang to say that I hadn't made the final selection, but I was next in line. Don told my parents that my enthusiasm and spirit were the reasons why I had got so close and that he was impressed by my keen attitude, so I suppose that was some consolation as I settled down to my 'A' Levels and club cricket in Hong Kong. Then, out of the blue, he rang the following March. Chris Lethbridge had been taken on by Warwickshire and there was a vacancy. My parents, even though they were teachers, didn't advise me about getting my 'A' Levels, because they knew that such an opportunity for a boy living in Hong Kong wouldn't come around again. After a frenzy of packing and last-minute organising, I arrived at Lord's at the start of a momentous season for English cricket – 1981, the year of Botham's Ashes. Ian Botham had been a member of the ground staff just eight years earlier and his achievements were a godsend to head coach Don Wilson as he tried various ways to inspire us. 'Just look at what Botham's done,' he'd tell us. 'That could be you.' That was stretching it a little, but typical of Don's positive thinking. Ian Botham was already a hero to me because of the way he approached the game. I'd only read one cricket book – 'by Tony Greig' – but I knew how I wanted to play the game, despite my respect for Geoffrey Boycott's disciplined professionalism.

Don Wilson was absolutely brilliant with us at Lord's. He was so enthusiastic, so knowledgeable and very funny. Every Friday night, after getting paid (£32 a week), we'd all go to the bar in the Indoor School and Don would hold court after buying us all a drink. One lad made the mistake of ordering a soft drink, which led Don to question his sexual orientation. 'Eee lad, there's a couple of other things that are as important as cricket – and one of them's having a drink! You'll have a pint!' Don liked us all to muck around together off the field as well, and he was brilliant at fostering team spirit, an aspect of the game that to me is very important and is one of the reasons for Warwickshire's success.

The MCC Young Cricketers had a huge fixture list, which was ideal for us – so much better than working the scoreboard or selling programmes during the big matches at Lord's. Although I was pleased to be selling scorecards one day at Lord's during a Test Match, because I got to speak to Mick Jagger. That's putting it a little strongly, I suppose. He said, 'Thanks' when I handed him the scorecard and grinned when I said, 'See ya, Mick!' as he walked away. I pushed my luck and asked him to sign a scorecard, and he happily obliged. What a life! Playing cricket every day, getting paid for it – and meeting Mick Jagger . . .

I struggled to make an impression in my first year. I found the bowlers far faster than anything I'd been used to – I soon bought a helmet! At last someone told me about where to place the wrist when you bowl, how to impart swing, when to bowl the bouncer; for someone from the cricketing backwoods of Hong Kong, it was a very, very steep learning curve when you consider the quality of the other young players on the staff. There were the Australians Tim Zoehrer, Wayne Phillips and Mark O'Neill, the great New Zealand batsman Martin Crowe and home-grown players like Phillip DeFreitas. Every day I'd be first in the nets to choose a good ball from the box, so that it would swing. I'd rub away at it to get a good shine, make sure I held up the seam properly, and keep trying to master the outswinger. None of that seemed to matter though when Martin Crowe batted against me; he was just on a different level, with awesome ability. I'd look at the gulf between those guys and me and never dream about playing county cricket, unlike all the rest of the ground staff. I'd look out over the hallowed turf at Lord's and daydream about playing just once on that immaculately kept surface. Just once – I didn't believe I could justify anything more than that. A first-class career was out of the question, but perhaps I could nip in for a friendly game in late September?

The height of my ambition in that summer of 1981 was just to be retained for another year. I savoured every moment of it,

I didn't find the atmosphere at all stuffy, not even when we had to bowl at the members. Don Wilson used to say, 'Right lads, you're finished for the day, but does anyone want to stay on to bowl at the members?' I was there like a shot, because I loved it all so much and it was bound to help my bowling. I even got tipped a quid now and then . . .

While I struggled to master the intricacies of swing bowling, I learned an awful lot about the mechanics of batting by watching players like Martin Crowe. I noticed how low he stayed while playing the cover drive, how he would bat for rhythm, getting accustomed to the pitch and the bowling before opening out. Even though I batted very low in the order that first year, I was taking it all in, telling myself that I'd put everything into practice if I ever got the chance for a long innings.

When I went back to Hong Kong after that first summer at Lord's, I broke some domestic records and a lot started falling into place for me. So much that I had picked up in England seemed to have been absorbed subconsciously and for the first time I felt I wasn't a bad player. I was then picked to play for Hong Kong against Singapore, one of the rare matches to be played on a grass wicket. I managed to take six wickets with the new ball, mainly due to my newly-discovered outswinger. I was then selected for Hong Kong in the ICC Trophy competition that saw us playing for a few weeks in the Midlands in 1982, and I loved that. For me, it was just a case of doing my best for whatever team I was in, enjoying the day and getting ready for the next match, wherever it was.

Not for the first time, my Mum had greater ambitions for me. She had watched me closely and decided that cricket in Hong Kong was no longer stretching me enough. Mum was very determined and she phoned her sister in Perth, Western Australia, to say that I wanted to play club cricket out there. I'd already met a guy from Perth called Tony Taylor in London who had told me his club, Claremont Cottesloe, had four sides: that was good enough for Mum. Off I went to Western Australia to find out just how good I was at cricket in a very tough environment. I was 19. Three times a week, my uncle Walter would drop me off at the nets and I'd cadge a lift back. Eventually, I moved into a flat with Tony Taylor and started to enjoy the Australian way of life. I started off in the second team at Claremont Cottesloe, following in the footsteps of David Gower, Norman Cowans and Nick Cook. Mind you, they'd played in the first team. They were England players, after all – what could I expect?

I quickly had to learn to play off the back foot on those fast wickets and my bowling needed more variety because the new ball soon lost its shine and hardness on the dry surfaces. I spent nine seasons playing grade cricket in Western Australia, and there's no doubt it was a vital stage in my development, not just as a cricketer pure and simple, but in mental terms. I really had to toughen up straight away. Before I went to Australia, the game of cricket was such a joy to me that I'd have a permanent smile on my face out in the middle, loving the privilege of playing a great game. In Australia, there isn't any room for such sentiments. It's hard, unrelenting and losing is not an option. Cricket out there was so much more vocal than anywhere else I had played. I was teased about being a Pom, first because I was based at Lord's (their attempts at a posh English accent were very amusing), then because they thought I was no good.

The sledging on the field never stopped, and I admit that I brought those experiences with me to county cricket as I became more self-confident. It was so intense. The midweek practice sessions were very organised and intensive, with everything geared up to 90 overs that coming Saturday, with the return innings of 90 overs the following Saturday. It took a while to get used to being out in the field for 90 overs in the heat of Perth, but it was all part of the toughening-up process for me. The sides would enjoy victory afterwards among themselves, but there was rarely a sense of enjoyment or pleasure on the pitch during the game. And the post-mortems could be very serious and bitter. One day, Robin Smith turned a game against us, winning it with a brilliant innings. In the dressing-room afterwards, the inquest went along predictable lines: 'We're just not good enough, we've got to work harder.' Yet we hadn't played badly, we just lost to a great knock, in my eyes, but they didn't see it that way. If you lose, there must be reasons for it. They also didn't believe in mixing with the opposition, whatever the result. They'd sing in the shower if they'd won, take it badly in defeat – and always go back to their own clubhouse and mix with all the teams from their own club. The Australian concept of 'mateship' is very strong and perhaps that's why they gel as a team more than in other countries. For me, it was just a case of getting used to a different cricketing philosophy. I didn't think one view was preferable to the other, just different.

There's no doubt that playing out there made me a better cricketer and, as I moved to a higher standard of cricket in Perth, I was pleased that my own game improved in the nine years I spent there. I was named Western Australia's Grade Cricketer of the Year for two seasons, and that meant a great deal to me. It's an award on the recommendation of the umpires for consistency throughout the season, so for them to give it to a Pom must count for something. Also, the State players like Mike Veletta, Bruce Reid and Graeme Wood (all Test cricketers) were regulars in the competition, so doing well against that lot was great for me. The same goes for Alec Stewart, who also won the award in Western Australia. Interesting that some English experts have sometimes accused Alec and me of going over the top on the field at times. Australians would just say we were fair dinkum cricketers!

My second summer with MCC Young Cricketers showed a distinct upturn and I put that down to my experiences in Australia. I was even more battle-hardened when I came back in 1983 after a season in Perth that saw me make a double hundred in grade cricket. I was beginning to think I wasn't such a bad cricketer after all, and I was chuffed when picked at short notice to go on an MCC tour of Holland and Denmark. Vanburn Holder had dropped out and I think they only chose me because it was convenient, but I wasn't complaining. It was a terrific trip. The cricket talk from the old pros was an eye-opener for me, and I took all the leg-pulling in good part. They called me 'Boy' as I fetched and carried their bags for them, but it was all in good fun.

Unknown to me, Sussex had made an approach to the MCC on my behalf when I was on that tour. It all came about in a way that's convinced me that luck is vital to any cricketer. At the end of April, MCC played the champion county, Middlesex, at Lord's in the traditional curtain-raiser to the English season. It rained all three days and not a ball was bowled. So the players needed some practice, and they went to the Indoor School at various stages for a net. Ian Gould was there when I was bowling and I offered to send a few down at him. Gould had been on the England tour to Australia a few months earlier, and as wicket-keeper/batsman with Sussex, he was highly regarded. So I tried my very best to impress and with a successful season in Perth behind me, I was full of confidence. I was mentally harder, physically stronger and I was doing more with the ball. My bouncer worked well against Gould, I rapped him on the pads several times with late swing, and made the odd one go across him. I bowled really well at Gould that afternoon, but thought no more about it after he'd gone. After the game was washed out on the third day, I happened to be walking past the pavilion door as the players were leaving. Gould, on his way to a county match, bumped into me, and when I said 'Cheerio', he stopped, recognised me and asked my name. He said he'd recommend me to his county, Sussex. I thanked him, but thought there must be far better young cricketers than me around to interest a county. Little did I know that Sussex were about to suffer a series of injuries to their seam bowlers and that a vacancy would soon arise.

After Gould's recommendation, I played a couple of second team games for Sussex. Then I went on the MCC tour to Holland and Denmark.

When I got back from that tour, I was summoned to the office of Donald Carr, the Test and County Cricket Board secretary. Sussex had offered me a contract but the question of my appearance the previous year for Hong Kong in the ICC Trophy was a worry. Mr Carr wanted to know how English I was. Would my Hong Kong birthplace count against me in registration terms? Well, I put on my most pukka English accent for Mr Carr, but it was more relevant that both my parents had been born in England. I was in the clear and allowed to sign for Sussex. Within a few weeks, I made my county debut – at Hove against Somerset.

Looking back, it was an unbelievable sequence of events that got me into professional cricket. Strokes of luck everywhere. Chris Lethbridge being signed by Warwickshire, allowing me a place on the ground staff. Don Wilson having faith in me because of my enthusiasm, nothing else. That MCC game against Middlesex being washed out. The fact that I was bowling when Ian Gould came into my net at Lord's. Bumping into him as he was leaving the ground on that last day. Would he have done anything about me if I hadn't said 'Cheerio'? The fact that his county suddenly became short of seam bowlers, so short that they had to turn to a 20-year-old who was just coming to terms with the basics of seam and swing bowling. They could have snapped up many more cricketers of the same age, with greater maturity and ability. I just happened to be in the right place at the right time. People say that you make your own luck in life, but that wasn't so for me in the summer of 1983. I should have done the pools every week!

3

The County Novice

If I was lucky to get on to a county staff, I was even luckier to slip into the Sussex first team within a week or so of arriving at Hove. They signed me as cover for some of their seamers, especially Imran Khan – not much of a challenge that! The great man had a stress fracture of the shin and was playing as a batsman. Adrian Jones, who ought to have been next in line from the second team, was also injured and then, after I had played just two games for the seconds, Ian Greig's freak injury gave me my first-team chance. Greig had played for England the previous year and was obviously a key all-rounder for Sussex. At the start of June, during the home county game with Kent, he had broken his leg, trying to get into his flat. The front door key had snapped off in the lock, and as he tried to climb in through the first-floor window, the ledge gave in and he fell. Greig only played eight championship matches that season, so within a couple of days of that accident, I was making my county debut, at Hove against Somerset.

I hadn't even met my county captain, John Barclay, until the morning of my debut. He couldn't have been nicer. He asked what I bowled and said, 'Don't worry, we'll work it out, just enjoy it – and good luck.' Johnny was like that all through my Sussex career, a marvellous enthusiast who made you want to do well for him as well as yourself.

We fielded first, I came on first change and bowled every ball as fast as I could. I wasn't confident enough to hold the seam up the right way, trying to swing it: all the Lord's Indoor School stuff went out the window, I just wanted to get it down the other end as quick as possible. I took five wickets in the game, which we won, and I was chuffed to bits. The wicket was superb, by the standards I had been used to, and I was pleased to have battled my way to 16 at number nine, after I had come in on a hat-trick. Those five wickets were a huge thrill though, even if Somerset were without Viv Richards and Ian Botham, who were playing in the World Cup at the time. I did my sums quickly and thought, 'If I carry on like this, I'll get over seventy wickets this season!' Then it dawned on me that it might rain, and I might get carted around, or get injured, or dropped. I was so naive – but thrilled to be playing county cricket, and not being humiliated.

The Sunday League game was terrific that weekend. There was such a buzz at the ground, and I remembered the advice of the coach, Stewart Storey – 'You've got to attack the ball in the field.' I was running around at full tilt, hurling the ball in, and the crowd applauded me: the adrenalin flowed and I was really pumped up. It was great fun and was the first time I'd played in front of a large, vocal crowd. I loved that atmosphere. That Sussex team had some excellent fielders – Alan Wells, Gehan Mendis, Paul Phillipson and, above all, Paul Parker. Only Trevor Penney comes near to Paul Parker as a fielder in my experience. He worked so hard at his fielding that he became, in effect, an all-rounder – someone who bats and fields, saving runs and taking wickets. You would put Paul where you knew it would be busy and just rely on him to intimidate the batsman. He'd worked out a new method of fielding, the slide/pick-up that was faster than picking up the ball, then throwing on the turn. I saw him outwit Richard Hadlee with that new method, tempting him for the second run and when Hadlee was coasting, Paul threw the stumps down on one knee. It was a brilliant piece of work and typical of Paul's professional approach to fielding. He never saw it as a chore and his displays would lift the whole side.

I stayed in the first team after my debut, playing 17 championship games that season. John Barclay said he couldn't drop me, because I had done so well, which was very good of him. I'm not sure how popular it made me with some of the second team, though. There was this feeling that you had to serve your time in the seconds before getting a chance in the first team, but here was I – a young sprog from Lord's – walking straight in, and staying in the side. I was also disappointed early on with the attitude of several of the senior players. There was a surprising amount of back-stabbing, an attitude that astonished me, because I thought it was just a privilege to be playing county cricket, and that everyone must feel the same. I realise now that my boyish enthusiasm must have annoyed some of the older guys. Whenever it rained, I was so disappointed, whereas most of the others were pleased. Sussex weren't going to win the championship and they saw little motivation in playing after the halfway mark in the season. Whenever I looked out of the dressing-room window and said, 'Great lads – it's stopped raining!' the only ones to share my enthusiasm were Paul Parker and the captain, John Barclay. Paul clearly bothered some of the senior players with his professional approach to cricket and his overall integrity. One night, early in that first season, I went out for a few drinks with Colin and Alan Wells and Chris Waller, and they spent some time putting the boot into Paul Parker, saying he was probably tucked up in bed early, reading a book. I said nothing, sipped my beer and within a week I was having dinner with Paul, asking his advice, respecting his approach to his profession. Clearly Paul's dedication disconcerted some of the senior Sussex players; they felt shown up by him. Paul wanted to be the best fielder and batsman, and so he worked harder than anybody, to graft consistency onto his natural talent. I soon realised that you have to be yourself, even in a team game. Do what suits you best in terms of preparation and don't knock those who have a different perspective.

I tried too hard to please in that first season with Sussex. I was so keen, so naive – I'd say the first thing that came into my head, and the senior guys would tease me. Soon I became the butt of their humour as my mouth tended to run away, with my brain ten minutes behind (a fault I still have, I'm afraid!). County cricket was a far harder school mentally than I realised. In my first season, I was bowling against Middlesex and, I thought, doing okay. Mike Gatting was at the non-striker's end, watching with exasperation as I kept Wilf Slack quiet. Gatt couldn't take much more of this and shouted out, 'Come on Slacky – this bloke can't bowl!' Some of my team-mates enjoyed that, but it was one of many harsh introductions for me to the county grind. I didn't forget that moment. Gatt has become a friend over the years, and we enjoy the jousts on the field, but whenever I get him out I shout, 'Huh! Can't bowl, eh? Take a shower!' It was sink or swim and I was going to toughen up, because I loved playing county cricket so much.

I was soon physically shattered in that first season. Garth le Roux couldn't bowl after August because of a groin problem, and soon the guys nicknamed me 'Jesus' (as in 'the Saviour'), because I was always so keen to bowl. From my debut in late June, I sent down 470-odd overs in the championship alone, stayed in the side for the Sunday League, and my body was very stretched. I was wiry, but not physically strong enough for all that bowling; and I relied on adrenalin to get me through, because I still couldn't believe my luck that I was playing for a county side so soon. John Barclay was a fantastically supportive captain. I felt he was a man who was genuinely interested in my career. He had a lovely way of dealing with his players. He'd sidle up and confide in me in that classy Old Etonian accent: 'I'd simply love it if you could possibly give me another over. Can you?' and you'd run through the proverbial brick wall for him. I lost respect early on for some of the senior players, realising that you do it for yourself, the captain and the club, not for the knockers in the side – but for John Barclay I had total respect. I'm not at all surprised he has done well in the England set-up on tours. He was so encouraging, he'd always pick up on some-thing positive. If you'd had a bad day in the field, you'd apolo-gise to him – he deserved that at least – and Johnny would say, 'Not at all, you did your best. What about that late outswinger in your fourth over – beautiful ball that one. If you'd got a wicket then it would've all been different. Keep going.' He'd leave you on a high, feeling better. Johnny had a marvellous cricket brain, a deep knowledge of where opposition batsmen liked to play the ball, and he was bloody-minded enough to fol-low the ball, by altering his field if he felt a batsman was going to keep playing the ball into certain areas. He was worth his place in the side as a gutsy batsman, who could bowl useful off-spin. Sadly his gutsiness with the bat reduced his ability to spin his off-breaks, as he kept getting hit on the fingers because of the way he batted. He would take a huge stride on the front foot, and the blows kept coming to the hand, but Johnny never flinched. I remember a 60-odd he made against Malcolm Marshall at his best, which was so impressive. Johnny's commitment and positive attitude never wavered and when I eventually became a county captain, I tried to instil his supportive, positive methods of man-management into the Warwickshire set-up.

Johnny's relationship with Imran Khan in the Sussex side was at times amusing, sometimes frustrating and always fascinating. When I joined Sussex, Imran was the most charismatic cricketer in the world. Imran wasn't just a top all-rounder, a successful captain with Pakistan, a player who would improve any side in the world, he was a classy guy – and I'm sure he wouldn't disagree with that assessment. We lesser mortals in the Sussex dressing-room would read about his playboy activities with a mixture of envy and admiration, but there were no doubts about his success with women, his prominence in London social circles that we could only read about, or that county cricket appeared fairly low on his list of priorities. Imran would decide when he was coming on to bowl, not John Barclay. There were times when I had just got a wicket and I'd be bustling in, full of my usual optimism and then I'd hear that familiar drawl, 'Johnny – bring me on now.' The captain would come up to me and say, 'You've done really awfully well to get us our breakthrough, but Imran's our strike bowler. Hope you understand.' I did, but I'd be pissed off – especially when Imran would then decide he'd had enough after four overs and I'd be brought back on to bowl at a guy who had been in for half an hour.

In my first season, I saw Imran's pride and his insensitivity at close quarters in one county game, at Edgbaston. We were playing Warwickshire and Alvin Kallicharran was batting like a millionaire. I came on to bowl and immediately had him dropped by Imran at slip. He didn't say a word to me by way of apology. Then I had two big shouts for lbw against Kalli, only for the umpire, Bill Alley, to say, 'I can't give him out – I've never seen

him bat so well, I'm enjoying this.' Thanks very much, umpire –
what ever happened to the laws of cricket? When it came to our
turn to bat, Imran copped a stack of bouncers from Paul Smith.
It was clearly 'payback time' for previous encounters, with Paul
realising this time that Imran wouldn't be able to retaliate,
because of his shin problem. He was in the side purely as a batsman, so Imran got bouncers and verbals aplenty. He was furious. When we fielded again, he was still fired up and called for
his bowling boots. 'I want to bowl, Johnny, I'm going to have
Smith.' Barclay said, 'Are you sure?' but that was just an irrelevance. Imran had decreed he would bowl.

He came off his short run, but still fired them down at the
speed of light. Every time a new batsman came in, we'd say,
'This is him – here's Smith!' and he'd snort and bowl bouncers
at everyone, as he suffered from mistaken identity. Winding him
up worked a treat, because he ended up with 6/6, including a
hat-trick, and the wicket of Paul Smith. Honour was satisfied as
far as Imran was concerned, and he looked forward to a comfortable victory, as we chased just over two hundred. Unfortunately, our batsmen failed Imran, despite his stylish 64. Soon we
were in danger of defeat, which did nothing for Imran's mood.
He was even less impressed when he walked out of our dressing-
room to find D.A. Reeve padded up. He stopped, stared at me,
took a look at the scoreboard and said, 'Oh shit.' He called for
our captain and, in front of the other guys, said, 'Johnny,
Dermot can't bat, put him in at number eleven and put Wally
ahead of him at ten.' With that he went back into the dressing-
room. Barclay said, 'Good idea, Imran', and as I fought back the
urge to say something derogatory to Imran, I was demoted to
last man and 'Wally' – Chris Waller – who boasted a career
average of eight and an aversion to fast bowling, went in ahead
of me. Sadly for me, there is no happy ending to this story. I was
given out lbw for nought – by Bill Alley, the umpire with a selec-
tive attitude to lbw appeals – and we lost by 21 runs. Afterwards,
Imran really made my day when he said, 'Johnny, I told you so
– Dermot can't bat.' I was almost in tears and I only wish I had
stood up to him. Imran's behaviour was something I would
never do to a team-mate and another lesson I took with me

when I became Warwickshire's captain – never belittle a colleague over his cricketing ability, or lack of it.

That incident might have destroyed me. Yet I realised that it was just Imran's way of speaking, reflecting his inbuilt confidence. He didn't mean to denigrate me, although it was hard to believe that at the time, especially as I knew I wasn't a huge favourite in the Sussex dressing-room because of my sudden arrival in the first team, with a few of their pals left behind in the second team. In fact, Imran went out of his way to help me after that Edgbaston game. He was very thoughtful about how to cope with the lifestyle of being a county cricketer, about the right type of food to eat and the need to avoid too much alcohol. Imran would call Ian Gould 'Lagerboots – you can hear Gouldy sloshing around behind the stumps', and Gouldy would have to take that from him. Imran told me that too many players succumb to the social pressure of drinking pints of lager because the others are at it and if you don't join in, they'll tease you. His advice was to drink mineral water if that's what you prefer and don't give in to mild bullying. He set a great example in that regard, looking after his physique. He would do weight exercises on his arms, because he felt that he needed strength for his heavy bat. That is one of the reasons why Imran could hit the spinners out of sight, because he was so strong. He also gave me some good advice about injecting extra pace into my bowling: jump higher. That was how he was transformed into a quick bowler. Mind you, Imran was always pretty keen on a jump, wasn't he?!

Imran had this massive self-belief. One day, he hit Jack Simmons for a huge six over long-off and his batting partner, Alan Wells, came down to congratulate him. Imran simply said, 'That's an easy shot for me', and he meant it. In a Sunday League game against Derbyshire, he came unstuck against Geoff Miller's off-spin and scored slowly. We only managed about 140 in our 40 overs and Imran just couldn't get Miller away. In the bath afterwards, Imran was, for a second or two, apologetic. He said, 'I had a nightmare. They're going to call for a stewards' and they're going to blame me.' He then walked into the dressing-room and called for attention. 'Guys, it's all my fault, I stuffed up. But Miller was bowling so well that I thought I'd see him off. If I couldn't get after him, surely no one else in the side could. My plan was to hit Michael Holding when he came on. I'm sorry, guys, but don't forget all the other games I've won for you.' That was typical Imran – a sincere apology by his standards, a kick in the teeth to the rest of us about our batting inadequacies and the conviction that he'd be able to smash Michael Holding around. And he believed it all!

He did it again at Ilford, when we were following on against Essex. I was nightwatchman, batting at number three, and the obvious danger man for us was their left-arm spinner, John Childs. Or, in the words of Imran, 'John Childseese'. The boys found it amusing to hear Imran mispronounce Childs' name. Half an hour before the start of play, Imran announced in his most imperious tone, 'Johnny, I must talk to the players – I have something really important to tell them.' Johnny Barclay, of course, agreed and we settled down at the feet of the great man. 'Listen to me, fellas, I grew up on these kind of pitches in Pakistan, so I know what I'm talking about. The danger bowler is this John Childseese, so don't leave your crease, otherwise you'll be stumped. The ball is turning too much, so just stay in your crease, wait for the short ball, and cut it for four. It's that simple – thank you, Johnny.' As Imran stood back, our captain replied, 'Well, Imran, thanks awfully for that – it was inspirational. Well, chaps, looks like we're batting all day, making around 400 and no one's getting out. Good luck then, do your best. On, on!'

I thought for a split second about the joys of running Imran out when we batted together but I decided against it for the good of the side. Anyway, it would be part of my cricket education to see the master at close quarters, dealing with a fine spinner. The Imran masterclass didn't last very long – he was stumped off John Childseese for just four. I was at the other end, as he skipped down the crease, missed the turning ball by a long way and was stumped by a yard. I thought back to his team talk and had to stop myself from laughing out loud. I was waiting for his explanation afterwards and wasn't disappointed. 'It was a half volley, I lifted my foot a little. That's all.' Not a word about trying to hit him over the top for six, something he had expressly forbidden in his inspirational team talk.

Imran did have a sense of humour, though. He was particularly taken with Cockney rhyming slang. When Ian Gould, a cheery southerner, used to say, 'Mornin' lads, I had a skinful last night. Sunk a few pints down the old Gregory', Imran would stare at him, trying to work it all out. Finally, he said, 'Gouldy, where is this pub, the Gregory – are there any nice chickies there?' Gouldy would sigh, 'I've told you before, it's slang – Gregory – Gregory Peck – neck. A few pints down the old Gregory! Geddit?' Imran slowly digested this and got the last laugh. 'Oh, thank you, Gouldy – my old china plate.' With that, we went out to field.

Imran went to fine leg and Garth le Roux started to bowl. As he was running up, Imran shouted, 'Stop, Garth! Stop!' He sounded so panicky that fielders, batsmen, umpires all stopped dead in their tracks and turned to Imran at fine leg. His advice to Garth was 'Bowl him a bouncer.' Someone shouted back, 'Why?' and Imran replied, 'To hit him in the Gregory!' We fell apart, Garth couldn't bowl for laughing and Imran was tickled pink for the rest of the day. For a time he really got into the Cockney slang. He'd stride into the dressing-room and inform us, 'Guys, I went to this fabulous Mori last night.' Someone would say, 'Mori, what's that?' and Imran would summon up his most arrogant stare and say, 'Mori – Moriarty – Party. God, you're so thick.' I found it hilarious to hear this proud Pakistani, born in Lahore, educated at Oxford University, speaking in Cockney rhyming slang.

Imran had a way of making you feel respected by him, then he'd bring you down without realising the impact of his words. I bumped into him one year in Australia, where I'd been playing grade cricket. He was with the Pakistan side, but he stopped to chat and asked how my cricket was going. I told him about the double hundred I'd just scored in grade cricket, an innings that really delighted me. He looked at me and said, 'You mean the whole team got two hundred?' I corrected him and he said, 'Dermot, why do you make these things up, to impress me?' A team-mate alongside me confirmed that I had actually scored a double hundred and Imran asked about the standard of the game, about the wicket. Finally he said, 'Dermot, you must be joking. I played grade cricket in Sydney and I never even got a hundred!' The following season in England, I got a fair number of runs in county cricket and for a time I played pretty well. Imran wasn't playing all that much for us – the society season was in full swing in London at the time and Ascot, then Wimbledon probably called – but he came back to play in one match, where I scored just 18. When I walked in after getting out, he said, 'Well played', and I answered, 'But I only got 18.' I told him to piss off, that I'd been playing well and scoring runs. Imran said, 'Have you really? I haven't seen the scores lately.' I resisted the temptation to point out that the county cricket scores aren't published in *Tatler*, but it was another example of Imran's thoughtlessness, that he was on a totally different plane to his Sussex team-mates.

To be fair to him, he often tried to make amends to me. I think he was genuinely interested in my cricket career. He knew it hadn't been easy for me when I first came into the Sussex side, and I knew he valued the fact that I was an individual and wouldn't go with the herd in social terms. I remember he was the first to try to teach me the intricacies of reverse swing, where the ball will go in the opposite direction to where it's expected. Imran knew all about this from playing in Pakistan, where the ball gets scuffed up early and is therefore difficult to swing traditionally. I just couldn't grasp what Imran was on about, even though I asked him several questions. In the end, he said, 'I give up – Johnny, he won't listen.' That day, Trevor Jesty hit me for 14 in an over and I wished Imran had got through to me about reverse swing. At least he had tried, though.

A few years after Imran and I both left Sussex, we played against each other on the biggest stage of all – the World Cup Final, at Melbourne, in 1992. On the eve of the game, I had first-hand experience of Imran's distinctive sense of humour. The England and Pakistani sides had been invited to a big bash, and the Australian hosts had put on a satirical show. Some Aussie came on, dressed as the Queen, and proceeded to satirise the Royal Family. That was too much for Ian Botham, who walked out during the soup. Our captain, Graham Gooch, followed him out, as did Alec Stewart, and soon it looked as if the whole England team would walk out. I looked at Allan Lamb and he joked: 'For goodness' sake, Dermot – we haven't drunk any of this wine yet, and it's good stuff, man.' I stayed there, as the Fergie and Diana jokes came out, and although it was close to the bone, because we were representing our country the next day, I thought the guy's comic technique was good. During the show, I couldn't help noticing that on the nearby table, Imran was in hysterics. I went over and sat down beside him, and the tears were flowing down his cheeks. Finally, he managed to speak and said, 'Dermot, it's so funny – only the real English have walked out. The colonials don't know what to do!' With that, he dissolved into more helpless laughter and I looked around to see which English players were still there. Sure enough – there was Graeme Hick, Robin Smith, Allan Lamb, Derek Pringle, Chris Lewis, Phillip DeFreitas, Gladstone Small and Dermot Reeve. All born abroad. Some from what might be termed a 'colonial' background. Of the English-born, only Neil Fairbrother and Richard Illingworth were still there. I thought it was very smart of Imran to spot that.

Next day, we lost the Final and you could see Imran's pride at the achievement as he stood on the podium, and his joy at the realisation that now he could get the financial support for his cancer hospital. Later I went into their dressing-room to congratulate the Pakistan team and Imran motioned to me to sit down beside him: he does have this regal manner! He said, 'Dermot, I must tell you, I'm very happy for you, you've done so well to get so far in the game.' Then a crucial pause and the killer phrase – 'for someone of your limited ability.' There I was, thinking for a fleeting second that he was being nice to me, then he takes away the compliment. He really knows how to make a guy feel special! The trouble is, he actually meant what he was saying. He had never rated me on talent, but he liked the way I had made a career for myself on application and character. I suppose I ought to have been flattered.

I shall always be grateful though to Imran Khan for one thing. That distinctive, aristocratic voice of his has given me rich pickings when I do after-dinner speeches. I'm lucky enough to have an ear for accents, and to be able to impersonate some. When I grew up in Hong Kong, there were 28 different nationalities at school and I could somehow manage a few of the accents. As a boy, I'd do impersonations in Chinese or Indian while reading poems out loud and they seemed to work. So when I heard a new accent, I'd try to do that one. When I joined Sussex, I'd walk around trying out new voices, and I was particularly taken by Imran's. So was everybody else in the dressing-room and Imran finally got very shirty about it. One day he shouted, 'Why do all of you guys think you sound like me? It's pathetic, just be yourselves. Dermot is the only one who remotely sounds like me.' I took that as a licence to impersonate him, but he still wasn't too happy about it. He finally cracked at Lord's, as I was going through my routine, trying to get his distinctive drawl just right. Imran said, 'Listen, you little shit, if you go on like that I'm going to punch you on the head!' John Barclay overheard him and said, 'Oh there's nothing like a great team spirit is there, chaps?' and disappeared to lunch! After that, I was wary about doing Imran in his presence, but I was extremely grateful to him in his absence one day in 1992. I was a guest at the dinner marking the Hong Kong Sixes event, and the master of ceremonies knew I was a bit of a closet mimic. Anyway, he sprung it on me, telling the audience I was going to do my impersonations. I was struck dumb with terror, because I had nothing prepared and genuinely thought I was there just for the fun. I managed to get through 20 minutes of Brian Johnston and Imran Khan impersonations, and although it was the longest twenty minutes of my life, it went fairly well. Since then, I have managed to organise some sort of party piece for my after-dinner work, and Imran features regularly. So thanks for everything, Imran – especially that voice.

Imran didn't play at all for Sussex in my second season, in 1984, but we soldiered on, rising several places up the championship table to sixth place. I was well aware that 'second seasonitis' might strike me, so there could be a reaction to my first, satisfactory season, but I did quite well. I averaged 27 with the bat and 25 with the ball in first-class cricket (compared to 12 and 28 the year before) and at one stage I managed to get as high as number seven in the batting order. A hundred against Surrey as nightwatchman helped, I suppose, but in the end, I had to be content with number eight or nine in a strong batting side. Looking back on those years now, I realise I tried too hard on the field. By that I mean I was too keyed up, too full of nervous tension, so that I didn't focus properly on the ball. With greater experience, I now understand that to do well as a batsman, you have to watch the ball as closely as possible, but you can't do that unless you're relaxed at the right moment. Your mind needs to be relaxed, yet focused when it really counts. You also need to be in an encouraging environment if you're a young player and that wasn't the case for me, with the exceptions of John Barclay, Paul Parker, Colin Wells and Gehan Mendis. There were too many petty jealousies, too much conformist thinking. If you expressed a contrary view, you were pigeonholed as a cocky youngster who had only been in the game five minutes.

In my early years at Sussex, a local radio reporter interviewed me, and asked my ambitions. I said what any self-respecting young professional ought to say – that I would dearly love to play for England one day. I didn't at any stage suggest I was good enough, but some of my team-mates heard the interview and used it as ammunition. I particularly recall the words of Alan Wells: 'You ought to just concentrate on staying in the first team, getting your cap, hoping for a benefit at the end of it all. You'll never play for England.' I just gave him a look but inside I was angry. I believe his attitude was wrong, that you have to aspire to a goal, even if you might fall short for lack of talent. I knew I didn't look all that special on the cricket field, that I wasn't the finished, polished article. When I first saw myself on video as a Sussex player, I wasn't at all impressed – but it was the best I could manage and I was more concerned about effectiveness than style. Alan Wells was far more elegant than me as a batsman, but he was a long way from England selection when he tried to cuff me down.

Years later, when I first played for England – and scored 59 on my Test debut – I recalled that quote from Alan Wells and smiled to myself. When I eventually captained Warwickshire, I tried to use incidents like that one with Alan Wells to get the guys properly motivated. I'd tell them at no stage should they even think about coasting. If you're looking to score a certain number of runs in a month and you get there with a week to spare, you revise your target and keep pushing yourself. Simplify the game, take it one over at a time, never look ahead to the last day. Don't conform or settle for your county cap and possibly a benefit ten years later. Make it happen for you. If I'd taken Alan Wells' words to heart, I probably would have drifted out of county cricket soon afterwards.

I seriously thought about retiring after a couple of years with Sussex. I was still the butt of a few influential senior players, and although most of it could be construed as the usual dressing-room banter, I was sensitive and no one ever said, 'Don't worry, it's just a bit of fun.' Ian Greig once threw my kit out of the dressing-room, which I found childish from such a mature guy, but also significant: I was obviously a threat to him in his eyes as the side's all-rounder. I remember being bitterly disappointed when he was picked ahead of me against the Australians in 1985 and John Barclay's consoling words ('You'll get a chance to play against them in the future') didn't cut much ice. Any young player surrounded by such experience would be a little sensitive, but I felt there wasn't enough encouragement. In one game against Essex, I got myself out badly – a loose shot to cover off Derek Pringle after I had batted away against Neil Foster, picking up sore ribs, but I left Ian Gould high and dry at the other end. As soon as I walked in, our coach Stewart Storey tore a strip off me, telling me it was a bloody awful shot. It dawned on me then that there was a right way and a wrong way to get out. I remember being caught at short leg off an off-break from Mike Watkinson that turned, only to be told 'bad luck' by the coach. Yet when Colin Wells swept Watkinson straight to deep square leg, he was told it was a waste of a wicket and a bad shot. Now to my mind, I was more guilty than Colin, because at least he was trying an attacking shot, while I was just defending. Yet my dismissal looked better than Colin's and I didn't get the rollicking. When I came to Warwickshire I decided I would bat with more freedom, that if I got out, at least it would hopefully come from playing positively. My experiences of being bawled out in front of my team-mates at Sussex also influenced me in choosing the right way to talk to someone who has been brainless on the field – in private, face-to-face, long after the heat of the moment has passed. That player doesn't need to be told he has stuffed up as soon as he walks off the field.

Stewart Storey wasn't always hard, though. He was aware of Ian Greig's attitude to me and he sympathised. He told me about one young player from his days with Surrey, who was finally hounded out of the game by the older pros. They were insecure about their own futures, the prospect of a benefit, their declining prowess, and they made this lad a whipping boy. He stood it for a time and then gave it away. Stewart said he was worried I'd be going the same way, and I admitted I was thinking about it, because I just wanted to enjoy myself and keep improving. I didn't need the back-stabbing. He told me to stick at it, that it was a hard profession and to develop thick skin. Of course, he was right, but I do think I was in an insensitive environment and I started to wonder if I would enjoy my cricket somewhere else on the county circuit.

Ian Greig wasn't retained at the end of the 1985 season, but that didn't necessarily smooth the way for me in my ambition to move up the batting order. The wickets at Hove were now so good that I didn't expect to get many innings there in championship matches, unless we were in trouble. After my hundred as a nightwatchman against Surrey, I put together a few good scores and I suggested to Stewart Storey that perhaps I could open if we were involved in a run chase, so that the better players could come in later, with the pressure eased if I managed to pull off a few shots. He made it clear that I would never open the innings, which disappointed me. It seemed a depressingly conformist attitude: did that mean you never open the bowling with a spinner? Young David Wood was trying to make his way as an opener for Sussex in those days, but even if he was short of form and confidence, he would still be the opener even in a run chase – because he was categorised as an opener. So I was pigeon-holed as a lower order batsman, whose main task was to bowl. There seemed little awareness that circumstances change, that you have to be flexible: the sort of dynamic attitude that helped Sri Lanka win the World Cup.

I loved the occasion of the big match and when Sussex won the Nat West Final at Lord's in 1986, I was in my element. I won the Man of the Match Award because I was determined to enjoy the day and not freeze. I wanted the ball to come to me all the time in the field, and when I made a good stop in the second over, I just felt I was going to do well. I took 4/20 coming on third change, including my old Sussex team-mate Gehan Mendis out lbw, and then I ruined the day for the Lancashire fans and the neutrals by getting Clive Lloyd out lbw for nought. It was big Clive's farewell game, and many hoped he'd sign off with a major innings, but umpire Ken Palmer wasn't to be swayed and he supported my appeal. Lloyd out second ball; I've always rated Ken Palmer as an umpire! We cruised to a seven-wicket win and I was so pleased for my Dad, because I got the award from his special hero, Sir Leonard Hutton, who was the match adjudicator. Dad was there to see it, so that was a great day for both of us to savour. I can't explain why I managed to do so well on such a high-pressure day, other than being able to relax at the right time and not let the tension drain me. I just smiled my way through the entire day, and I felt fresh as a daisy. If you go with the flow, and manage to switch on the concentration when it's needed, you can do yourself justice on big occasions like a Lord's Final. I find that if you are too tense, nothing happens when you press the button.

A year after that Lord's Final, I had decided to leave Sussex. It was purely a case of ambition, certainly not money. I wasn't enjoying it at Sussex as much as I had hoped. It was more fun playing as an amateur, when I used to look forward to every game as if it was going to be my last. When you do it for a job, all that changes and it becomes hard work every day. I could understand how so many of the senior players at Sussex had become jaded by mid-season, and that only increased my admiration for John Barclay and Paul Parker, who were still so enthusiastic. They must have been superb actors, because I rarely saw them listless, apart from one day when Paul Parker got himself out. He was in a rich seam of form at the time, batting for hours, and playing really well until he had had enough. When he finally got out, he almost crawled back to the dressing-room and said, 'Dermot, for the very first time, I'm glad I'm out.' He was dead on his feet because of the daily workload, a rare admission from someone like Paul Parker. I could sympathise with that, but I wanted a fresh challenge if I was going to stay in the game and face days like that one which exhausted Paul so much.

Basically, I left Sussex because I wanted to improve as a cricketer and I wasn't getting very far. When I first went there, the wickets encouraged the faster bowlers and I did quite well behind the likes of Imran, Garth le Roux and Tony Pigott. I learned to swing the ball, because I swiftly realised I lacked the physique to be able to bowl flat out, over after over, day after day. Gradually the Hove wickets changed in texture; they became abrasive, and you couldn't keep the shine on the ball essential for the traditional swing bowler. This was my main reason for leaving Sussex. It was literally a case of the grass being greener elsewhere. In those days I was playing more as a bowler than an all-rounder, but I was struggling to get wickets in the home games. My 1987 bowling statistics make the point: my average at Hove was 46 which would have placed me 128th in the national averages, while for away games it was 21.07 which would have placed me 12th. My overall average was 29.52 placing me 65th. It wasn't just one freak season either, in 1986 the statistics were alarmingly similar.

I was also getting little chance of batting. In the Nat West Final of '86, I was down to bat at number nine. I honestly thought I was a better player than that, and that I could get a thousand runs a season if I went up the order. Yet, after five years in the first team, I was still going in at seven and lower. After five years of championship cricket, I was averaging 25 with the bat, but getting only one innings per match. I wanted to improve as a cricketer, to see how far I could push myself towards my dream of playing for England. When the news came out that I had asked to be released, there were some daft rumours flying around that I had fallen out with the captain, Paul Parker. That was nonsense, I had the greatest respect for Paul. In fact he rang me up asking me to stay, offering me the new ball for the following season. I had to point out to Paul that I wasn't an opening bowler any more, that I wanted to go to a home ground where the ball would still swing after a lot of overs and where I could bat in the middle order. We parted on the best of terms as far as I'm concerned, and I shall always be grateful to the example set by Paul Parker in my early years in county cricket. It was typical of Paul that he was still playing county cricket for Durham at the age of 38, still fielding brilliantly, batting stylishly and supporting his team-mates to the hilt.

Kent and Warwickshire were two counties who expressed keen interest in me and I plumped in the end for Warwickshire. I felt that Kent had enough seam and swing bowlers on their staff, which might have restricted my first-team chances, and I liked the potential at Edgbaston. I'd played a second team game there in my final season with Sussex, and I noticed that the ball was still swinging after 60 overs. The outfield was lush, helping to keep the shine on the ball and I felt that it would be a good place for a swing bowler. Andy Lloyd, the Warwickshire captain, seemed very keen to sign me and I liked that. It was time for a change of scenery. It proved a good decision.

4

A Change of Scenery

I came to Edgbaston at just the right time for my career. I was 25, ambitious, eager to learn more about the game, but I didn't want to be dragged down by the old-stagers in the dressing-room who had seen it all before and didn't take kindly to lippy lads with views of their own. There was a freshness about life at Edgbaston at the start of the 1988 season. Players like Norman Gifford, Alvin Kallicharran, Dennis Amiss and Geoff Humpage had given great service to the club, but they had either just retired, or were drifting out of the game. Warwickshire had finished third bottom of the 1987 championship table and at the foot of the Sunday League, so the only way was up as far as I was concerned. The new brooms – the captain Andy Lloyd and the coach, Bob Cottam – felt the same way. They knew we weren't a great side, but they were determined to be more positive in their approach. It seemed that avoiding defeat had been the main priority in previous seasons, but Andy was having none of that. A keen gambler on all sports, particularly on the horses, he was the right guy to captain us. He knew that you could draw every game and finish bottom of the table. He was very keen on group discussions to analyse how we could win a match, how we could maximise our assets, rather than worry about the opposition. At least we'd have a go.

Judging by the way Andy Lloyd negotiated with me to persuade me to come to Edgbaston, I was his type of player and that meant a lot to me. I had been frustrated by the selfishness of some of my Sussex colleagues and I wanted greater input in team discussions. I felt there were a lot of cricketing conventions that should be challenged; too many senior players just conformed in the way they approached and played the game. The wickets and conditions at Edgbaston would also be beneficial to my bowling, compared to Hove. When you're a swing bowler and the ball comes back off the boundary boards without any alteration in shape or shine, you feel you've got a chance of swinging the ball consistently, especially with lush outfields like you get at Edgbaston. In my last year with Sussex, I had taken 7/37 against Lancashire in conditions that were ideal for my type of bowling: low cloud, moisture in the air, green outfield. That was at Lytham, though – not at Hove. I couldn't keep hoping that a few times a season I'd encounter conditions that suited me, I wanted to enjoy the prospect regularly on my home ground. Edgbaston seemed perfect for that, and I knew that the policy towards the pitches there was going to change under the new captain. They would help the faster bowlers more than the traditional Edgbaston featherbeds which favoured batsmen, yet gave little hope of positive results.

It was no coincidence that Warwickshire hadn't won a trophy since 1980, or the championship since 1972: their pitches just didn't lead to a positive, dynamic approach. Lloyd had experienced all that in his ten years at the club, and he was determined to see a fresher attitude, with the bowlers getting more encouragement from the home wickets. It was something that many other county sides had done for years, and become successful as a result, and I saw no reason why we shouldn't do the same. That's been the general policy at Edgbaston since I've been at the club and although traditionalists and other counties moan about our 'result' pitches, it's not as if we have been the first to prepare pitches that play to our strengths. We've also won a lot of matches away from home, in all sorts of conditions, but that is conveniently overlooked.

We finished sixth in the 1988 championship season and only the champions, Worcestershire, picked up more bowling bonus points. It was a great season for our fast bowlers – Allan Donald, Tony Merrick, Tim Munton and Gladstone Small – but, sadly, I played little part in our bowling revival. I could only bowl less than 300 overs in championship matches, because of a shoulder injury that has proved a worry over the years. In my last month with Sussex, I had a cortisone injection in my right shoulder, but within six weeks, I couldn't even brush my teeth or lift a tea cup. I had a scan in Australia, and that showed an abnormality of the joint and a tear to a tendon. By the time I reported to Edgbaston for the next season, it had healed, but I still needed an operation that August. It took a yard off my pace, and I bowled just under a hundred overs in the 1989 championship summer. It was very frustrating, at a time when I was looking to bowl a lot of overs, and it hampered my throwing in the field as well. After a season with Sussex, I realised that I'd never be a tearaway fast bowler, but I still had to bang the ball in to take advantage of the indifferent bounce that Edgbaston offered. Losing that yard of pace was a blow, but I still worked at my swing bowling. I used to watch and admire the techniques of Ian Botham, Kevin Cooper, Terry Alderman and Richard Ellison, as they timed the release of the ball, using their wrist and fingers to control the late swing, experimenting at either end of the crease. But that shoulder injury delayed my progress as an all-rounder at Edgbaston, at a time when I should have been developing.

I was lucky, though, that Bob Cottam was an exceptional bowling coach. He did a great deal for the likes of Tim Munton, helping him to learn how to swing the ball. Munton became an absolute rock to Warwickshire after that, a reliable, hard-working bowler who could get the best players out because he could now swing the ball late. Cottam was the ideal coach at the time for Warwickshire. He liked guys who would get stuck in at the crease, who didn't flinch at the short stuff, and played the hook shot whenever it was on. He thought it was fine to show disappointment when you were out, because that meant you cared. Diving around in the field was also a must for Cottam; as a former England bowler himself, he knew the need to encourage the bowlers with a high degree of commitment in the field. I knew I was Bob's type of cricketer, visual and hyperactive. Bob warmed to vocal, aggressive cricketers and didn't have much time for anyone moping around, feeling sorry for themselves.

Within two years of coming to Edgbaston, Bob had made me

the vice-captain, but not before we had a few disagreements. Bob's a very hot-blooded guy, who wears his heart on his sleeve. As a coach, he was bursting with knowledge and opinions, many of them stimulating and imaginative, but he wasn't a calm watcher. At times he would get too emotional when viewing a game and that didn't help the players relax. His successors, Bob Woolmer and Phil Neale, have been able to cope with that in different ways – Wooley would take himself off to the gym and eff and blind at us out on the field, while Phil is a very relaxed guy in those situations, rightly pointing out that it's now the captain's responsibility.

Bob Cottam was more vocal, he judged players very quickly, in black and white terms: he would always be a Gooch man rather than a Gower man, for example. One day I was very upset at Bob's emotions running away from him. It was a Sunday League game against Northants and I was bowling at David Ripley. I had bowled five 'dot' balls in a row at David Ripley and as I walked back I thought, 'The last thing he'll expect now is the slower ball.' It had been working well for me that summer, so I tried it – out of the back of my hand. Ripley smashed it for six. Well played to him, I thought – he'd spotted it. In the dressing-room immediately after the end of the Northants innings, Bob tore a strip off me in front of the others, demanding what the hell I thought I was doing against Ripley. It was all done in front of the team and I asked to see him in his office. He was still red in the cheeks as I explained quietly yet assertively that I'd done my best and there was no need for such confrontational action, especially with my team-mates sat beside me. He calmed down and we got on fine after that, but it was another lesson I took with me when I became captain. Rollickings should be handed out calmly, in private, without the player being denigrated publicly.

As well as Bob Cottam's expertise as a bowling coach, he was excellent at spotting young talent. As long as they played with guts and energy, Cott would push them forward. He spotted and developed many of the players who came through the ranks to become regulars in our successful sides, when we picked up six trophies in three seasons. The likes of Keith Piper, Roger

Twose and Trevor Penney were all spotted and signed by Bob Cottam. I was particularly impressed with Bob's coaching of the bowlers, including Allan Donald, who was fast but erratic in his early days at Edgbaston. Cott put him on the road to streamlining his action and adding control to that natural talent to bowl fast. He topped the national bowling averages in 1989, and it was a major plus to have him firing away on pitches that helped him.

Slowly things were starting to gel at Edgbaston and it was a huge boost to our confidence to win the Nat West Trophy in 1989. It took the pressure off Andy Lloyd, who had been coming under fire for our erratic performances earlier in the season, and it brought a thawing in the relationship between captain and coach. They were both strong-minded characters, not afraid to voice their opinions, and there were times when we weren't totally focused in the same direction. The batting let us down consistently, but it all came good on a dark evening at Lord's in September, when Warwickshire won a Final for the first time in 21 years. I got the Man of the Match Award for a tight spell of bowling and 40-odd in a low-scoring match, and that pleased many of cricket's statisticians. It meant I had become the first player to pick up the award for two different counties. I didn't set much store by that, because it was only because I had moved to another county, but I was happy with two finals, two victories and two "Man of the Match" awards.

It was much more vital to win, especially as we were up against Middlesex, one of the best one-day sides in the game, on their home ground. On a slow pitch, we only needed 211 in our 60 overs, but against the likes of Norman Cowans, Angus Fraser and John Emburey, that was never going to be easy. I was run out by an inch at the bowler's end, and although *Wisden* and the TV commentator said I was backing up too far, that was because my partner, Asif Din, said, 'Yes', then 'No', and therefore I didn't have time to beat the throw from mid wicket. Never mind, it's one of those things that regularly happen in one-day cricket and, due to the cool head of Neil Smith, we got home.

Smith was a great selection by Cottam and Lloyd. Roger Twose, a left-handed batsman, had pushed hard for selection but Neil had made 161 the day before against Yorkshire, batting as a nightwatchman, so he was in confident form with the bat. Although only 22, he was a very mature cricketer. His father, Mike (better known as M.J.K.), was chairman of our cricket committee, but as you'd expect from a former captain of England and Warwickshire, was only interested in what Neil could do on the field, rather than adding to the Smith family name. Neil had bowled his off-spin very well in their innings, bowling the dangerous Desmond Haynes, but when he came in to bat, it was a situation that would have tested the most experienced player. I had been run out, with 20 needed off 18 balls, and after Neil Smith, we were down to the bowlers. He and Asif Din had to do it – and it was so dark now! The last over was to be bowled by Simon Hughes, a good choice at the death, because he bowled a full length, and for variation possessed an excellent slower ball. With ten needed in that last over, you would have backed Middlesex. Neil got the strike for the second ball and he made contact with Hughes' slower one. Bob Cottam was sat alongside me on the dressing-room balcony and shouted, 'Where's it gone?' For some reason, I saw it clearly: 'It's six, it's six!' Neil had hit it superbly and the ball soared back over the bowler's head, to hit the covers, a good 20 yards over the long off boundary. What a shot, at the perfect time! Then Hughes bowled a legside wide, and fumbled a straight drive from Neil, and we were home with two balls to spare. It was a great party that night!

The heart we had shown to win that Final must have made a lot of people in the game sit up and take notice. On paper, Middlesex were clear favourites, with the experience and the quality in their side. We were in transition, but we fielded well and supported each other all the way through. It was particularly gratifying to see a young player come in at the death and play with such calmness. The environment at Edgbaston was beginning to suit those with a bolder approach, and that great win was an important staging post for the club and those players who went on to share so many trophies a few years later.

We didn't build on that famous victory straight away, though. The following season was a good one for me personally, as I at last made a decent contribution as an all-rounder, with wickets, slip catches and a batting average of over 50. Batting as high as number 5 gave me more opportunity and I made almost 1,500 first-class runs, but the side still wasn't clicking, even though we finished fifth in the championship. Our record in the one-day games was dreadful, and that ought to have been the area where we did well, considering the ability the players had but our fielding was letting us down and we played spin poorly. The cricket committee boxed itself into a corner about our two overseas players, Tom Moody and Allan Donald. Only one could play at a time, and for the following season, only one could be registered – so which one would it be? There was a lot of shilly-shallying around, complicated by Tom Moody's awesome batting form, but in the end the cricket committee made the right decision to keep faith with Donald. That had to be right. Tom proved a top player for us, a great guy in the dressing-room, but it's well-known that a class fast bowler wins you more matches, especially on pitches like Edgbaston where speed through the air and off the pitch can be deadly with uncertain bounce. Looking back now on Warwickshire's record under my captaincy, I can only thank those on the cricket committee who saw the sense of keeping Allan Donald. He has been a model professional for us, an inspiration to the rest of the staff – and a matchwinner consistently.

Soon after the 1990 season, Bob Cottam left. He had several run-ins with the cricket committee over policy matters, and he didn't want to stay. It was no secret that his relationship with the captain, Andy Lloyd, wasn't all that harmonious, but I was sad to see Cott leave. His part in Warwickshire's resurgence shouldn't be forgotten as he breathed new life into the playing staff in his three years at Edgbaston and his successor, Bob Woolmer, was grateful for his legacy.

Of all the coaches I have worked with, Bob Woolmer has been the best. He was also great fun to have around in his four years at Edgbaston. Bob had the knack of being apart from the players at the right times, giving them their space, but he was accessible and ready to laugh at himself. No one ever spent more time with the hairdryer in our dressing-room than Bob, and the amount of work he put in at the gym did nothing for his splendid paunch – all he managed was a very strong pair of legs! Bob took all the ribbing in good part and he helped foster a great team spirit, where young players were encouraged to debate the pros and cons openly, without being talked down by the elders.

Bob's passion for cricket was only surpassed by his love of food, and we spent many evenings down at T.G.I. Fridays restaurant in Birmingham, talking about the game, hatching plans, and bouncing ideas off each other. I was a single guy at the time and Bob's family were usually at home in South Africa, so we had time to spend with each other to shoot the breeze. I loved his bright, open thinking, his readiness to take on new ideas, to take a more scientific approach to professional cricket. Andy Lloyd deserves a lot of credit for recommending Bob Woolmer. Obviously Andy had played against Bob, who was a fine batsman for Kent and England, but he got to know him particularly well out in South Africa. He recognised a coach with imagination, hunger to succeed and the ability to put over his ideas. His greatest asset is that he has a very young nature – he'd say, 'Come on, I'm learning as I go along as well, you guys can come with me.' That was appreciated by the Warwickshire boys. His relaxed way concealed a formidable cricket brain, a terrific memory and a passion to improve. Bob Woolmer's part in our success at Edgbaston cannot be over-estimated. England lost a great coach when they overlooked him, allowing him to go to South Africa as the national coach. I find it amazing that Bob was never even offered an 'A' tour, despite his excellent record at Edgbaston in such a short space of time.

As soon as he arrived, Bob made an immediate impression on me for his innovative attitude. At Trinidad, of all places, we had a team meeting that was to have significant repercussions over the next few years. I had studied our statistics, talked to Bob and we came to the conclusion that the side had to change the way we batted against spinners. Bob said we all should learn how to play the sweep shot, and also the reverse sweep. We pointed out that players such as Mike Gatting, Graham Gooch and Chris Cowdrey were superb players of the sweep, bringing them thousands of runs in their careers. It was all very well thinking about

playing defensively with a straight bat against the sharply turning ball, but that kind of delivery may still get you out and if
you're playing defensively you've got little chance of scoring
runs. By sweeping, you can actually take the ball on the full or
smother the spin and still be in your crease, avoiding the chance
of being stumped. We also talked about playing the reverse
sweep if there was a gap behind square on the offside.

The first time I saw that stroke played was in 1984 by, of all
people, Malcolm Marshall. John Barclay was the bowler and
Marshall's two strokes turned the game. Barclay wasn't
impressed, saying the stroke should be banned, but I remember
thinking, 'There's an off-spinner who doesn't like that shot, so
that must be a good option.' It made sense to combat an off-
spinner who's bowling to a right-hander with six men on the
legside and three on the off. If you play it well, a man has to be
brought over from the legside to plug the gap on the offside –
and then you can pick up runs in the orthodox manner, playing
with the off-break on to the legside, finding the gap. For years,
off-spinners like Nigel Cowley, Jack Simmons, Geoff Miller,
Eddie Hemmings and John Emburey had been some of the
most economical bowlers in one-day cricket because they had
been played mostly in orthodox fashion. The ball would be fired
in around middle and leg, and the batsman would only get a
single if he managed to pierce the legside field of six. The bowler
would make sure he didn't bowl with a short legside boundary,
so was rarely hit for six. It was about time the off-spinner was
played in a different manner.

Of course, there were many diehards who were totally against
the reverse sweep. Peter May, the chairman of selectors, was very
unimpressed when Ian Botham played it against Greg Matthews
in 1985 and got himself out against Australia in a one-day international. The chairman said sniffily that it wasn't a shot in the
MCC Coaching Book, the implication being that it therefore
shouldn't be played. That ignored the fact that Peter May would
have needed to find different ways of scoring quickly against
tight spin bowling if he had been playing in 1985, more than 20
years after his retirement. It also insulted Ian Botham's daring,
positive qualities that made him such a great player. Take away

Botham's bravado and you dilute his effectiveness.

Mike Gatting also got a lot of stick for playing the reverse sweep in the 1987 World Cup Final, getting out to Allan Border as soon as he came on. It was suggested by many that Gatting lost us the World Cup with that single stroke. There was nothing wrong with the principle of the shot, just the execution. You can look a prat when the reverse sweep gets you out, but what about the countless times you see batsmen bowled by an offspinner giving themselves room for the cut shot? I reckon I've got out three times in my career to the reverse sweep, two of them on successive Sundays in 1993, but that didn't stop me playing it if the circumstances demanded it. Too many people are worried about getting out the wrong way. It's acceptable to be caught at short leg from an off-break but dismissal from the reverse sweep has the journalists rushing to their laptops and the committee members shaking their heads. Effectiveness ought to be the crucial factor, not style.

Bob Woolmer struck a chord with me as we debated the issue in that first meeting in Trinidad. A few of the lads were against changing the way we batted against spin, but I had felt that since I came to Edgbaston we had been missing out. Our top batters played the quicks very well, but we were too passive against the spinners. We didn't work the ball around, we were content just to wait for the loose ball, but against a good spinner it seldom comes. A good finger-spinner would just toy with us as we played him from the crease. Woolmer said we had to look to dominate the spinners from the first ball, that no longer do we look to play out maidens, even in championship cricket we should be more assertive. Andy Lloyd was equally concerned about that, and from then on he played very positively, with the side's best interests paramount. At a late stage in his career, he started to sweep the spinners quite well, and that was important; the younger players could see a senior batsman having success with a new approach, and that would help persuade them it was the right way to play the spinners.

After that Trinidad meeting, we tried a bolder approach in our next match on that tour – and we lost! They had two spinners and we struggled against them on the matting surface, especially as their wicket-keeper kept loosening the mat when the spinners were on. I was out lbw playing the sweep, and in our next team meeting we had an interesting difference of views. Gladstone Small, who had been sceptical about the new approach, pointed out that I'd got out to the sweep, only to be told by Andy Lloyd that I was also the top scorer, having got a few runs with the sweep shot. It was all a matter of degree, of stroke selection, of intensive practice. The cricket management were adamant that this was the way forward but it was obviously going to take time to implement. I'd seen the likes of Gatting and Gooch destroy spinners over the years, and Bob Woolmer felt the same way. He had seen Alan Knott, Chris and Colin Cowdrey sweep and paddle the slow bowlers to distraction and he was convinced it was a vital tool in combating tight bowling and the increasingly athletic fielding in the county game. The players needed to be educated, and it took some time to win over the likes of Gladstone, and Neil and Paul Smith – but over the years they came to admire the way the boys played the sweep and the reverse. When Tim Munton played it during the game against Hampshire when we won the 1994 championship, I was very chuffed. It was great to see such a positive, flexible approach from our number eleven batsman. As long as you practise it before using it in a match, I see it as a business stroke with little more risk attached than any other.

It became a personal crusade for me and Bob Woolmer over the next few years, and we knew that we had to win over influential people on the Warwickshire cricket committee, as well as some sceptical players. After Dominic Ostler had worked hard on the reverse sweep in winter practice, he played it at last out in the middle, and it got him runs. We were delighted with that, and so was Dominic, because the hard work had paid off for him. He could see the point of the shot, how it messed up the bowler's field and improved his run rate. As we talked about it in the dressing-room, Dennis Amiss walked in. He was chairman of the cricket committee at the time, having retired after a great career when batting had been more straightforward on flat Edgbaston wickets. He said, 'Dominic, I don't like you playing that shot. I used to try to come down the wicket and play the off-spinner over extra cover.' Bob Woolmer and I weren't impressed by what we saw as interference by Dennis, and we asked him not to raise it again with Dominic. We didn't want Dominic to face a dilemma – does he listen to his captain and coach or to the chairman of cricket, who had scored a hundred hundreds, and would have a big say in deciding whether he was going to get a new contract? Fortunately Dennis saw the point and I was impressed with Bob's assertiveness, as Dennis was a very good friend. I knew that guys play better when they're not getting too much strife. It was important for me to get this across to Bob, so that he could help create a relaxed ambience, where players aren't chastised strongly for making a mistake. Bob enjoyed a meeting of minds over cricket matters, and he would take enormous amounts of time to get his message across. The insistence on playing spinners differently was, in my opinion, the most vital element in Warwickshire's subsequent success. You can forget all that stuff about 'Larashire', and my captaincy, and Allan Donald's brilliant example: getting after the spinners set us apart from other sides, because we all did it, not just a few batsmen who were fine players of spin. There was a collective approach which stemmed from the cricket management encouraging everyone to play with spirit and freshness as long as the hard work had been done in the nets.

Bob was excellent on non-cricketing matters such as nutrition and a scientific approach to fitness. He brought with him not just a thorough knowledge of cricket and its techniques, but also the breadth of practical experience that would make us better cricketers. I had been concerned at the standard of fielding since I'd been at Edgbaston and Bob was onto that straight away. He knew that your skills suffer when you get tired, so he demanded greater levels of fitness, so that our fielding would stand up to a long day out in the middle under the sun. He brought in experts from Birmingham University to advise us on the proper diet, how to improve our flexibility, how to maintain stamina – all the things that other counties are embracing now, several years on. Bob was shrewd enough to realise that if he talked on and on about such matters, the lads would get bored, because they heard enough from him anyway, so an expert on such matters would automatically get their attention and the message would get home.

In cricketing terms, Bob would talk to every player on the staff at the end of the season, asking them what area constituted a weakness. He would identify it, then tell them to go away to work on it, and come back for next season, with that weakness turned into a strength. Roger Twose is just one example of the success of that approach. Bob felt he had a weakness against the short ball and told Roger to work on it in the winter. He came back with a revised technique and greater confidence against short-pitched bowling. By the time opposition bowlers had realised he was no longer vulnerable against that line of attack, Roger was scoring a lot of runs and enjoying a great season. A weakness had been turned into a strength by hard work and imaginative coaching.

When I first came to Warwickshire, Asif Din was our best fielder – yet in the modern game, Asif would only be classified as an average fielder, not an outstanding one. That was an indication of how far we needed to improve as a fielding side, even allowing for the inevitable weeding out of some senior players who weren't very good at that discipline. Bob Woolmer worked us hard in improving our catching and he did it in a typically imaginative way – with a tennis racket. He knew that a tennis ball is harder to catch than a cricket ball when you're working in close. A tennis ball can bounce out of your hands, and taking it cleanly really teaches you how to give with the ball at the moment of impact. Constant catching practice with a hard cricket ball can give you sore hands, so that when the chance comes out in the middle, you might subconsciously fail to go all the way for the snick. Bob would hit 50 catches a time to your left hand with a tennis ball, then another 50 to your other hand. He would advise you to go for a catch in the middle with both hands whenever possible, but his reasoning behind one-handed catching in practice was that it was harder: you would feel safer and more relaxed going for the chance with both hands in the field after gaining confidence with one-handed takes of a tennis ball. We knew that if the team's percentage of catching was high, it would be easier to win the championship. The high standard of our close catching in recent years has given us a head start over other counties and when I saw the Lancashire coach, David Lloyd, using the tennis racket in practice in the 1995 season, I felt proud that Warwickshire had been ahead of them by several years in that respect.

Our first season under Woolmer's coaching, in 1991, saw an immediate improvement. We batted much more positively, even if we didn't score massively. Our seam bowling attack of Allan Donald, Tim Munton, Gladstone Small and myself brought us 244 championship wickets between us, and I was pleased with my all-round efforts, averaging almost 49 with the bat and 21 with the ball. I relished batting as high as number five, and I was beginning to think my burning ambition to play for England wasn't as fanciful as I had thought, especially with Ian Botham in decline, as injuries piled up for him. It was more important, though, for the side to do well and we finished second in the championship, 13 points behind Essex, who were admittedly a stronger all-round unit with top quality spinners. The fact that we pressed them so hard, leading the table for three months, was a great consolation to us, justifying the positive way we played our cricket. We won as many games as Essex and our 11 victories would have brought us the title in five of the previous six years. Our tally of five away wins was the same as at Edgbaston (the other coming at Coventry), so we couldn't be accused of relying on favourable home conditions to get so close to the championship. At least, so we thought; we would have to get used to generalisations about the Edgbaston pitches and their effect on our continued success. That 1991 season was the first time we encountered the reluctance of so-called experts to give us credit for being a good side, rather than one which needed home advantage to win matches.

Andy Lloyd set the right example as captain in the field, always looking to force a win with positive field placings, keeping Allan Donald under wraps till he was needed, rather than over-bowling him. When he batted at number three, Andy played shots right from the start, making sure we had enough runs at speed to get among the opposition with our strong seam attack. Four-day cricket demands you get a fair quantity of runs at a good pace, otherwise you will struggle to get 20 wickets for victory especially if rain intervenes. I think Warwickshire realised that quicker than most counties, and Lloyd and Woolmer sorted out the correct strategy right from the off.

They also had no qualms about giving young players a chance. Jason Ratcliffe, at the age of 22, opened the innings most of the games in the championship, while 20-year-old Dominic Ostler was given the chance and the encouragement to bat at number four, and he responded magnificently. The fielding also improved greatly with so many young players coming through. That helped us in one-day competitions, with some success in all of them, even though we fell down at crucial times. Still, it was a very important season for this developing Warwickshire side. We responded eagerly to Woolmer's innovative ideas, to Lloyd's bold captaincy, and we were starting to gel as a unit. There was a lot of fun in the dressing-room as well, with the players enjoying the tension-free atmosphere – but we were also learning when to dig in and really concentrate at key moments in the match.

For me, it was a pleasure to be part of such a positive set-up, with plenty of give and take, easy banter, but a professional approach when needed. I hadn't regretted my move from Sussex at all, and I was sure Warwickshire were on the verge of great things. Success doesn't just happen overnight, and the contributions of Andy Lloyd, Bob Cottam and Bob Woolmer won't be forgotten by those of us who sprayed a lot of victory champagne around a few years later.

5

County Captain

At the end of the 1992 season, I succeeded Andy Lloyd as Warwickshire's captain. The news leaked out in a rather messy way, with two championship games left. Andy had been struggling with his form and fitness, and the club felt an announcement had to be made sooner rather than later, to avoid speculation. It didn't do much for morale in our dressing-room, though, and the way we subsided in our last match, against Kent, showed there was much to do. They got over 600 in their innings and bowled us out cheaply to win by an innings and plenty. We needed to show guts to hang in for a draw, but all we did was play shots and get out, as if we had given up. I felt our younger players needed to be harder mentally: Keith Piper seemed more pleased with the six he hit than anything; he seemed to ignore the fact that he had got out cheaply in the first innings and we had lost badly. It seemed as if we didn't care in that Kent game; that attitude would have to change.

I had been attracted to captaincy in my Sussex days and John Barclay had encouraged me, telling me to keep thinking and make contributions. I hadn't forgotten the stick I took for voicing my England ambitions, though, so I just kept making mental notes and trying to work out what my captains were thinking of when they made key decisions. I enjoyed the bluff and counter-bluff of captaincy, trying it on with the opposite number, feeling each other out in the negotiations you often had with three-day cricket. In the short game, you often had to rely on nods and winks, especially if rain had interrupted the game. You'd agree a target on the third and final morning, with the batting side scoring runs to set up a target for the fourth innings. One game at Edgbaston when I was playing for Sussex showed up the dilemma.

Asif Din and Alvin Kallicharran tossed up some stuff that was supposed to give us 150 more runs before the declaration. Unfortunately for us, we lost wickets and when Tony Pigott and I came together we were seven down and still 80 short of the target before declaring. Suddenly, Warwickshire's captain, Norman Gifford, realised he could bowl us out cheaply, leaving them to chase around 200, rather than the negotiated 250, and he started to play proper cricket. He took off the part-time spinners, dispensed with the attacking field, daring us to take risks. I blocked out two maiden overs from Gifford and he started to chunter. But I knew what he was trying to do. Tony Pigott continued to swing his bat, as Gifford said, 'You're doing the right thing, Tony – but what about the other bloke?' Pigott said, 'I agree with you, Giff' but I chipped in, 'I know what you're trying, Giff', and he eventually threw the ball back to Asif Din in disgust. Pigott was happy – he got his maiden hundred – and we ended up setting them exactly the amount agreed. My captain, Paul Parker, said I was absolutely right to play it the hard way, to have spotted that Gifford had changed his tactics.

I had definite aims when I took over the Warwickshire captaincy. The aggression that Andy Lloyd had instilled into the side, and his desire to go hard for the win, were qualities that I had valued. We needed to be fitter, though, and Bob Woolmer and I decided more attention to detail in that area was needed. Fielding had to improve, and that begins with increased fitness. I also wanted the players to be more respectful of each other in certain areas. Racist remarks have always annoyed me; I've never understood why people think racist jibes are funny, and sometimes in our dressing-room I had seen that one or two of our players had been upset at a few comments that were tactless and disrespectful. To me, that affected morale and it had to stop. I also wanted us to stop mickey-taking on cricketing matters. Now I'm all for leg-pulling and lively banter, but I don't think it's good for team morale if a player's defects as a cricketer get highlighted and he is denigrated in front of others. It's a fine line, I agree, but players are more sensitive about their game than they usually let on.

There'd been times when I had to keep the peace in the slips between Dominic Ostler and the wicket-keeper Keith Piper over the responsibility for a catch. I'd be at first slip, the edge would travel between myself and Keith and Dominic would say, 'Don't you want to catch them today then, Keith?' Now Keith has a quick temper and I worried that he wouldn't be focused on the next ball because of Dominic's remark. Incidentally, Dominic would only be retaliating to Keith calling him 'Costus', when he had dropped a catch earlier – 'Costus' as in 'That could cost us the match'. It all seems fairly trivial but I have seen many a young player's composure suffer because of mickey-taking. I also didn't like it when Jason Ratcliffe came up with a new nickname for Roger Twose – 'Boards,' as in 'The ball keeps getting hit to the boards.' This came after Roger had been carted around during a bowling spell. That one soon spread to any suffering bowler. On the face of it, a guy might take it well and spit back with a cutting remark of his own, but what was it doing inside his head? Was it reducing his morale and effectiveness as a cricketer?

Early on, the new attitude to cricketing defects didn't work all that well. The brain often lags behind the quick mouth – it certainly does with me at times! – and I'd be pulling the guys up all the time. 'That's a cricketing issue,' I'd say, 'you can't take the piss on that.' I then went the other way, saying it was open season, and I'd go round the dressing-room sledging everyone for their cricketing frailties. The point of that was to underline that we all have cricketing defects and it was up to all of us to overcome them – together. It was all designed to protect a player's confidence: when that ball's in the air for a vital catch, I want that fielder to be shouting 'Mine, Mine!', wanting the ball to come to him, not pulling up the ladder to leave the responsibility to someone else.

At Sussex, I had seen how a negative atmosphere can affect a cricketer, so that he doesn't give of his best. Underneath that macho bravado, every professional cricketer is sensitive. We all question our ability. I certainly do it all the time. One day, when I was knocking up on the outfield, I was playing a few front foot drives, and Keith Piper came over to look, only to end up sniggering. Being laughed at while you're practising doesn't exactly help anyone's confidence and I told Keith so. I know I don't look pretty: I've gone into the indoor nets, armed with a video camera, and tried to bat like Mark Waugh, but it hasn't worked, it's not me. I used to suffer badly from fear of failure, even though my reputation is one of being supremely confident. I'm sure even the most confident and gifted players have flashes of self-doubt. For me, it was crucial that the Warwickshire players would be encouraged in those areas, in a supportive environment rather than one where everyone was on their guard, waiting for the next jibe.

The players needed to feel there was a genuine desire in the team for individuals to do well. It's hard for a senior player to change his attitude, as he becomes more introverted, worried about his form, whether he'll be kept on long enough to qualify for a benefit, with so many bright youngsters knocking on the door. We were lucky at Edgbaston with the senior players when I started as captain: they wanted success as much as I did, and we worked to create an atmosphere in which the younger players weren't intimidated, but made to feel equal and encouraged to speak their minds at team meetings. I wanted the younger guys to feel totally focused on winning the game for the team, rather than shining as individuals.

Early in his career, Keith Piper was too worried about what others were saying about him off the field. He'd want to impress the opposition with his batting, or the press when he kept wicket. We'd have to tell him just to forget what anyone else might be saying about him off the field. He's now a top wicket-keeper, not just because of his great natural talent, but because he's concentrating better.

In one of my early games at Edgbaston, Asif Din was at fault when running out Paul Smith in a tense one-day game. I was next man in and as I came to the wicket Asif said, 'What are they saying in the dressing-room about that run out?' I had to tell him to forget it, that was history, to focus on the rest of the game. Asif is a lovely, sensitive guy, but in those days he took too much notice of his cricketing environment, he was looking over his shoulder too much. Norman Gifford hauled him over the coals one day when he tried to hit the spinner over the top and holed out to mid-on, so he was afraid to try it again for a long time. He wasn't made to feel comfortable about his game, and above all he needed to be encouraged and backed by the management.

To me, it was a matter of self-esteem. I wanted my players to feel good about their efforts towards their game, and feel comfortable enough to speak up on cricketing issues in a team meeting. I didn't want anyone feeling they were too inexperienced to be entitled to make a contribution. I'd loved the way John Barclay had handled me at Sussex. He really wanted us to do well, he didn't have an ounce of professional jealousy in him. He'd create a framework whereby he'd encourage us as individuals in the desire that the team would gel as a unit. It wasn't Johnny's fault that some players were too selfish to go all the way with him. He'd talk so enthusiastically to me about my future: 'Yes, I really think you could play for England, and captain a county. Come up to me and talk any time, give me your views.' I couldn't believe that he was so interested in what I had to say when I wasn't exactly setting the county scene on fire, but he was so warm and supportive. At Edgbaston, I wanted to forge that kind of atmosphere, where the players were delighted for the individual who did well, where petty jealousies were absent, leading to an encouraging, successful environment.

I've been amazed at how slow some counties have been to cotton on to the necessity for a strong team spirit.

In 1995, I saw at first hand a terrible piece of man-management, and a young lad called Carl Crowe suffered. We were playing Leicestershire and young Crowe dropped a catch at cover off Gordon Parsons. The bowler shouted, 'Come on, what's going on!' and Alan Mullally said, 'How are we going to win games when you blokes can't catch?' Parsons eventually calmed down when Paul Nixon, their wicket-keeper, pointed out, 'Does he think we don't want to catch it?', but the damage was done for a lad making his first-class debut. He slunk around in the field, and you could tell he didn't want the ball to come near him.

That night, I went out for a drink and Mullally hinted that he'd like to come to Warwickshire. I said there was no way that I'd want him at Edgbaston with his attitude, because of the way he, a senior player, had treated a lad making his debut on the field. I told him, 'You made him feel inadequate and he's gone home, probably thinking you don't like him or rate him.' Mullally ended up apologising to me about the way he had treated his own team-mate! I told him not to apologise to me, because he had helped Warwickshire, but he ought to apologise to young Crowe next morning. I was also disappointed with Nigel Briers, the Leicestershire captain, over that incident. He clapped his hands and said, 'Come on boys, keep going', but he didn't seem to offer much consolation to Crowe. That wouldn't happen at Warwickshire. You must allow your players to relax, to feel you're all going in the same direction. No one drops a catch on purpose. County cricket can be very frustrating because of the bowlers' attitude to the batsmen and vice versa. That can develop camps and rifts in a team, as well as the destructive 'fear of failure' syndrome.

I was determined to eliminate tension as much as possible. So we brought in a 'smile break'. I'd read about laughter therapy classes, where psychologists have explained that laughing eases stress, relaxes the class, and leads to contagious laughter in the group. You feel good about yourself and upbeat about life if you laugh a lot. Presumably laughter releases a chemical in the body, it acts as a relaxing agent, and it helps you approach the job on an even keel. Instead of feeling tense about our lack of wickets when fielding, I'd say, 'Come on fellas, they've put on a hundred', and start laughing. We'd all join in, the opposition batsmen would look at us, puzzled, and it gave us a boost. Shouting didn't relieve the tension, but the team laugh certainly did, especially when we'd catch sight of Gladstone Small refusing to laugh out loud, but happy to compromise by smiling broadly.

Sometimes we'd play football with an imaginary ball, as the bowler walked back to the mark. Extra cover would chip the ball to mid-off, who would then control it on his chest and boot it over to mid-on, and so it would go on around the field, till the imaginary ball would come to Gladstone, who would kick it out of the ground – and that would start us all laughing. Sometimes it would be a basketball move, with the fielder spinning the imaginary ball on his finger. It may have looked daft at various times, but the trick is to laugh at yourself. On a hard day, when you're looking for some luck and a breakthrough, that feeling of togetherness, of fun, can lift the bowlers. You're sharing an experience, having a laugh – plus the opposition don't know what to make of it all.

I've always liked to win as a cricketer, because I also like to have a party, have a good time and relax with my team-mates. So when I became captain, I didn't have to alter my attitude to winning. But I had to become a better actor when we lost. It was important to avoid getting too morbid after a bad day, and here again I'd learned a lot from John Barclay's sunny attitude. The captain needs to act out the part, to say the correct upbeat things after a bad performance. So I'd say things like, 'Gee were we unlucky today! I can't believe it. Never mind, fellas, a better day tomorrow! Well tried! Have a good night out, and we'll be fresh for them tomorrow, a fresh start!' It sounds trite, but I felt the captain had to be up tempo, I didn't want the guys creeping around, feeling sorry for themselves.

I also wanted a lot of physical contact among the players out in the middle – lots of hugging and hand-slapping when we got a wicket. I know the old-stagers tut-tut and say, 'You're only doing your job, what's the big deal?' but I wanted to show that enjoying the game was important to us. It's great when the fielder at fine leg runs up to the bowler and says 'Well done', rather than sitting on the fence by the boundary, having a rest, looking around. I wanted us all to share in our successes, to be happy to be out there playing for Warwickshire, sharing the good moments.

To me, it was just a case of fine tuning when I took over as captain of Warwickshire. The raw materials were there. We had some fine young players coming through, and our fielding was getting better as a result, although it had to improve even more for my satisfaction. I was conscious that Allan Donald, our matchwinner, had to be handled as well by me as Andy Lloyd had done. When I first captained him, at Old Trafford, he really threw me. After two overs, Allan said he didn't want to bowl any more. I was astonished, because the hallmark of Allan Donald has always been a willingness to bowl. My strategy that day was to start with a good blast with the new ball by Allan and Gladstone Small, and I had to be firm with Allan. I was club vice captain at the time and it wasn't easy telling him he had to bowl. That was the only time I ever had a problem with him. Under the expert tutelage of Bob Woolmer, he grew in stature as a fast bowler and gave us a marvellous cutting edge.

I was disappointed in my first season as captain that we lost Allan's services for the last six weeks of the season. He had to go to Sri Lanka with South Africa, and with Tim Munton and Gladstone Small both suffering injuries, our seam attack was greatly reduced in effectiveness. Compare the statistics in 1991, when those three plus myself took 244 championship wickets. In 1993 the figure was down to just 95. So our cutting edge was blunted, and we were short of quality spinners as well, even though Neil Smith was developing impressively. With four-day cricket now the norm in the championship, we needed greater depth and variety in spin to make a serious challenge, a fact underlined when Middlesex outplayed us at Edgbaston on a wicket ideal for John Emburey and Phil Tufnell.

I was nervous the first time I led Warwickshire that season, because although I had captained the side a fair amount before that first game against Northants, this was the real thing: I couldn't shelter behind being just the stand-in. We beat Northants by eight wickets and I enjoyed an unbeaten 87, and then we went to Kent and beat them. So that was a good start against two of the strongest county sides. But it didn't last. We tailed away in the championship after Donald left for Sri Lanka, and injuries to key bowlers didn't help either. No one averaged more than 40 in the championship, only two got over a thousand runs and the young players were having to learn rapidly. But I was glad to get the likes of Trevor Penney, Neil Smith and Michael Bell playing, because they would learn more in the hard world of the first eleven, rather than chugging along in the seconds. Although we finished second bottom of the championship in my first season as captain, there were encouraging signs. We just needed to sharpen up our approach, be more influential in the spin bowling department, keep the seamers fit and get more from our batsmen. The competition for places was increasing, and the 'comfort zone' was being eliminated.

With half the season gone, it was clear to me that we needed a good run in the Nat West Trophy to give us confidence and an incentive for the rest of that 1993 season. We had gone out in the Benson and Hedges Cup in the first round, we were nowhere in the championship and struggling in the Sunday League. I decided to rest Munton and Small as they battled against injuries, and keep them fresh for the shorter games in the Nat West. Our semi-final win down at Taunton showed the kind of resilience I wanted. Somerset, a dangerous one-day side, must have fancied a target of 253 at just over four an over, especially when Gladstone Small limped off after bowling only five overs. He had already taken two key wickets by then, but I then had to fiddle some overs from bowlers who would possibly not have been used. Jason Ratcliffe and Roger Twose gave me six overs that only went for 24 as our tight fielding and overall discipline made up for the loss of Small. I was really pleased with that effort, and so we had got to Lord's after falling at the semi-final stage in the last two seasons.

Our remarkable win against Sussex in the Final was a triumph for positive thinking, a refusal to think we would lose. It's been called the greatest one-day Final, and it's hard to argue with that. We had to chase 322, the highest total yet in a Lord's Final, and we finally did it in the dark, playing with great heart and aggression. Our bowlers had been carted around by David Smith and Martin Speight and a lesser side would have been demoralised, especially after losing both openers at 18, and Dominic Ostler at 93/3. But everybody kept going, scoring at nearly a run a ball. Asif Din and I enjoyed a record partnership and Asif's hundred in as many balls was remarkable. Even then, when he was out in the penultimate over, we weren't fancied, but we won it off the last ball. It was a fantastic win, against the odds, with the lead coming from two of our most experienced players – Paul Smith and Asif. We won it without our overseas

player, Allan Donald, and with our other two Test bowlers –
Gladstone Small and Tim Munton – going for a lot of runs.
Young players like Neil Smith and Roger Twose kept their
heads, bowling very sensibly, while Roger faced the most important delivery of his life, getting the necessary run off the last ball
of the match and the only delivery he faced. For me, there were
heroes everywhere as I looked around that deliriously happy
dressing-room at Lord's.

I'm not sure my joy was universally shared around Edgbaston,
though. Soon after, one committee man said, 'Even though
we've won a trophy, it's been a disappointing season.' I thought
that harsh. We'd struggled with injuries, a team in transition,
with a new captain and our star bowler away for the last six weeks
of the season – yet we had pulled off a miraculous victory in a
Lord's Final. I thought at the time it was a highly significant victory, a vindication of our positive approach and the collective
strength of our team spirit. The players took enormous pride in
that win, and you could see our confidence rise as a result. Next
year, we created history by winning three trophies and coming
second in the fourth. Brian Lara was with us then, and his fabulous batting meant a great deal to us – but the win we snatched
at the death the previous September at Lord's was hugely significant. It allowed me as captain to justify our aggressive style of
playing, it brought self-belief to the younger guys, and revi-
talised the older ones. We came to believe that no game was ever
lost by us until the facts said otherwise. If we could beat Sussex
in those circumstances, we could take on anybody. Only those
who don't play modern first-class cricket underestimate the
importance of self-confidence. It comes and goes, but the
crucial thing is to hang on to it as long as you can, and if it's
waning in an individual, you need supportive team-mates to
revive it. I felt we were getting there at Edgbaston by the end of
the 1993 season.

I found captaincy stimulating and satisfying, but it was difficult to switch off mentally. I tend to be very analytical and at the
end of the day's play I like to dawdle in the dressing-room,
mulling over the events out in the middle, wondering if I'd got
it right. There are times when I don't want to talk cricket, as my

Mum sometimes finds when she stays with me for home games. Richard Illingworth had me caught at mid-off once, when I was trying to hit him over the top. That dismissal annoyed me, and when I got back home, I could see my mother wanted to discuss something with me as we sat having dinner. I asked her what was wrong and she said, 'I thought it was a bit early to try hitting him over the top.' I started to explain I was trying to push mid-off back, so I could pick up singles, that I just got too close to the ball, but then I told her, 'That's it! No more cricket talk tonight!' Yet sometimes I'll happily talk cricket with her or chat about it on the phone to my brothers. Normally, though, I prefer to switch off if I can, take in a movie with a huge box of popcorn or nip along to Ronnie Scott's Jazz Club in Birmingham and listen to some quality music. It's important to engage the brain because that shuts off cricket.

But it's not easy. I dream about cricket. Tactics actually come to me in my sleep! I also have nightmares that the boys won't follow my instructions when we're out in the field: that fine leg won't go out there, and the bowler shouts, 'Where's the fine leg gone?' I actually have a recurring dream that I can't put my pads on and it's my turn to bat! Cricket is such a dominant factor in my brain that I'll stop mid-sentence when I'm discussing something else if I've thought of something I should have done on the field. Sometimes it's impossible to get away from it.

Bob Woolmer was a constant support during my early period as captain. We'd adjourn regularly to T.G.I. Fridays restaurant in Birmingham, and while I chewed on my pasta, Bob would demolish a huge rack of lamb, polish off some red wine – and we'd talk cricket. He had such a passion for the game that we'd go into all sorts of areas, finding out different ways to motivate the players, to stretch them. Bob would tell me where I'd fallen down in the job, but always in a constructive, understanding manner.

My communication skills have sometimes let me down as captain. At times I've been in my own world, with my brain going at a hundred miles an hour – so that I've forgotten to talk to a player about something that was important. I really ought to have got into the habit of writing things down that need to be attended to, but I never get round to it. I don't always put in the necessary hours after close of play, because I feel I must get away from an atmosphere that can become claustrophobic. That's also selfishness on my part, I should be more thorough and professional in my dealings with players. Roger Twose, a forthright character and a man I respected, used to tell me that I ought to have more one-on-ones with the guys, rather than talking collectively. That's all very well, but there are only so many hours in the day, and I also had to think about my own game. I saw how John Barclay got ground down by all the minutiae of captaincy – the committee meetings, the gripes from players, the earbashers in the bar – so that he had to take a couple of games off by the end of the season. I didn't want that to happen to me, but I admit there have been occasions when I've been distracted and not told a player something important to him. When I first became captain, I told the guys that if someone was going to be left out, I wouldn't go into detail at the time. I'd tap the player on the shoulder half an hour before the start, tell him the score and say that we'd talk in detail later, or to go and see the coach for further explanation. I had to be hard-nosed about it on the first morning of the match, because I had my own preparations to organise, and also the rest of the team to consider. It sounds harsh, but the dropped player isn't much use to us at that stage, and the last thing I wanted was to have ranting and raving when I was trying to get everyone motivated for the match ahead. The players just had to accept that was to be the way of it, but I'm sure some were upset at the way things were done.

I've got a quick temper and at times I do lose it in front of the guys. It happened when I dropped Paul Taylor at slip off Tim Munton's bowling in that fantastic championship match against Northants in 1995. That was the best four-day game I ever played in, and with both sides locked at the top of the table, tensions were running high, when I dropped the ball. I felt awful, because runs were precious and that might have been an important miss. Straight away, Keith Piper told me, 'You're falling back', which really threw me. He was trying to give me coaching tips, ten seconds after I'd dropped the ball, instead of offering the usual encouragement I'd expect from a team-mate.

Keith and I are great mates – we used to share a house together – but he can flare up at the wrong times or say the wrong thing, and this was such an occasion.

Soon after that we came off at the end of the session, and as we walked into the dressing-room, I saw my helmet on the floor. I kicked out at it, it sailed across the room, and hit our coach, Phil Neale, on the back of the head. It must have looked very funny, but I shouted, 'Sorry, Phil!' and went straight into the showers area. I undressed, stood under the shower for a long time and cooled down. It was important for me to get away from the rest of the team and conceal how upset I was. At other times, I'd go into the kitchen and have a cup of coffee if I thought things were getting on top of me – just to get away from the players, to ensure harsh words weren't uttered in the heat of the moment.

Out on the field, I think I'm quite good on tactics. I like trying to be one jump ahead, to juggle the resources and keep our spirits up. I'm quite firm with the bowlers when they want a certain field and I disagree. Tim Munton likes to have a third man, but there are times on certain wickets when I'd rather have a fifth slip. You can see a bowler's disappointment when they don't get the field they want, but in the end the captain carries the can for results, so he should have what he thinks is best. I liked the players to express their views and play with aggression, but at times I needed to dampen things down. Keith Piper can be difficult to handle, but I liked his infectious, bubbly character on the pitch. Roger Twose was another challenge at times. I really admired Roger's approach to cricket – he was full of guts and passion, yet cool in a crisis, an absolute godsend. But he was very vocal and could get the red mists very easily. When he came on to bowl, he would often ask for a defensive field and if I overruled him, he'd say, 'You always get the field you want when you're bowling.' I'd have to point that I was the captain and he'd spit back, 'You're a crap captain', and then I'd say something like 'And you're a fat buffalo, Roger.' The cut and thrust of sophisticated debate!

In my early days, I noticed how strong-minded captains had to be if they were to be successful. Mike Gatting was very hard when he led the Middlesex side. It was sink or swim with him, if you were one of his players or an opponent. I've heard some amazing bust-ups on the field between Gatting and his two spinners, Phil Edmonds and John Emburey, especially when Gatt wouldn't give them the field they wanted. I once heard Embers tell him, 'Put someone there who's quicker than you – you can't run any more, you're too fat.' Gatt doesn't find it personal, even when we have a laugh at his expense on the field. It's no secret that Gatt likes his food, so whenever he's batting, and the interval is coming up, we'll start shouting, 'Come on fellas – it's getting near to lunch, Gatt's concentration's going', or 'Great line that, Allan – Gatt likes a nibble, he can't stop having a nibble.' Gatt is so competitive in everything he does that he won't let things like that bother him. I really admire the way he has kept up his standards over the years as captain. When I took the Warwickshire job, I asked his advice and he told me, 'Don't forget about your own game. If you're playing well, it'll help you in the job.' He was absolutely right, and on a personal level, our success in 1995 meant more to me than our historic season of '94, because I contributed more as a player.

Graham Gooch was another who set the highest personal standards to the rest of his side as captain. He came from a tough school at Essex, where he and Keith Fletcher made sure the players knew what was expected of them. However I felt Goochy's body language did let him down whenever a catch was dropped, or his bowlers didn't get the right line. That was because it meant so much to Goochy and he had difficulty understanding why others in the team lacked his dedication and desire to succeed. He was terrific to me when I played for him with England; I think he liked my bubbly attitude and I found him very supportive. He used to tell me to play the way I did for Warwickshire and I was impressed with the way he led by example and trained so hard. Goochy was quite right to say that times had changed, that you couldn't have a good night out and then expect to turn it on at full power next day in a vital game. He felt you had to treat your body like an engine, putting the best oil in it, with regular services. Goochy's image as the unsmiling Roundhead was a total travesty of the man. On my first England tour in 1992, to New Zealand and the World Cup, he was great company. He loved a laugh, enjoyed a drink at the right times and encouraged the players fully. Goochy was right to ignore those who didn't know him and just looked for the generalisation; he concentrated on his own self-esteem and won the respect of the players because of his self-discipline and professional standards.

Another hard captain was Allan Border. He was as tough as nails on the field, and happy to hand out the verbals. When Warwickshire played the Australians on the 1993 tour, he sledged me for playing the reverse sweep, asking me what kind of a (expletive deleted) shot that was. I was more impressed with his tactical grasp, though. When I batted against the off-spin of Tim May, he started off with a slip, short leg and silly point. After I'd got to 16, he had just one man round the bat at silly point, and he had sealed off all the gaps. He'd taken a good look at where I played the ball and I was stuck. I thought, 'Where the hell am I going to get a run?' and I just dried up. May had me caught at silly point for 23, but it was the shrewd captaincy of Border that did it for me.

Chris Cowdrey was chalk-and-cheese to Border, but I always admired the forceful way he led the Kent side. He was like John Barclay in the way he'd rush around the field, shouting 'Come on chaps', full of verve and encouragement. I warmed to him as a person and a captain and thought he was the kind of guy I'd love to play for. I thought about going to Kent when I left Sussex, and it was because of Chris Cowdrey. His achievement in taking Kent to within one point of the championship in 1988 was remarkable. Worcestershire had all the big guns – Botham, Dilley, Hick, plus some emerging England players – while Kent had no stars, yet missed out by a single point. They were a brilliant fielding side, with Cowdrey setting the perfect example.

Mike Brearley was a fantastic captain in his tactical awareness, with the knowledge of when to squeeze the opposition batsmen. When I first came to England as a teenager and joined the MCC groundstaff, I'd watch how he calmly manipulated his Middlesex bowlers and fielders while I was working the Lord's scoreboard. You always knew who was in charge, even though

Brearley would just wave a hand or clap quietly. His fielders looked towards him all the time, and he seemed to know the geometry of the field so well. I loved the way he used his spinners, Phil Edmonds and John Emburey. His two best fielders, Graham Barlow and Roland Butcher, would be at mid-wicket and extra cover, covering huge areas of ground between them, and then he'd have a short leg, a deep mid-wicket, a mid-on and silly point. It was an in-and-out field, so that the batsman couldn't go for the big hit because he had the man out at deep mid-wicket, and there were no quick singles to scamper with Barlow and Butcher on either side of the wicket. Brearley seemed to know just when a batsman was going to be positive, so he'd send a man out into the country, or if the batsman was being passive, he'd call up Clive Radley to silly point and often he'd snaffle one.

That Middlesex side under Brearley were streets ahead in terms of aggression and tactical skill on the field, and the captain pulled the strings so capably. No wonder he was such a great captain of England, especially with so many superb bowlers to choose from. All the talk about Brearley's supposed defects as a batsman seemed irrelevant to me. Middlesex and England won more games than most under his captaincy, and there was a common thread running through their confident performances: they had a masterful captain who knew how to get the best out of his players. Clearly he had thought deeply about the art of captaincy.

6

The Winning Habit

In the space of two years, and over three seasons, Warwickshire created cricket history by winning six trophies. We came to regard Lord's as our second home, winning three of the four Finals we appeared in. From a professional point of view, being the county champions in '94 and '95 gave us all the greatest pleasure and if I had to pick one trophy that pleased me most of all, it would be retaining the championship. My contribution was more satisfying than in '94 when I played in only eight championship matches, through injury and poor form: the following season, I averaged 34 with the bat and 17 with the ball, and I missed only two games. Above all, though, that title win in '95 was a fantastic achievement. There had been a lot of gripes around the county circuit and in the media that our first championship win stemmed from the brilliance of Brian Lara and the erratic Edgbaston wickets. Yet our batsmen all scored runs in 1994, and at a good speed, and the fact that we recorded more wins than any other county since 1979 surely indicated our all-round strength, home and away. Taking the title by a margin of 42 points didn't seem to cut much ice: it was far easier just to dub us 'Larashire'.

Next season, we were still undervalued even though our percentage of victories was the greatest in the history of the county championship, 14 out of 17. Of course, the long, hot summer helped, and it's daft to try to make comparisons with other sides from different eras, but surely Warwickshire deserved more praise than we got? Eventually, it came, grudgingly, in the face of some persuasive factual evidence on our behalf. Half our victories came away from home, on pitches that were prepared to draw the sting from Allan Donald, and the margin of those victories was very wide – three by an innings, two by ten wickets, one by nine wickets and the other by 111 runs. Yet we still had to face criticism that we won the title because the Edgbaston wickets favoured our seam attack. That might have been relevant if our three international seamers had operated together on those pitches, but Gladstone Small and Tim Munton suffered injuries, so that Donald, Small and Munton were in harness together for just one championship match that season – and that, at home, was drawn. With Brian Lara no longer with us, our allegedly weak batting seemed to get along, with six batsmen averaging over 40. Only Middlesex scored more batting bonus points than us, by a matter of two points.

Eventually, I found it rather amusing that so many so-called experts kept shaking their heads at the supremacy of a side with average players, and just one world-class performer – Lara in '94 and Donald in '95. With a bit of luck, we might have swept to the full hand of trophies in '94, when it could be argued that the toss of a coin thwarted us at the Nat West Final, forcing us to bat with the ball seaming all round the place. As we only lost the '95 Sunday League by run rate, after recovering from a bad start to post ten successive wins, we might have collected seven trophies in two seasons. Now that would have been a difficult one for our detractors to sort out!

We even seemed to take some of our fellow professionals by surprise. When I joined the England tour party in South Africa in 1995/96, I used to enjoy winding up some of the lads who still couldn't fathom out why we had been so successful. Darren Gough and Mark Ilott were particularly stubborn about our successes. Darren used to say, 'You're not the best team', and so the debate would begin in the team bus as we travelled somewhere. I'd point out the facts, yet he and Mark would keep saying, 'Lancashire are the best team, they've got the best players. I didn't need any invitation to stick up for my players, especially with so many Lancashire guys on the trip, who would be listening to me as we debated the issue. It was always good-humoured, though, and Goughy made us all laugh with his dogmatic stance, in the face of overwhelming statistical evidence. In the end, he compromised – he said we didn't have the best players, but we played best together as a team. Surely that was all any county captain could ask for. I was quite happy with that grudging admission from Goughy and in fun told him, 'You and the other lads are very welcome to come down to Edgbaston and polish our trophies. If you're very good, we'll let you lift them up!'

Others in the first-class game were more generous, though. When Nick Knight, Dominic Ostler and Keith Piper toured Pakistan with England 'A', the coach, John Emburey, made it clear to his players that they had to approach their cricket like the Warwickshire side. I was very pleased to be told this on the grapevine, especially as Embers had been in the Middlesex team that came second to us in our '95 championship win. He also made some appreciative remarks in Wisden: 'They are now way ahead of other clubs in terms of talking out a game plan and at stretching their players, making a team of average players a highly successful unit. Other clubs, note.' I do, however, disagree that we were a team made up of average players. Some of Dominic Ostler's strokeplay was at times breathtaking and Trevor Penney and Keith Piper have been quite excellent in the field, better in my view than any other cricketers in the country in their specialist positions. I could go on all day about the aspects of individual brilliance possessed by each player in that successful Warwickshire side – but let's say that 'average' isn't the word to use. Mark Nicholas, the Hampshire captain, came into our dressing-room after we had won the '94 title by beating his side and asked our secret. He later wrote about us in very interesting terms, saying that he couldn't think of another team who wanted each other to do so well, with no hint of rivalry. Mark felt that the supportive environment that had been created had allowed positive cricket to flow. He was right!

So what else was the secret of Warwickshire's success? Luck for a start. Cricket is not an exact science, that's why it's so fascinating. I hear commentators say, 'You get out what you put in', but I don't buy that. Devon Malcolm bowled his heart out for

England at Perth in '95, yet they kept dropping catches off him, and he took 2/198 in the match. Wasim Khan did very well for us in his first season in '95, yet he was dropped several times in his early innings. He ended up averaging 46 in the championship. Luck comes and goes at bewildering times in a cricketer's career, and you make the most of it when it comes. We were very lucky that Manoj Prabhakar's injured ankle meant we had to turn to Brian Lara to replace him in April 1994. When he scored 375 against England a few days after agreeing to join us, we felt even luckier. He then scored six championship hundreds in his first seven innings for us, including that amazing 501 not out against Durham, and we were on a roll. Brian's positive example only matched the way we were going to approach our cricket that season, but the speed at which he scored his runs was crucial. Throughout that season, he scored his championship runs at the rate of five and a half per six balls, an amazing performance. That rate gave our bowlers more time to bowl out the opposition twice, a vital asset in four-day cricket.

Apart from our great fortune in having Lara with us, our success owed much to planning and attitude. The seeds had been sown by Andy Lloyd and Bob Cottam in terms of attitude and getting in some good young players. That 1989 Nat West gave us some breathing space and I saw our 1993 triumph in the same competition as justification of the work put in by Bob Woolmer and the cricket management.

The first time I met Bob I told him I felt it was the cricket management's job to make sure the players at Edgbaston were better prepared than any other county – surely this would give us a better chance? Bob was receptive and I appreciated his honesty when in his first team chat he told us he was still learning as a coach. His efforts could not have been greater. He ensured we became better prepared than ever before. He brought in specialists – psychologists, doctors of nutrition and sports scientists – to help with the fitness. The truth is that Bob knew enough about all these areas of expertise to educate the team himself, but he realised that players pay more attention when it's being explained by outsiders with letters after their names. Bob was such an innovative coach and encouraged all the players to communicate at team discussions. We had more meet-ings and fun when Bob arrived than in any other previous season. It was important to sit down and discuss regularly how we could improve, how we could surprise the opposition. It's a common complaint from older cricketers that young players don't talk enough cricket, they prefer to be off quickly after the day has ended, but Bob Woolmer and I didn't want that. It was very gratifying to see the young lads talking about the game in the bar, in the dressing-room, or during the day when we were batting. They became deep thinkers, ready to challenge the views of the senior players, and that democratic atmosphere was good for team spirit. Bob Woolmer had once told Andy Lloyd, 'You don't realise how important it is for the captain to set the tone of the day', and I realised that it was up to me initially to make sure we weren't going to be lethargic. A fair degree of bluffing was needed at times – you can't always feel like cracking jokes and smiling – but I think Bob Woolmer and I managed to make our dressing-room sound chirpy and bubbly. The sound of laughter does wonders for morale in any team environment.

We didn't go in for regimented things at Edgbaston, but some matters are important, and I was very keen on communi-cating my thoughts. At the start of each season, I would stand up at the first big team meeting and emphasise the points that to me were vital: 'You're not under any pressure to win a trophy. I want you to enjoy it, above all. Get behind your team-mates, do your best every ball and you can be proud of yourselves. Sorry, guys, but I'm going to get a big philosophical and spiritual here. Seriously, I don't care if we don't win anything this year. Fellas, we chase a ball around a field for a job. We're not important. We don't save lives. We're entertainers. In 20 years, no one's going to really care how we did this year! Someone might be talking about it around a dinner table, but you're not going to be there. It's really not that important. Cricket will come and go in your lives, so enjoy it while you're here. What you will have forever is your self-esteem. Now winning games doesn't help that, but doing your best every day does. Guys, let's really enjoy this year!' It would then tend to be a bit quiet for a few seconds before Roger Twose or Keith Piper would appear moved, and shout something like, 'Yeah, let's do it!', and slap each other on the back. Roger's favourite saying was, 'I love you great guys,' and that would always get a laugh, but he was trying to show how much it meant to him to be part of a team that was giving a hundred per cent. I really meant it when I'd tell the players to forget about the pressure of winning trophies – that was the responsibility of the coach and the captain, they were the ones who had to get the best out of the players. I wanted them to feel as relaxed as possible, as I believe you play your best cricket when you're relaxed and confident. I was trying to take the pressure off them by making them realise it's just a game. I believe in total encouragement, enthusing about the most complex sport in the world, hopefully lifting spirits and motivating tired bodies if necessary.

I'm also quite keen on group communication before each session. Sometimes, it'll be a quick word along the lines of 'Come on fellas, that wicket's going to deteriorate, first innings runs would be nice.' If we'd been batting and we'd got to lunchtime, I'd question the batsmen who'd been in, and ask them to tell us about the pitch. What pace is it? Is there any turn? Most would elaborate and discuss particular strengths and weaknesses. Roger Twose used to be the most in-depth: he was a fine communicator as well as an intelligent cricketer. Dominic Ostler's descriptions of the condition of the wicket were always good for a laugh. In his early days, he would blush and shrug his shoulders, before stuttering a few words. He's such a nice bloke, and at times I felt sorry I had to put him on the spot, but I knew in the long run it would help his confidence. After a while, Dom would come up with comments that appeared to the point and arrogant like, 'It's flat, there's nothing going on, just smash it!' – as if he'd rehearsed his words. He has now matured into a very self-confident man, with a certain presence at the crease that shows his increased confidence and he communicates as well as anyone now in the dressing-room.

Team meetings can also be good fun. At times Roger Twose would go totally over the top, eyes bulging, veins in the neck throbbing, roaring out, 'Yeh! Let's go for them, come on!' You had to tell Roger that the bell hadn't sounded yet, and we still had five minutes to go! Then he would call me 'Big Ears' to take the attention away from himself and that would raise a laugh. The trick, I feel, is to blend information with informality. At the close of play, we might have a de-briefing as the players change. It depends on how the game has gone. If we've had a bad day or session, I'll keep the conversation to the minimum and leave it for the following morning. I'll make sure my voice is pitched in a positive fashion when I tell the lads not to worry about it tonight, because if the captain sounds depressed, that can be contagious. Time for a spot of bluffing.

Out in the middle, I like communication in a group at the fall of each wicket. I want to know what the ball is doing, how we feel the wicket is playing, what to do about the next batsman. I'm all for celebrating a wicket, but after that, I want us to use the precious few seconds constructively when the new chap is on his way out. It'll be something like, 'Right, boys, Gatt's in next. Now he likes to play his shots right away, but he's an lbw candidate going half forward. Try to get the ball to come into him, because he leaves an open gate. He loves spinners, so let's keep them away from him for a time. So Neil, you're coming off – Allan get loose.' If it's a bowler who can bat a bit, it'll be along the lines of, 'This bloke's a compulsive hooker. Let's put a man out for the hook. But it's a slow wicket, so let's do some double bluffing. Keep the ball pitched up all the time, we've got a mid-off and mid on. Keep looking at the man on the hook, but don't bounce him. Let's try and get him bowled or lbw, half forward, because he's expecting the short one. Right, good plan, let's go!'

I might be concerned about the lack of shine on the ball, that it's not swinging much, so I'll tell the guys to work harder on it. More spit and polish. Possibly the ball has started to reverse swing, so I'll tell the guys to watch for the signal. To help the reverse swing, players must keep their sweaty palms off the rough side and dampen the other side of the ball. The fielders will then know to leave the rough side alone, throw the ball to mid-off and let him do the work on the ball. I don't know the scientific reason why the ball goes into reverse swing, but it sure helps to get batsmen out. The ball will reach a certain condition and then late swing can be achieved. In the past, fast bowlers didn't like to bowl with an old ball, as they didn't realise the technique used to make the ball reverse swing. Watching the Pakistani pair of Wasim and Waqar destroy the England batting in 1992 has helped cricketers understand reverse swing and now most England bowlers can use the technique. Unfortunately, English bowlers are rarely as effective as this brilliant pair of Pakistanis because they don't have their pace.

I expect concentration when we're out in the field. We became one of the best fielding sides in the championship by hard work, imaginative practice sessions by Bob Woolmer and going for young lads who could field well. Trevor Penney's work in the covers has been remarkable in recent seasons. He can be classified as an all-rounder, because in addition to a career batting average of over 40, he saves around 15 to 20 runs in a normal innings, and runs out batsmen all the time. Yet that didn't happen overnight for Trevor. He practised day after day back home in Zimbabwe and his work before play starts every day is an object lesson in professionalism. Roger Twose and Dominic Ostler gave us great athleticism in the field, and Nick Knight's arrival in 1995 was another boost – he's a terrific catcher close in and very quick and athletic everywhere.

We have taken a high percentage of catches at slip, absolutely vital in both successful championship campaigns. It was a real challenge on some cold days when Allan Donald was motoring in – those snicks would really fly. We'd get the twelfth man to bring out hand-warmers, which would be kept in our pockets. You definitely stand a better chance of hanging onto the ball with warm hands. We'd feel jealous on a cold day that Keith Piper had his nice warm gloves on and we'd hope all the edges were thin and go to him. Some of his catches in recent seasons have been unbelievable, and they have turned tight games for us. Keith is particularly good at taking low snicks in front of him that wouldn't have carried to slip. I can't believe there is a keeper on the circuit who is more naturally gifted, and now that his concentration is improving, he is even more consistent. He sets the standard for the rest of the guys in the field.

There are times, though, when I have to remind some of the

guys about the need for concentration. Sundays can be a test for me as captain. It can get very noisy, and that's when you need your fielders to be looking in your direction all the time, because they can't hear you out on the boundary, with the crowd roaring in a tense finish. It's a club rule that the boys don't sign autographs when they're on the field in Sunday games, because they must be concentrating. Dominic Ostler can be very frustrating to captain in such situations. I like the fielders to bustle into position, keeping an eye on me for late changes of mind, but Dominic turns his back after ten yards and plods to his position out in the deep. It's very frustrating to have to wait for all your fielders to get into their positions, and Dominic is the worst offender. I know he thinks I pick on him, but he hasn't improved that area of his fielding. I want urgency on the field, for the opposition to think they just can't take liberties, and showing poor body language is more annoying to me than any technical deficiencies. I want all ten to shout 'Bad Luck!' if someone drops a catch, even at a crucial time, because that's the sort of thing which underlines a good team spirit, and the batsmen are reminded that there are 11 players out there, determined to get rid of him. You need to impose yourselves on the batsmen, to give them no peace at all.

For all his brilliance, Keith Piper needs to be given sharp reminders at times. Sometimes Keith is too keen and gets too vocal and I have to come out of the slips because he's saying too much. He won't skirt around the subject: 'Skip, he's bowling crap – take him off.' If a snick has gone between second slip and gully, he'll tut-tut and say, 'Third slip'. At times like that, I feel like throttling Keith, even if he is such a good mate. You always wish you had one more fielder, but you must go with your hunch and hope the team is going in the same direction and following your thought processes.

At Warwickshire we encouraged our batsmen to learn every shot in the book and then in matches choose the correct ones for the conditions. It's about having the right game plan. The best players in the world adapt their techniques to suit the conditions and the players were told to aspire to be the best, not to set attainable, moderate goals for the season, but aim for the top.

We tried to instil the right environment, where batsmen wouldn't be castigated for getting out. If we were sitting watching our innings and a player made a mistake, you used to hear someone say, 'That's a bad shot – what's he doing?' so Bob Woolmer and I would turn it round and say, 'Just hang on – he's playing that shot for a reason. OK, poorly executed but the right idea'

I didn't want people talking negatively when they were watching. It only puts the next batsman due in under pressure. He feels he will also be analysed by his team-mates and if he were to play a poor shot, you could be sure his mind would think back to the boys watching and then wonder what they'd be saying. Bob and I put a stop to any negatives being blurted out impulsively and instead made the guys say things like, 'Bad luck, missed out on four there.'

We wanted the players to work things out, to think deeper about their game. In a Benson and Hedges Cup game, Asif Din got himself out against the off-spin of Surrey's James Boiling. The bowler had seven men in the ring, saving one and Asif was caught at mid-off. When he came in, he said, 'Sorry, Skip – bad shot', but I made a point of saying that it was only the execution that was wrong, the idea was good. The ball wasn't turning much, and Asif was trying to hit over the top, so that Boiling would then go on the defensive, putting men out in the deep. Then Asif would have been able to milk the bowling, playing him into the gaps, pushing it around for four or five an over. That would have been thoughtful cricket with little risk attached. It was the correct game plan, but he just got too close to the ball in executing the shot. If, on the other hand, a batsman gets himself out by hitting into the wind, with two men out for the lofted shot, that is poor cricket, because he ought to know that the ball might hold up in the air, despite the powerful execution of the shot. I would talk to him privately, perhaps the next day, after he's had time to cool down. He would know straight away that he'd made a mistake, otherwise he shouldn't be playing professional cricket. The important point is that he shouldn't be made to feel worse than he already does in front of his team-mates.

Dominic Ostler sometimes gets bored with just picking up the singles. He likes to play big shots, to dominate the bowler, and sometimes he chooses the wrong option, but I'd rather he erred on the side of being positive. Yet some days it's hard to play expansively on wickets that need more graft and attention, and this is where communication within the team is important. Before we bat, I'll say, 'I think this pitch will help the seam bowlers, so we might have to be a little careful. Make sure you're all watching, chat together out in the middle and tell us what's happening when you're out.' The trick is to settle for, say, 180 in a 40 overs game on a tricky pitch, but to avoid finding yourself 60 for 6 when you think you can get 260 by playing your shots all the time. It's a matter of judgement, of trusting your partner's view of things. Roger Twose was always great to bat with, because he was so confident and cool at the big times. He'd say, 'Skip, I'll go into positive mode now, you just knock it around, I'm ready for them.' I'd look at it a little more cautiously: 'Hang on Rog, this guy's only got one over left, then it's the off-spinner. I reckon I'll be able to sweep him to that short boundary because I've got the wind behind me', and we'd come to some sort of compromise. But I'd expect all my batters to keep looking at the options, and going for their shots when the situation was right.

You must think as a team, help each other and forget about individual statistics. How many times have you seen a player get to 99 in a limited overs match and start playing differently? That's bad cricket – he is wasting vital deliveries that ought to be adding to the team's score. If you've got to 99, there can't be much wrong with the way you've played that day, and you shouldn't alter, even for an over. You'd settle for 99 every time you went out to bat, wouldn't you? Even Nick Knight, a great team man, got sidetracked by his desire to get a hundred in his first season with us. He had played superbly for us, yet he narrowly missed his century at various stages of the season, and started to tighten up whenever he got near to the three figures. But he should have been playing better in the nineties than in the early stages of his innings.

There are many statistics in the game of cricket, and you have to assess which ones are the most relevant. I think runs per ball faced is more important than if you have scored a hundred, rather than ninety, especially in limited overs matches. At Warwickshire, we try very hard to keep the game plan uppermost in the mind, rather than individual landmarks, and that was one of the reasons why my efforts with the bat pleased me so much in the 1995 championship season, after poor form the season before. Often when I came in, we were going for quick runs, after a good start and – following the necessary format for the four-day game – the need was to crack on to give us time to take the wickets. When we played Hampshire, I managed to get a few in the slot as we chased quick runs before the declaration. I'd made up my mind that I was going to try sweeping Kevin James, and although he had a lot of fielders around the boundary, I was hitting out, rather than picking up the singles that were available everywhere. I ended up 77 not out, and as I came into the dressing-room, Roger Twose said, 'Well played, Skip, nice innings. Great to see you not playing for the not out, but for the team.' I was pleased Roger had spotted I was going for the runs, that being not out was an incidental – and I was even more pleased that he had spoken about that in front of the rest of the side. That was exactly the sort of team spirit Bob Woolmer and I had been looking for since we came together in 1993.

Professional cricket can be a very selfish exercise unless the captain and coach nip that in the bud. You are, after all, dealing with people's livelihoods, and there is the temptation to play for yourself, to get to a level of competence. At Warwickshire, we expect that competence but we also look for unselfishness within the framework of efficiency. Neil Smith is the best example of the team man. In championship games, he can bat as low as number ten sometimes, and he'll play either sort of game, depending on the circumstances. In the one-day matches, we decided to open with him as a sort of wild card – they came to be known as 'pinch-hitters' after the 1996 World Cup. Neil took to the job straight away; he was happy to open his shoulders and play his shots right from the first over, because that was the best option for the team in those types of games. If he got out for nought early on, it didn't matter, because we knew the risks attached. Another player might have muttered about having to throw his wicket away, but not Neil. We call him 'The Iceman' because of his cool temperament; ask him to do anything with bat or ball and he'll try it without any fuss.

That unselfishness among the players was very heartening whenever one of them was injured. Every professional wants to play, rather than sit on the physiotherapist's couch, or do weeks of rehabilitatory work alone in the gym – wondering if you can get your career back on the line, and if the guy who has taken your place is now the automatic choice. Senior players like Tim Munton, Gladstone Small and Andy Moles were terrific in that respect. In the two seasons when we won so many trophies, all three of them had various worrying injuries, not the niggly type that soon clear up. All of them must have been concerned about their futures in the game, but they kept their concerns to themselves. They worked hard on their own and showed the right, positive attitude to the rest of the squad. In another team, the frustrations those guys must have felt could have become corrosive, but they gave all they could to the first team effort when not playing. They came on the away trips, for physio treatment and to give support, and they took all the mickey-taking in good heart, even from the younger guys who had taken their places. Andy Moles suffered a bad Achilles tendon injury, but he wasn't seen moping, even though he must have been desperately disappointed at missing out. Tim Munton had to have a back operation, a very serious setback for a fast bowler, yet he appeared cheerful when he surely wasn't. Gladstone had the assorted knee, calf and thigh injuries a fast bowler gets after a long time in the game, yet he and these senior players would talk to the younger players, offering advice and showing joy at their team-mate's successes. Gladstone also had to put up with Ostler and Twose bantering with him, calling him 'Grandad', and constantly pinching his backside, telling him he had the best bottom in the championship! Glad is brilliant for team morale!

It was terrific to captain Allan Donald during this period of success, not just because of his matchwinning ability, but the way he supported the rest of the guys. When he first came over from South Africa, he'd come straight out of national service and he hardly said a word. He wasn't all that fluent in the

English language – he's an Afrikaaner – and he'd sit in the corner of the dressing-room, taking it all in. He matured as a person, and marrying a local girl, then having a daughter helped put him on another level of maturity. Having grown up with most of the lads, Allan really wanted to do it for the team.

Before I became captain, I used to try motivating him with daft things like, 'Al, I was having a drink with this batsman last night and he said he was really looking forward to facing you – says he played against you in the second team a couple of years ago and doesn't reckon you're very quick,' but when I kept repeating it every game, Allan soon rumbled me! He never really needed motivating, though: he had his own high personal standards and his regard for the rest of the team. He's gone from being a nice, young lad who could bowl fast but erratically, to a great professional who wants his team-mates to do well. He's never arrogant when he's successful and didn't complain if he had to do something that might reduce his effectiveness – like bowling him into the wind in a one-day game. Allan realised he was harder to hit than a slower bowler therefore it was best for the team for Allan to bowl from the worst end. He was so focused in the 1995 season that I just needed to wind him up. Having missed out on the 1993 Nat West Final and the 1994 season because of his commitments with South Africa, Allan was hungry for success with us. He was also hurt that Warwickshire had decided to go with Brian Lara as the overseas player for the 1996 season, a decision I thought was wrong. Allan was determined to show they were making the wrong cricketing decision, and when he forecast that he would take a hundred championship wickets, I was delighted, because he is not given to boasts. He ended up with 88 championship wickets, getting one every six overs, a fantastic strike rate. If he hadn't missed three games because of a broken bone in his foot he surely would have got the hundred.

He was remarkably fast, accurate and consistent throughout the '95 season, but I shall never forget his spell on the third evening of our home match at Edgbaston against Derbyshire. It was the penultimate game and we had to win. There was rain about, and although our first innings lead of 118 was satisfactory, we had to make early inroads on that third evening when Derbyshire came out to bat. They lost three wickets in that final 40 minutes, all to Allan Donald in an awesome display of clinical fast bowling. He knew what he had to do and he was inspired. He said it was the fastest spell of his career and he was so pumped up with adrenalin that even after the close of play he sat in the dressing-room, eyes wide open, wanting more. He had put so much in those six overs because he knew it was a vital phase of the game. Derbyshire could have easily avoided defeat on the final day, but due to Allan's inspiration we wrapped it up and went to Canterbury to clinch the title. It was absolutely right that Allan should get the final wicket to beat Kent and bring us the title, and the emotion he showed at that moment made us realise what it meant to him. I've seen some great overseas players in county cricket, but I can't believe there's been a better professional and a greater team man than Allan Donald. Warwickshire are very lucky that he's a big enough man to swallow his disappointment at being passed over in favour of Brian Lara and come back as our fast bowling coach and fitness trainer. Many other overseas stars would have sulked, then flounced off to another lucrative county deal. I like to think the atmosphere we've had in our dressing-room had something to do with Allan staying with us.

Looking back on that amazing 1994 season, when we lost just four out of 43 games in the four competitions, it's clear that we did it by stealth. All the early headlines were dominated by Brian Lara's arrival, then he continued to grab the attention for the first two months of the season with his brilliant batting. Meanwhile, we kept on winning cricket matches, and it stayed that way. Brian Lara only managed five half-centuries in the one-day competitions, but the other batsmen more than made up for that with bold displays. We had kept quiet about our aims for the '94 season, other than the usual platitudes about trying to play attractive, winning cricket, but we were very bullish about our prospects, even before we signed Lara. We took a lot of strength from that historic win at Lord's the previous September, our younger players were looking impressive, the fitness levels were excellent, and Roger Twose had come back from

New Zealand full of confidence after working on a couple of weaknesses.

His 277 not out in the first championship match against Glamorgan was overshadowed by Brian Lara's terrific hundred, but it was more significant to me. Roger was to prove an absolute rock over the next two seasons before he emigrated to New Zealand to try to forge an international career. He was a fantastic competitor, chockful of confidence – the sort of confidence that really annoys the opposition – with a cool brain in the heat of battle. Roger was also invaluable to me in getting over the message about how we should play spin. We both agreed that our batsmen had been too orthodox in previous seasons against the spinners and that we had to improvise more, play the reverse sweep, the paddle, getting the ball where the fielders weren't. We also believed these shots against the spinners should be premeditated, and we hammered home to the players that they'd be expected to extemporise. I believe our success in 1994 was more than any other reason down to our effectiveness against spin. Bob Woolmer and I stressed the need to practise the reverse sweep long and hard before trying it out in the middle, and the results were very gratifying. In the Sunday League and Nat West competitions in 1994, we got out just 24 times to the spinners, averaging 5.5 runs an over. We faced 8 overs of spin less than the opposition, scoring a staggering 238 runs more. In these competitions, the opposition only scored at 3.8 runs per over against Neil Smith and Richard Davis, losing a wicket every 16 runs. We lost a wicket to spin every 44 runs and scored at nearly 6 an over. Our success against seam bowlers was no better than the opposition, in fact it was slightly inferior. We scored at 4.6 runs per over against seam and pace bowling and lost a wicket every 23 runs. Our seamers conceded 4.6 runs per over, but only took a wicket every 26 runs. On those statistics, you would finish mid-table in the Sunday League, but our superior batting against spin took us to nearly all three of the one-day trophies in '94.

Before the 1994 season, Dominic Ostler and Trevor Penney didn't want to play the reverse sweep, but Twose nagged away at them. He was batting with Penney in a second eleven game down at Taunton, and the off-spinner came on with a 6/3 field, with six fielders on the legside. Trevor wasn't keen on trying the reverse sweep, even though the field was open for the shot. He had practised it in the nets, and played it well, but he was wary about trying it out in the middle – the old syndrome of 'getting out in a bad way' I suppose. Roger Twose was having none of that. He marched down the pitch and simply ordered Penney to play the reverse sweep, saying, 'Look at the field, Trevor – do it, just do it!' He hit four off the first reverse sweep, then a couple more next ball. Trevor couldn't believe how easy he found it.

Soon after that, he was in a partnership with Twose against Yorkshire, and two spinners were in tandem. I saw Roger walk down to talk to Trevor and it was clear what advice he was giving him. He played the shot, scampered three and I could see how pleased he was. That was great; another dimension to Trevor Penney's batting. Earlier that season, he had played out a maiden at Guildford to James Boiling's off-spin and he told me that he hadn't thought about the reverse sweep, even though it was a 6/3 field. Yet Graeme Welch, in one of his early games for the first team, had come in and played it first ball! The young players in the second team were all playing it now, in contrast to a few years earlier when Neal Abberley, their coach, had told Roger Twose, 'Do that again and you're out of the net.' To be fair to Abbers, he had come to see the point of the shot and he was as keen as Woolmer and myself to see it practised, then played in a match whenever it was needed. When Phil Neale succeeded Bob Woolmer, he was staggered to hear us nominate where our batters would play the spinner – 'He won't do it now, he'll knock it square for one, because a man's there to block it. Hang on, it's there for him now, the bloke's been moved.' He was amazed that we knew each other's game so well. I took that as a great compliment.

I was very grateful to Roger Twose for banging on about the reverse sweep to the guys during the 1993 and '94 seasons. Roger's a highly intelligent, articulate chap and he would put the message over clearly in team nettings: 'Listen fellas, it's easy, you've just got to practise it. We should all be playing it, you'll get one run at the very least.' I was delighted my beliefs had rubbed off on another player and it became almost a mission to Roger. When we played Glamorgan, Matthew Maynard congratulated him on having the bottle to play the reverse sweep to the first ball Roger faced, and it was music to my ears when I heard the likes of Gladstone Small and Neil Smith say, 'That's great cricket' as they watched Roger play it, or premeditate a shot against the spinners. Neil and Gladstone had taken some persuading about the new way of playing the spinners from the time we had our team meeting in Trinidad, back in '91, and it was terrific to see they had been won over.

We kept stressing the importance of practising the reverse sweep before trying it out in the middle, though. In 1993, in a Sunday League game against Surrey, Jason Ratcliffe played it in desperation against James Boiling after he and Andy Moles had got stuck. We had needed a positive start from our two openers because we knew that Waqar Younis would come on late in the innings, and it would be very difficult to score at more than six an over off a world-class reverse-swing expert. But they couldn't get the ball away, and the asking rate escalated to ten an over eventually. We duly collapsed to 176 all out, losing by 18 runs, because of the poor start. Boiling got away with 2/40 in his ten overs. Everything I had asked for in our team meetings had gone out of the window and I was annoyed. I told Jason afterwards that it was poor cricket to play the reverse sweep when he had never practised it. I believe he took that on board and that he's a better player of spin these days than he was in 1993.

Nick Knight had the right attitude when he joined us in 1995. He said how impressed he had been by our batting in one-day games the year before, and that he wanted to broaden his range against the spinners. He came up to stay with me before the season started, I showed him a video I had compiled about batting against spin and we went into the indoor nets to practise. Phil Neale joined us, and he coached the reverse sweep for the first time that day. It was a good session, Nick was very receptive and adaptable as we worked on premeditated shots. He wore the helmet and grille, because you can easily get a top edge.

In the 1995 season, Nick played the spinners very well, and he ended up playing for England. He would play the slog/sweep in front of square and if that was blocked off, then he'd go for the reverse sweep or the paddle. He wanted to play those shots well and he worked very hard in the indoor nets. Nick has a very quick brain and fast hands: I saw him one day set himself for the sweep, notice the ball had been dropped short, change his mind at the last instant and go for the cut instead. Normally I would say, 'Don't cop out – once you're down there, you've got to go through with the shot', but Nick's reactions were so sharp he got away with it.

Despite our success at Warwickshire with premeditating spin, I think there is still a resistance against it in some circles. The England captain, Mike Atherton penned an interesting article for my benefit brochure, about our match against Lancashire, when they scored 305/2 and we fell short of the target. It was a Benson and Hedges game and we didn't play the reverse sweep well that day, with Trevor Penney eventually getting out playing the shot. That night I went to a supporters' forum and the first question I took was, 'Why did Trevor Penney play that ridiculous shot? It cost us the game.' So I got on my soapbox, gave him all the statistics and explained how valuable the reverse sweep and premeditating spin is in modern cricket and concluded that we simply had a bad day. He apologised profusely, I got a nice round of applause and there was no harm done.

Mike Atherton obviously felt the same way as that supporter. In his article for me, he called it a 'Get Out of Jail' shot, referred to Warwickshire's 'obsession' with the stroke and pointed out that Brian Lara never had to play it, nor wanted to. Well for a start Brian Lara is a genius, but even he was starting to play the paddle towards the end of his great season in '94. I also believe he would be an even more destructive player if he mixed up his shots against the spinners, because there were times when he got tied up by them in the Sunday League and indeed was regularly dismissed by spin. In fact, Brian Lara and Paul Smith were responsible for one third of our dismissals to spinners in the Sunday League and Nat West and both hardly ever premeditated. I don't expect Atherton to know that, he was usually fairly busy elsewhere on Sundays. It was nonsense, though, to suggest that great players like Lara don't need it in their locker.

Desmond Haynes played it regularly and he scored more hundreds in one-day internationals than anyone else. Mike Gatting, Ian Botham, Javed Miandad and many other top batsmen have played the reverse sweep productively. I'm fairly certain that Mike Atherton didn't score one-day runs as quickly as Roger Twose in '94 and '95, so perhaps he might think about broadening his range. As for it being a 'Get Out of Jail' stroke, I never wanted it to be played that way, as Jason Ratcliffe had found out two years earlier. In the vast majority of cases, our batsmen have played it safely and productively, and I was disappointed that the England captain seemed so rigid and orthodox in his thinking. In fact several of Atherton's Lancashire team-mates now play the shot, among them Graham Lloyd, who is one of the best players of spin in the country. At Warwickshire we see it as a safe, controlled stroke and it has helped us win trophies.

Our bold approach against the spinners also benefited us in championship matches, when we were on a run chase on the final day. In 1994, we won two games against the clock, when we were, in effect, into a one-day game, with the asking rate around six an over. At Northampton, we got 230 off 37 overs to win by four wickets, with Nick Cook's left-arm spin going for nearly six an over, and at Scarborough, we rattled along at five an over to beat Yorkshire by eight wickets, with Jeremy Batty and Richard Stemp taking some stick. I was delighted with Andy Moles that day. He had worked really hard with Bob Woolmer to widen his repertoire of strokes and he premeditated superbly, making 48 in as many balls. Because Andy was receptive to the new methods at an advanced stage of his career, he was now playing with far greater freedom than in his early days, when he was a little stodgy. He was now worth his place in a one-day side just as much as in the longer games.

Paul Smith was another senior player who eventually worked hard at the reverse sweep in the indoor nets, so that at the start of the 1995 season, he was playing it successfully against Leicestershire's Adrian Pierson. Poor Adrian was badly mauled by us in a Sunday League game later in the same year. Roger Twose initially reverse swept Pierson fine and when the fielder at backward point was moved to short third man, Roger then struck boundary after boundary with the reverse hit. Now the reverse hit is more complicated than its brother, the more conservative reverse sweep. In playing the reverse hit, you put your back foot forward, which turns your shoulders into a left hander's position (if you're a right-hander), and this allows a full swing of the bat. I actually came across this shot accidentally while coaching the Hong Kong side in 1993. I was trying to coach the reverse sweep to Stewart Brew, Hong Kong's premier all-rounder, but he kept putting the wrong leg forward and smacking the ball square on the offside. It looks a high-risk shot and is more difficult than the reverse sweep, but if practised properly, can be effective. I had shown it to Roger at the start of the 1994 season and he took to it immediately. Poor Adrian Pierson didn't know what to do that day at Leicester, eventually going for 1/79 in his eight overs. Afterwards, as we commiserated with our former team-mate, he asked where he had gone wrong. Roger replied, 'You did nothing wrong, mate – I just wouldn't have bowled you.' He wasn't trying to put Adrian down, just pointing out that Warwickshire's prowess against spinners is so good that we fancied ourselves against any of them.

I was absolutely delighted that we didn't stand still after our great season in '94, when we took everybody by surprise. We didn't lose anybody to the Test team in '94, only Keith Piper made it on one of the England tours that winter, and we had little national media coverage until the second half of the season, with the earlier focus on Brian Lara – so we just cruised along, enjoying the fact that not many rated us until we had won three out of four competitions. Then it was time to revise a few rigid opinions. The next season was even more satisfying, because we buried the myth of 'Larashire'. The team continued to evolve, with Neil Smith blossoming into an England player and young lads like Wasim Khan, Ashley Giles and Dougie Brown coming into the side and playing with great freedom and confidence. I was anxious to prove there was still some life left in me as a cricketer, after fitness and form worries reduced my effectiveness in the '94 championship, and I was pleased with my contribution. All through that '95 season, players from other counties were coming up to me, saying they would like to play at Edgbaston, which was a nice compliment. It was also flattering to see more county sides premeditating against spin in 1995 and I knew that most observant sides would eventually catch us up. In the 1996 season, Northants played our spinners brilliantly and one of their batsmen, Mal Loye told me afterwards that they'd had a team meeting in 1994 after losing to us in a Sunday League game. Their coach, Bob Carter had pointed out Warwickshire's superiority that day in playing spin and he suggested they copy our unorthodox methods.

In my time as captain, I was more than happy with the players available to me and was delighted that Nick Knight strengthened us in 1995. It meant a lot that he would choose to leave a successful outfit like Essex to join us. I had been impressed by a hundred by him against us in our first championship season and Nick told me that he liked the way we approached our cricket. He moved for the sake of his career, for ambition not for financial considerations, and he was impressive right from the start. He was hungry for success, a very bright, personable guy who spoke eloquently about the game and wanted to learn. He adapted very swiftly to the Warwickshire way of thinking, and reacted well to the encouragement. In his very first game he sidled up to me and said, 'Skip, do you think we might try a leg gully?' I liked the way he acknowledged the captain's authority, while at the same time showing his own independent style of thinking in a pleasant manner. Nick Knight has definite leadership qualities and he has proved a great signing for us.

It was a terrific feeling, sitting in the Lord's dressing-room in 1995, after another successful Final, to see the pleasure all the lads felt in each other's performances. There was Keith Piper hugging everyone, Roger Twose – in his last big match for us – singing loudly and tunelessly. That warm feeling of camaraderie can only be understood by a team that has gone through so much together, and getting a call from our former coach, Bob Woolmer, from Cape Town made it all the more sweet. Six trophies in 24 calendar months was the best possible answer to those outside the game who couldn't understand how a side lacking household names could be so supreme – and to those on the circuit who chose to ignore the facts and continue denigrating us. They kept harping about the pitches at Edgbaston, the unreliable bounce, the fact that we had a huge advantage with our seam attack. Mike Brearley, writing in the aftermath of the '95 Edgbaston Test, when England were overwhelmed by the West Indies, suggested that such pitches were the reason why we won championships. I was disappointed that a man of Brearley's stature hadn't bothered taking a deeper look than just one Test Match. For a start, Steve Rouse, our groundsman, is very much his own man and doesn't take too much notice of the observations of the coach or captain once the season starts. He has his own idea about what constitutes a good cricket wicket. Mike Brearley might also like to consider that in our first championship season, we were unbeaten away from home and next season lost one game on our travels and ended up winning as many matches away as at home. We can't have been that bad then! After a time, I decided to let the carping comments just slide away. I'd say to our players, 'Listen guys, in ten years' time, no one will talk about the quality of the pitches at Edgbaston, they'll talk about you making history. The public have short memories, and you're just a conversation piece around the dinner table or in the pub. The most important thing is that you do well for each other, and your very best as an individual. Focus on your own self-esteem. Ask yourself after each day's play if you did your best? If the answer is 'yes', that is good enough for me.

I tried to avoid a set routine in how I dealt with players individually, even though I'd look for a collective attitude. Some players get keyed up when a big game approaches. Keith Piper gets more nervous and vocal on the morning of a big match, and I have to tell him to relax and not to vary his preparations, just maintain his high standards. Sometimes, a flash of anger from Keith can be counter-productive. He showed his intense disappointment in a Sunday League game against Glamorgan that we had to win and looked like losing as we defended a small total. Neil Smith bowled five 'dot' balls at David Hemp, then gave him a really slow delivery that was swept to the boundary. Keith put his hands up in horror and said to me, 'What's he doing? That's stupid cricket!' and I then tried to calm him down. We soon got a wicket and as we gathered round, Keith had a go at Neil, saying things that were totally out of order. Luckily Neil's a calm character who knew that our keeper was just pumped up, but I had to pull Keith aside and have a strong word. He's a great lad, but can be a little combustible at times, so he has to be treated in a certain way.

Paul Smith has to be handled in the right fashion too. He's a maverick, a free spirit, and if you put your arm around him all the time, and be nice to him, you won't get what you want. In most situations, you want him to bowl with fire in his belly, and to achieve this I'll deliberately try to rile him. As he's walking back to his mark, I'll shout out, 'Come on Smithy, get your arm up, they're playing you off the front foot. You're bowling like a girl!' He's the one cricketer on the staff for whom I'll ignore my rule about not denigrating for cricketing reasons. He could lose his energy quickly because he'd lose his adrenalin and that would result in a reduction of pace and effectiveness. He did, however, respond well to the big occasion and was at his best when he bowled 'effort' balls, on a wicket of uneven bounce. In the 1994 Nat West semi-final against Kent, he bowled medium pace early on and he was treated dismissively. He slunk away to the boundary, disgusted with himself, showed poor body language, and didn't walk in with the bowler. The crowd suddenly woke up, the atmosphere suddenly galvanised Paul, and when I brought him back he bowled like a demon. He was almost as quick as Allan Donald that day, and with the crowd on his side, he helped win us a match that we really should have lost. He did it again that season, at Lord's in the Benson and Hedges Cup Final, when he picked up the Gold Award for a terrific all-round performance.

I think the right mental attitude is a very important ingredient in winning cricket matches. It's about fine tuning, getting yourself prepared in the way that suits you, so that when you start the serious business, you feel 'I'm looking forward to this, I'm ready.' Cricketers tend to look for excuses when they fail, so I don't want a regimented approach to the preparation for the day's play. I tell the guys to do what they want, as long as they're prepared to their own satisfaction. I don't see much point to all those throw-downs to the batsman on a slow outfield, where the surface is so different from the actual middle. I like to bowl on the edge of the square, at a single stump, rather than be enclosed in the nets. To me, the environment for practice must be similar to the actual match. Most of your technique has been ingrained in you as a teenager, and if you practise too much before the start of play, you can lose your edge, and your ability to maintain your concentration for the day can be impaired. These days, my preparation in the morning tends to be a shower, a cup of coffee, a session with the physio (to get loose), and a few catches thrown at me. It all depends on what's best for you. We are probably the only county that doesn't have a regimented warm-up. Routines can get monotonous and boredom makes you tired. You can get stiff after a warm-up and for me, the key time to be warm is when it's actually needed – out in the middle.

All I ask is that the players are mentally confident and physically ready when they take the field, and I don't care how they've achieved that. I had to bite my tongue one day when Neil Smith was run out without facing a ball, going for the second run. Neil admitted when he came in that he wasn't quite loose enough, and he should have been. I once ran out Gladstone Small in a one-day game, and although it looked my fault, it wasn't, because Glad wasn't backing up properly. These little subtleties can change a game. Look at Dean Jones: he's terrific at backing up, and he turns so quickly for the second or third run. Cricketers should copy him. I expect my players to attend to details like that without needing to hammer home the point.

I'm fascinated at the variants you can encounter in a team game like cricket. It's an evolving sport, with so many new ideas coming through every season. It was significant to me that more opposition batsmen played the reverse sweep against our bowlers in 1995 than the year before. I like to think we were among the first to use a 'pinch-hitter' in Neil Smith to open the innings. We were also happy to be flexible in the middle order, putting bold strikers like Paul Smith and Dougie Brown in early for the one-day games and leaving a fine player like Trevor Penney till later in the innings, when he's so good at scampering singles and running twos to the fielders on the boundary. You

Top left: Dermot was winning trophies from an early age. Here he is in Kowloon, 1973, aged 10. *Top right:* Aged 7 months – already enjoying life. *Middle and bottom:* The four brothers (from the left) Philip, Mark, Dermot, Paul in 1967 and 1990.

Top: Dermot with his beloved daughter Emily and *(bottom)* with his mother on Boxing Day 1991.

Right: Dermot in his first season at Sussex in 1983, aged 20 and *(below)* making his first appearance for England as sub in the Texaco Trophy game against the West Indies at Old Trafford in 1991.

Monica Reeve

Roger Wootton

Roger Wootton

Batting against Kent whom Warwickshire beat in the Nat West semi-final in 1994, before losing in the final – one of only 4 games that they lost all season.

Roger Wootton

Reverse sweeping in the final AXA Equity & Law match against Gloucestershire in 1994 which won Warwickshire this trophy to add to their County Championship and B & H Cup.

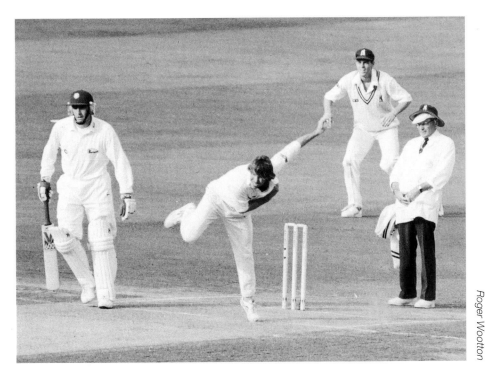

Roger Wootton

Bowling in the Nat West final at Lord's against Northants in 1995, which Warwickshire went on to win.

Roger Wootton

Taking a sharp catch to dismiss Vikram Solanki of Worcestershire off Neil Smith in 1995.

Roger Wootton

Victory celebrations after their Nat West Trophy win against Sussex in 1993.

Roger Wootton

With Tim Munton, the vice-captain, holding their three trophies for 1994, an unprecedented feat.

The boys celebrate winning yet another Lord's final to take the Nat West Trophy in 1995.

Receiving the winner's cheque after winning the Britannic Assurance County Championship in 1995 at Kent in Canterbury.

Dermot displaying his O.B.E. outside Buckingham Palace in March 1996 which he was awarded in the 1995 New Year's Honours list for his services to cricket and *(below)* unwinding at Lord's having won the Nat West Trophy in 1995.

don't have to hit boundaries to achieve a run rate as high as 7 an over, and Trevor knows this; often he saw us home with sensible, intelligent strokeplay. I'll also open the bowling with a spinner if it's justified. To me cricket is the art of the possible and you need to be flexible to stay on top. I like to think that Warwickshire have won so many trophies in recent years because they kept one jump ahead of the rest. Success didn't suddenly happen in 1994 as if by magic. We were creeping up on the rails, hoping no one would notice, but in the end they did. It may still be a mystery to Darren Gough, but our methods in winning so many trophies contained no dark secrets. It's amazing what you can achieve in a team sport when everyone feels relaxed and privileged to be out there, playing for each other.

7

Getting Up Noses

'I don't like you, Reeve. You get up my nose and if you come anywhere near me, I'll rearrange yours.' Not the usual after-match banter you experience in a committee room when the players of both sides mingle for a drink. But Lancashire's David Lloyd was in no mood for genial niceties when we gathered in the Old Trafford committee room in May 1995. Clearly, a few things had been festering with the Lancashire coach during this particular game, but he probably chose the wrong time and place to have a go at me. Lloyd's outburst was in front of some Lancashire committee including Chairman Bob Bennett. It was another indication that on the county circuit, there is no love lost between Lancashire and Warwickshire. And that incident was further proof of how I can get under people's skins – and sometimes I even mean to.

That bust-up with Lancashire had been on the cards for some time. We had known that some of their players and David Lloyd had resented our success, that we were making more of our assets than they were at Old Trafford, and Lloyd's early season comment of 'How can they win three trophies in a year with that side?' wasn't enjoyed in our dressing-room. Whenever we played them, you could see how important it was for them to take us down a peg or two, that they felt we were up ourselves and arrogant. We thought that was rich, coming from Lancashire. I thought both sets of players were very similar in approach, but clearly our continued success bothered David Lloyd. In his capacity as an excellent summariser for BBC Radio, David never

missed a chance to have a dig at Warwickshire for the quality of
pitches at Edgbaston and once, when he was covering a semi-
final involving Warwickshire, he referred to us as 'strutters'.

The roots of that incident involving David and me had obviously been growing for some time. I know I had really annoyed
Wasim Akram the year before with a daft remark that I instantly
regretted. It was the summer when Imran Khan had admitted
publicly that he had altered the condition of the ball with a
bottle top when he played for Sussex. When Lancashire came to
Edgbaston, Wasim was fielding down on the boundary and he
signalled to his twelfth man for something. I was standing at the
door to the players' entrance and shouted out, 'Bottle top?' As
soon as I said it, I realised it was tactless and Wasim looked furious. It was a remark made in jest, to entertain our lads, but it was
one of umpteen cases when my smart mouth was running away
from my brain. Soon, half-truths were circulating around the circuit and it was being said that when I went out to bat, I brought
on a bottle top and presented it to Wasim Akram. Not true, but
I was told that Wasim was out to get me and I could understand
why I wasn't the most popular opponent to the Lancashire lads.

Then, a week before the Old Trafford bust-up, Lancashire came
to play us at Edgbaston in a Benson and Hedges Cup game. That
led to David Lloyd alleging that I had tried to 'out-psych' him and
his twelfth man in the viewing area when Warwickshire were batting. Lloyd thought I was deliberately trying to belittle his off-
spinner Gary Yates by making derogatory remarks about his
bowling, putting unfair pressure on Lloyd, who was sitting a few
yards away with his twelfth man. That was rubbish. I was so
involved in our efforts to match a big score of over 300 that I was
babbling to the boys about how we had to get after the spinners.
I blurted out, 'Come on fellas, we've got to take him for six an
over.' I just blurted it out in front of the guys in the viewing area,
because I knew the importance of getting at least a run a ball on
such a good pitch against the spinners. We played spin so well in
one-day games that I wanted to remind the lads who were due to
bat that we simply had to get after Gary Yates. It wasn't meant to
be derogatory at all to Yates, who is a fine all-round player in one-
day cricket, or a slur on Lancashire cricket in any way, it was

simply a gee-up to our boys – but David Lloyd saw hidden meanings. I also found out that David didn't like my impersonation of Lancashire accents. I have this habit of copying people's voices and at times walk around in my own world, babbling away, doing impressions. Now David's voice is very distinctive and when I hear it, I can't help myself and try to copy it. I can see how it could be construed as mickey-taking, but I have honestly never done anything like that off the field, to deliberately upset someone. I actually love listening to David Lloyd, I find his enthusiasm infectious on the radio or in after-dinner speeches, he is brilliant. Presumably, though, I must have been working on my Lancashire accent on the day that David heard me, and he must have concluded I was taking the mickey out of his part of the world.

All of that came to a head at Old Trafford when we played Lancashire in a championship and Sunday League match. The atmosphere had been highly competitive right from the start. On the Sunday, when John Crawley was given out caught by Neil Smith on the mid-wicket boundary, the lumpy stuff hit the fan. Crawley was walking back to the pavilion after ascertaining that it was a fair catch, when David Lloyd shouted from their balcony, 'Stay there, Creepy! He had his foot on the rope!' I went over to Neil Smith, and he told me that he took his foot off the rope before he took the catch and that it was fair. John Holder, the square leg umpire, saw the incident much more clearly than the Lancashire guys on their balcony and confirmed that Crawley was out. But the shouts from the Lancashire balcony incensed the crowd and Neil Smith and the rest of us got some real stick after that. Unfortunately for John Crawley, he bore the brunt of some anger. As he walked up the stairs to the Lancashire dressing-room, Gladstone Small, who was not playing that day, came out and gave him a mouthful. A few minutes later, as we got on with the game out in the middle, David Lloyd came downstairs and stated that none of our players were welcome upstairs. So, if any of our team got injured over the next two days, or wanted to use the gym, it was off limits. In the committee room after the game, I tried to have a word with David to explain that Neil Smith did have his foot on the rope, but lifted it off as the ball came his way. I was however annoyed that one of my players was being blatantly accused of cheating, but it probably wasn't the best time to try to talk it through. I had naively thought that David and I had got on well, so I was surprised at the volley of abuse that greeted my approach. The following day, Bob Bennett asked me to join him and David Lloyd in a meeting and that was when it became apparent to me that I had severely upset the Lancashire coach. We worked out our differences and I hope that David sees it now as a misunderstanding, rather than deliberate mind games.

In my early days at Sussex, I thought it was important to be liked and to be popular. I was over-sensitive to people's comments and tried hard to fit in. It's honestly not worth the effort! It's funny, but people I tend to warm to, and spend time with, are often categorised as arrogant or show-offs, a couple of allegations that are regularly thrown in my direction. It's water off a duck's back now! I focus on my own self-esteem and am more content now that I ever was when I made an effort to impress in the past. It's sad, but I'm not as trusting as I used to be, or as sociable. There are too many who dislike you because of petty jealousy. As soon as you are successful, people suddenly judge you, and some love to try knocking you down. I have made a few friends through cricket and shared fun times on the county circuit and England tours. It's not imperative, though, to be liked by people who don't really know me. I would far rather have the respect of my players and that of the opposition as a cricketer. I've seen a few sides full of so-called nice chaps that never won anything. I treasure Allan Donald's quote about me: 'I'd hate to play against Dermot Reeve, he must be a pain in the neck, but he's great to have in the side.' That's all that matters in the tough school of professional sport. I was also delighted by a comment Robin Smith made to me during our first England tour together in 1992. After a fortnight, he said to me, 'I have to apologise to you, Dermot. For years, I've thought you the biggest shit in county cricket, but now I've got to know you, you're okay.' It was nice to know that I had got under the skin of such a nice guy when we were in opposition, because I don't see it as my function to be nice to the opposition. I stand by the quote: 'You're out there to win matches, not friends.' On that tour of New Zealand, I got annoyed at Robin Smith indulging in genial chat with Mark Greatbatch as Robin was fielding at silly point. Now I know that's part of Robin's charming nature, but I had to tell him he should try to make Greatbatch feel uncomfortable at the crease, not ask him where he was dining out that night. If that meant some verbals, give it out.

I learned a lot about being mentally strong during my nine years of grade cricket in Western Australia. Out there, the Aussies don't even think about passing the time of day with opponents, and they rarely spend more than a few minutes together after the game, preferring to go back to their own club and drink as a unit. I learned to give it back if anyone had a go at me on the field, but I wish I could have come up with the kind of reply I heard one day from a guy called Peter Capes. Peter had played for Western Australia as a bowler who could also bat usefully, and one day in a grade match he came up against a typical, cocky young Aussie fast bowler, who clearly felt that sledging was a vital part of his armoury. After beating him with one good delivery, he shouted derisively at Peter, 'And you're a State player!' When he almost got him again with a good delivery, the lad got even more abusive. Peter looked down the pitch at the quickie and said, 'If you're going to have a verbal go at me, you'll win that battle, because you know who I am. But I haven't got a f***ing clue who you are!' That really brought the bowler down a peg or two, because the clever implication from Peter was that he was a nobody.

When the red mists descend out there on the field, there are times when I wish I could summon up a quip like Peter Capes managed that day. But it's more important not to be fazed by anything that's said out there, to show you won't be overwhelmed. It's a test of character, and that was hammered home to me right at the start of my career with Sussex. I was so happy to be playing county cricket that I was determined to enjoy it all the time, and hoped to be popular. But I soon realised it was a very hard school and your nerve and heart were tested as much as your skills. Early on, Mark Nicholas baited me as we were holding out for a draw against Hampshire. I was blocking successfully, so Nicholas shouted out in that familiar public school drawl, 'That's it, I've had enough – this chap can't bat. Come on, Macco, finish it off.' And with that, he threw the ball to the great Malcolm Marshall. Well, Nicholas' arrogant manner had succeeded in annoying me, and that made me even more determined to see it out. I held out for the draw and was very pleased to thwart Mark Nicholas. His subtle form of sledging hadn't worked and to cap a great moment for me, Malcolm Marshall said, 'Well played, lad' as we walked off.

I had an early run-in with Ian Botham in my first season that helped me. At that stage, I was totally in awe of Ian. He had been my hero when I was on the Lord's ground staff as I watched him take so many wickets for England with some brilliant swing bowling. I loved his confident, visual manner and thought him a fabulous advert for the English game. So when I first faced Ian in a county game, it was all I could do to stop myself asking for his autograph! I came in to bat just before lunch against Somerset and even I realised, naive as I was, that it would be a good idea if we faced as few deliveries as possible before the interval. In the last over before lunch, with Somerset trying to squeeze in another over, I kept pulling away from my crease, gesturing towards the sightscreen as some imaginary spectators walked past. Ian was standing at slip and knew what I was up to and he growled at the young sprog, 'Get on with it, I know what you're trying to do!' I almost blurted out, 'Yes, sir!' but calmed myself and stuttered: 'You'd do the same'. I thought I'd passed a little test in the great man's eyes.

A few years later, I was sufficiently self-confident to come off best in a sledging bout with Botham. It was an incident that has gained a lot of exaggerated mileage, so much so that various cricket magazines and newspaper articles over the years have maintained that I called Botham that day 'a fat has-been'. Not true. What is true is that I wouldn't be brow-beaten and intimidated by him and made that clear. The undercurrent to the flashpoint was that Ian was beginning to be under pressure for his all-rounder's spot in the England team by the time we had our spat in 1990. After his back operation, he hadn't made the England tour party to the West Indies in '89/'90 and that had hurt him. I was one of several players putting in decent performances in county cricket as an all-rounder and although none of us could compare with a great player like Botham in his prime, he was still having to rack up some performances to get back in the England side – and he knew it. His pride was hurt by the England selectors, he knew his body was beginning to let him down and he was eyeing up the pretenders to his crown. His magnificent competitive instinct wouldn't allow him to acknowledge those rivals to his England spot and I'm sure he didn't think much of me.

So when I came in to bat at Edgbaston against Worcestershire in May 1990 I'm sure Ian wanted to blow away this upstart with the annoying manner. Although I was batting well, he kept telling me how lucky I was and I took that as a compliment, because I must have been getting to him. Ian kept throwing his arms up, going through the complete repertoire of hard-luck stories and histrionics (I could recognise them all, because I did the same stuff when I was bowling), until he got me out. Or rather, he prevailed on umpire Nigel Plews to confirm an optimistic lbw shout. I'd taken a big stride forward, got an inside edge on to the pad when the appeal bellowed out of Botham. I was given out, and as I walked away disappointedly, Botham shouted at me, 'F*** off!' I turned back, stared at him and was rewarded with, 'Go on, f*** off!' All the Worcestershire players then joined in as they gathered round Botham and I stopped ten yards from them and said to Botham, 'Pick your dummy up and put it back in your mouth.' Botham roared at me, 'I'll ram it down your face!' and after walking a few yards back to the pavilion, I turned and said to him, 'You've had your day, mate.' With that, I was off. Afterwards my captain, Andy Lloyd told me, 'Beefy's after you, he wants to fill you in. What did you say to him?' I wasn't bothered at all by the incident, it was a moment that should have stayed on the field, not for public consumption. Somehow my remarks to Botham were picked up and recycled though. It's still printed that I called him a 'fat has-been'. For all my faults, I've rarely had a go at a fellow cricketer about his physical shape – and all I did was to show to Ian Botham that I wouldn't be intimidated by anyone on the field. I think he respected that, because we had a chat about my alleged remark some time later and we got on fine when I first toured with him for England in 1992.

If you took all the cricketers I've annoyed out in the middle, you'd have a pretty handy team. Curtley Ambrose would take the new ball for a start. I hope he wouldn't bowl beamers, though – as he did at me in 1990. That match at Northampton was memorable for me because I made the highest score of my career – 202 not out – and because Ambrose decided the way to get rid of me was with a beamer. The trouble started just after I reached my hundred, when I played forward to Mark Robinson. I hit the pad with the inside edge of my bat, the ball went through to the wicket-keeper and all the slips went up for the catch. I was given not out and Greg Thomas, a fiery character, came up from second slip and gave me a real mouthful. The umpire, Don Oslear, was quick to intervene and said, 'Greg, he never hit it, the bat hit the pad, go back to slip and shut up.' Well Greg bowled the next over and I hit him for a couple of boundaries. The last ball was a well-placed beamer and I got out of the way just in time. Thomas said, 'Sorry, it slipped', a likely story from someone good enough to bowl for England.

Thomas came off and I continued to enjoy myself on a beautiful batting pitch. Ambrose came on and I hooked a bouncer past square leg to the boundary. I stood there watching the ball go to the fence, enjoying the moment, and when I turned round, there was Curtley towering over me. He stared at me and said, 'Be careful.' Through my grille I started back, but never said a word. I honestly wasn't fazed. It was such a slow wicket that I was looking forward to facing probably another bouncer. The next ball I never saw – because it didn't bounce. Curtley had beamed me. He then bowled me another two and somehow I stayed calm, telling myself to keep on batting. Although it wasn't the end of the over, I wasn't going to carry on batting without a chest and arm guard so I called for the protection as Barry Duddleston, the umpire at Curtley's end, seemed stunned by it all. Geoff Humpage came on with a chest pad for me, pausing only to give Ambrose a piece of his mind. I thought, 'Gee, thanks Geoff – I've still got to bat against this bloke!' After the over, Ambrose left the field.

At the close of play, I sat in the dressing-room and got angry. Those beamers could have killed me. It doesn't matter that the Northants guys believed I was out: what Ambrose did was in-excusable. What disciplinary action would be taken? I found out next morning, when I was asked into the office of Northants' chief executive, Steve Coverdale. There was my captain, Andy Lloyd, his opposite number, Allan Lamb – and Curtley Ambrose. Lamby had missed the incident – he wasn't playing through injury – but opened up by saying, 'Honestly, Dermot – I've got to believe that Curtley didn't mean it, because he's a great bowler and the beamers missed you.' I was trying to work that one out when Lamby brushed it aside: 'It doesn't matter, because Curtley wants to apologise. Curtley, say you're sorry.' And Curtley uttered his one word of that meeting: 'Sorry'. Lamby ushered him out of the office: 'Okay, Curtley, go off and warm up now', and closed the door. He then turned to me and said, 'Don't worry, the bloody wanker bowled me two in the West Indies, as well'. With that, Lamby donned his sunglasses, ready to walk out. I was dumbfounded. It was hardly a fulsome apology. Lamby also added, 'What do you expect, running down the wicket to fast bowlers?' I had done no such thing and the myth also grew that I had gone down on one knee to sweep Ambrose for six, and that had got his dander up. Has anyone ever seen Curtley Ambrose swept for six by a batsman on one knee? Strange how these rumours grow and become truths in the eyes of people who weren't actually there.

I do seem to have this ability to annoy West Indian fast bowlers, as Winston Benjamin would surely agree. He bowled me two beamers one day at Hinckley after a close lbw decision went against him. I could see he was angry at Merv Kitchen's decision and he bowled me two bouncers in a row. The first I hooked for four with a proper stroke, the next was mishooked over the wicketkeeper. Next ball was a fast, accurate beamer and I saw it just in time, getting the ball on the splice of my bat in front of my face. It could have killed me, and it wasn't pleasant to turn round and see all the slips laughing. Next ball was the same and Merv Kitchen thankfully took action and said, 'That's it, captain, have a word with your player', and David Gower did the necessary. Next ball – a bouncer. Benjamin was then warned for intimidation and he then threw all his toys out of the cot as he finished the over off three steps. After I took a single, Geoff Humpage played the last ball of the over back to the bowler. As it bobbled back to him, Benjamin hoofed the ball over cover point's head and third man had to chase after it. 'Yes, run,' I shouted at Humpage and we got three extra runs from his pique. I thought that was very funny, which I'm sure didn't endear me to the fielders or Winston Benjamin.

There is a fine line between justifiable needle and unfair behaviour on the field and I wouldn't want anyone to think I'm blameless. I admit I have transgressed sometimes. Even though I deplore the use of beamers, I admit I bowled one at Gehan Mendis once. We were playing at Old Trafford against Lancashire and Mendis, my old team-mate at Sussex, had given me some fearful stick, fielding at silly point when I batted. That didn't worry me, all part and parcel of the game. When I bowled at Mendis and Graeme Fowler, my first delivery swung prodigiously and I said, 'Oh, great – it's swinging' and Mendo then gave me some more verbals from the non-striker's end. It then dawned on me that Mendo had worked it all out. He was trying to rile me, to get me to drop it short in my anger, rather than pitch it up, looking for late swing. Mendo was a great cutter and puller and he was looking to pick me off if I tried to bang it in. Anyway, his constant sledging finally got to me and I proceeded to bowl some attempted beamers. The first was a knee-high full toss, the next a waist-high full toss and the third a beamer at head height that Mendo avoided. My next ball led to a big shout for lbw from me; the umpire, Dickie Bird, shouted 'Not out' instantly, threw my sweater at me and walked away. It was the end of the over and Dickie was quite right to show his displeasure at me. I had lost my rag for once and he let me know it wasn't to happen again, in the right way. That's the only time I've ever tried to bowl beamers.

I know the reputation about me that's grown on the county circuit and how it seeps into the media, and I only worry about the factual inaccuracies, rather than the general image, which, I think, is one of a guy who wants to win, who will try hard to stay on the legitimate side of the game's spirit, but will push the opposition as hard as possible. So it's felt that I'm always spoiling for a set-to on the field and that there are certain players looking out for me. Kevin Curran and I often have a laugh at people's expense in that sense. He and I are similar types on the field and whenever Northants play Warwickshire, we try to live up to the myth that we can't stand each other, that it wouldn't take much for us to come to blows on the field. At times one of us will give the other a little shoulder barge if either is in the way, or one will point the bat at the other if he's hit a boundary. It's become a laugh with Kevin and me and we try to see if the press reports will pick up the next day on alleged hostility towards each other. I have tremendous respect for Kevin as a cricketer, and we get along fine socially, but it's funny when I hear that commentators have said, 'There's no love lost between Curran and Reeve on and off the field.' How do they know?

The worst verbals I've encountered on a cricket field came from the New Zealander Mark Greatbatch, and I admit I was amused at how easily I managed to wind him up. He's known as 'Paddy' by his team-mates because he easily loses his temper and gets in a 'paddy', and I got him going during a one-day international at Dunedin in 1992. It was a very slow pitch, a low-scoring game, and when I came in to bat the game was anyone's and tensions were bubbling nicely. Greatbatch wasn't happy with me at all: I'd got him out in the previous one-dayer, caught at deep square leg, and in this game, taken behind by Alec Stewart, a decision that did not please our 'Paddy'. When I came in, I started trying to extemporise on the slow wicket, using the slog sweep to try to break free of some accurate bowling. I was trying to put pressure on the fielders with my partner, Chris Lewis. The ball would go to Greatbatch in the short extra cover and short mid-wicket regions and I'd be skipping down the pitch, daring him to throw at my stumps, hoping for some overthrows. That was annoying him, so I said, 'Go on, then, try it', and he started swearing at me, giving me a right earful. I found it very funny, and proceeded to ask him how many he had scored. It proved a red rag to this particular Kiwi bull and the air was blue.

By now, I was really pumped up, loving the tight situation and that I was getting under the opposition's skins. I hit Rod Latham for two boundaries to relieve the pressure, each time shouting 'Yes!' in exhilaration, and that really annoyed Greatbatch and his captain, Martin Crowe. Crowe snarled at me, 'I don't know why you're laughing, let's see how you are when you lose.' For a time, it looked as if we might. Greatbatch caught Lewis, he showed the ball to me in triumph and Crowe shouted at me, 'Just f*** off.' Tempers were fraying as Derek Pringle came in, and he worked the ball around superbly to bring us victory in the last over with five balls to spare. I had the satisfaction of hitting the winning runs and as I walked off the field with a huge smile on my face, Martin Crowe came over, shook my hand and said, 'Well played.' I considered that the gesture of a true sportsman, despite what went on between us a few minutes earlier. To me, that's how the game ought to be played – give nothing to the opposition, try all legitimate ways to unsettle them, and forget about it when the game is done.

My problem is that my mouth runs away from me sometimes, and I can see how that can really annoy opponents. And umpires, too. John Hampshire stopped play once against Essex, because he took exception to something I shouted from gully. I'd just got back from grade cricket in Australia, so I was still full of all that breezy cockiness you expect from Australian cricketers. When Allan Donald was about to bowl, I shouted, 'Come on Al! Let him have one!' John Hampshire walked over and told me I was over the top. I said I was only trying to sow seeds of doubt in the batsman's mind, so that he might go back to a ball that proved to be pitched up. John thought it was against the spirit of the game, but to me there was nothing wrong with encouraging our strike bowler, and getting the batsman thinking.

On the whole, I think we get on well with umpires, because at least we play with spirit at Warwickshire and don't moan at them. I'm sure they have to turn a deaf ear sometimes to some of the things we say on the field. For some reason, the chemistry between Kent and Warwickshire has never been right during my time at Edgbaston, and I dare say I've contributed to that. In one match, Allan Donald fired out Neil Taylor second ball, and as the batsman walked slowly away, our captain, Andy Lloyd, shouted, 'That's good enough for that ****' That set the tone for the game, which was hardly cucumber sandwiches and strawberry jam in spirit. When I batted, Richard Ellison stuck out his foot and tried to trip me up as I looked for a second run, and when I bowled, my mouth got the better of me again. Matthew Fleming was batting, a player who likes to play his shots and does in a very positive manner. Well I made a great fuss about setting a fielder out for the hook on the backward square leg boundary – and Fleming fell for it. As he passed me on the way to the pavilion, I said loudly, 'What a bloody idiot!' A daft thing to say, I know, but you get carried away in the heat of battle, and my self-confidence that borders at times on obnoxiousness does me no favours.

We really enjoy putting one over on Kent, particularly when the adrenalin flows. We've had more verbal battles with them than any other side in recent years and we had great fun down at Canterbury in the last weekend of the 1995 season. On the Saturday, we had wrapped up the championship by an innings and our celebration must have stuck in their throats in the adjoining dressing-room. That defeat meant they were bottom of the table for the first time this century, so they really had to pick themselves up for the Sunday League game next day. Kent were favourites to win the title, and at best we could be level on points, but sadly lost out on run rate. Worcestershire could still win the title but unfortunately for them, their game was abandoned due to rain. Midway through our innings the news spread through the packed Canterbury crowd that Kent had won the league. It was their first trophy since 1978 and the players were quite rightly celebrating on the field. I knew that I'd get some stick from the Kent players when I batted but, I was determined they weren't going to win this game. I wanted to ensure that their Sunday League title would be theirs only on a faster run rate, with Warwickshire runners up. If you're going to relinquish your title, do it with style, I thought. I knew that if our game the previous week hadn't been abandoned with Warwickshire in a great position, we would have retained the title. As far as I was concerned, all that adrenalin out in the middle galvanised me. As I walked towards the stumps, Graham Cowdrey stayed at the crease, and shouted to his fast bowler, Martin McCague, 'It's Reeve, Martin – come on, knock his head off.' That was all I needed to get me going. I bellowed loudly at Cowdrey, 'F*** off, you stupid prick!' and that really pumped me up. My partner, Roger Twose – who never needed a second bidding to get stuck in – joined me in the middle and shouted, 'Yeh, come on – let's get aggressive!' Roger loved situations like that, even though we were in a tight spot. He loved to goad the opposition, and Kent got the full works from him. As we got nearer to victory, he shouted to me, 'Remind me, Skip – what was our bonus for winning three trophies last year?' and then an over later, 'Come on, Skip – you've been in this situation before – like when we won the Nat West a few days ago!' It would be fair to say that Roger used to go over the top occasionally and in his last match for Warwickshire, he was more vocal than usual. With 25 runs still required for victory, Dean Headley asked the umpire to save him a stump. I shouted over, 'Don't worry, Deano – I'll save you a stump!' He said, 'Thanks,' before he realised I was taking the mickey by insinuating that I'd still be there at the finish. I was determined to see the job home, and enjoyed handing that stump over. That night, we left Kent's supporters to their celebrations at the ground, and went off for our own fun, enjoying the memories of six trophies from September '93 to September '95.

I know that Warwickshire aren't a popular side under my captaincy. This despite having some really nice guys on the staff in recent years, who were very well liked on the circuit, but as veterans like Asif Din and Gladstone Small will confirm, we were winning nothing for years with a popular bunch of players. I'm employed to get the best out of the players and I enjoy my cricket more if I'm aggressive. I know there are many people in the game who don't like me and that we are seen as a brash side, over-confident to the point of cockiness. Honestly that doesn't bother me, as I've been employed to get the best out of the team and believe this is helped by our boisterous attitude. Just before the start of our historic season in 1994, I attended a captains' meeting and a few umpires were present. One of them said that the game was becoming too noisy and vocal out in the middle, and he cited Warwickshire as the worst offenders. I replied that in my opinion English cricket was in danger of being too soft, that we needed a sharp, competitive edge, that we're too friendly to the opposition out in the middle.

Before every season, I tell my players what's expected when we're in the field. I want them to be positively vocal, to address their comments about an opposition batsman to each other. The tone of comment is crucial, it mustn't be half-hearted. I want the boys to be positive and upbeat in their encouragement. There is a fine line between strong vocal encouragement and the kind of sledging that questions a batsman's parentage or mocks his physical shape, and although we all fall from grace sometimes, I insist the boys don't get personal. I think it's fair enough if a guy plays an unconvincing shot against Allan Donald that I shout out from the slips, 'I'm not convinced, Al' or 'He's not happy against you, Al.' That's encouraging your bowler, letting the batsman know that we think he's on borrowed time. I don't think that's sledging. I tell my players that it's a war out there, to forget any friendships with opposition players until close of play. I want the opposition to feel uncomfortable against us, that it's our turf they're on – even when we're playing away – and that the odds are eleven of us, against two of them when we're fielding.

You can make a batsman lose his composure by letting him think he shouldn't be out there. When Nick Knight joined us from Essex, I liked his attitude right from the start in the field. He'd stand at silly point, staring at the batsman, and shout to our spinner, Neil Smith, 'Come on, bring me in the game. You and me, Neil, you and me!' In other words, 'I'm not afraid of being in here, I'll take the knocks. Are you up to it?' Nick claps his hands loudly and puts pressure on the batsman, something he obviously learned at the hard Essex school, where many trophies were won under Keith Fletcher and Graham Gooch. Such vocals can inhibit a batsman. I've seen their hands shake or their feet twitch when I've been close in. It's a tough game, and provided those things are kept under control, I see no harm in putting psychological pressure on the batsmen.

Our games against Worcestershire are always red-blooded

affairs, and not just because they are local derbies and both sides have jostled each other for trophies in recent years, but because they've got some tough characters on their side as well. Richard Illingworth and Steve Rhodes always bait me, and I've had a few four-letter words flung in my direction when they've got me out, but it's forgotten when the boundary line is crossed and the pavilion gate closed behind me. The important thing to me is that you shouldn't show that you are bothered by all the vocal stuff. That was Tim Curtis' mistake.

Now Tim's a cricketer of the old school, and a very charming bloke, but he got exasperated at us when he was batting one day. I stopped a ball, the rest of the side shouted, 'Great stop, Derm!' and there was a lot of hollering, designed to gee us all up. Tim stopped batting, tut-tutted and said, 'It's just like a zoo out here.' That did it. I performed my best sea-lion impression and some of the other lads joined in.

Sometimes we have gone too far on the field. No one's perfect and I'm certainly no angel – but Roger Twose has been a real thorn in the flesh of some opponents. Next to me, Roger must have been the most unpopular Warwickshire player in the opposition's eyes, because he can appear so bumptious, arrogant and over-aggressive. One day, Alec Stewart said to me, 'That Twose is a pain in the neck, isn't he?' I said, 'Actually, Alec, he's a really nice guy. He's intelligent, sensitive, cares about the outside world – and he's a hell of a guy to have on your side because of his aggression. I'm glad he's in my team.' I thought that was an interesting comment from Alec, bearing in mind that he also played a lot of grade cricket in Western Australia, and has the reputation of occasionally getting up people's noses on the field, but I let that one pass.

I agree that Roger can go over the top, though. I had to speak to him when we played England 'A' early in the '95 season. Paul Nixon, the opposition wicket-keeper, had broken his hand, but he was brave enough to carry on batting, although in obvious pain. I was well aware at the start of that season that we had picked up a certain reputation for verbals and that we were being closely monitored by the umpires. Allan Donald bowled one that beat Nixon for pace, as he went for the hook. It passed harmlessly down the legside as Nixon played far too late. Roger Twose at mid-on just burst out laughing and shouted at Nixon, 'Nico, what are you doing?' I thought that was a little disrespectful of Roger, because Nixon was battling away with a broken hand, showing a lot of guts. A quiet word did the trick afterwards, but that didn't stop Roger getting stuck in when he felt the need. He and Kevin Curran had an interesting conversation later that season, which alerted the umpires, but those two could look after themselves.

I'm sure that one of the reasons why I get up some people's noses is because I don't conform to the stereotype of an English cricketer. Having lived in Hong Kong, played so many years in Australia and enjoyed travelling all my life, I suppose I see life and my career in colonial, rather than typically English terms. I'm not all that sentimental about the public school attitude to cricket – all that 'for the good of the game' stuff, and that false modesty. I don't care about looking stylish on the field, I'm more bothered about effectiveness and succeeding. Because I'm hyperactive and talk quickly, I do blurt out some tactless remarks at times and I have upset some people. I'm an extrovert who enjoys life, who likes to party, who makes no pretence at shyness. I have developed a thick skin, and become more selfish with my time. I'll make an effort to be with those I'm interested in, but walk away from anything that doesn't appeal to me.

I suppose I'm vain, although I still dress like a student, and don't bother about buying expensive clothes. I don't gel or blow-dry my hair, unlike many, but the general feeling about me is that I'm very keen on myself. I've been headbutted in a night club just because I was Dermot Reeve, with a fairly high profile in the Birmingham area, and I've also received death threats. I've heard the rumour that I once said to a friend in a night club, 'Come on, let's get out of here – nobody recognises me.' That's a total fabrication, laughable.

I took more seriously the gossip item in a Birmingham newspaper that I walked into a Birmingham night club wearing my England World Cup shirt with 'Reeve' on the back of it, so that everybody would know who I was. The truth is much more mundane. One Sunday lunchtime, my brother and his family came up to Birmingham and we went out to lunch at one of my favourite restaurants, T.G.I. Fridays. In my usual panic to find something clean to wear, I pulled out a pair of jeans and the cleanest T-shirt I could find. It was one of the powder blue polo shirts we were issued with for the tour to New Zealand in 1992, with the word 'England' on the chest, and nothing on the back. Someone mentioned this to the local press and the next thing the public read is that I'm prancing around a night spot one evening, with my name on the back of the shirt I wore in the World Cup Final. I managed to get a retraction from the paper the following week, but that didn't stop the lie appearing later in the *Cricketer* magazine. I mentioned it in conversation to the England captain, Graham Gooch, who said in his dry way, 'Yeah, Derm, I heard about it – but didn't you have your phone number under your name?' It was nice to have a laugh about something that had got under my skin.

I find it amazing how these myths get recycled – like the 'fat has-been' one about Ian Botham, the brush I had with Brian Lara at Northampton, and this nonsense about my World Cup shirt. Is it because the journalists just wade through the cuttings and don't bother checking the revised facts, or is it the case that an image needs to be consolidated?

I suppose everyone who is successful in some profession has to put up with it. I'm only a minor sporting celebrity in one area of England, but I wouldn't want to be any higher in profile. I worked it out that as long as I'm happy with myself, I won't worry too much. I've got some very good friends with whom I clicked straight away, who understand my idiosyncrasies. T.G.I. Fridays and Ronnie Scott's Jazz Club in Birmingham are second homes to me, where I can hang out with people who don't care about how I'm doing on the cricket field. My loving, supportive family are even more important to me, we're always there for each other, taking a keen interest in our respective careers. As for those players I have annoyed on the cricket field, I admit I must be a pain to play against, but hopefully the guys I've played with have always found me supportive.

8

One-Day Cricket

I've been categorised as the ideal one-day cricketer, full of ingenuity and cheek, pulling the strings in the field and smashing a
few runs in the hectic final stages to sweep my side to victory. All
very flattering, I suppose, and there have been times when I've
got it right. I'm also pigeonholed as a 'bits and pieces cricketer',
someone who isn't outstanding in any one particular discipline, a
handy man to have in your side, they say. Now I accept many
people get carried away by statistics, and that it appears I make a
more important contribution in one-day games for Warwickshire
than in first-class cricket – but I believe my record in the longer
form of cricket isn't as ordinary as many believe.

When I arrived at Edgbaston from Sussex in 1988, I averaged
25 in first-class cricket with the bat and 28 with the ball: since
then it's 38 with the bat and 24 with the ball. Just to take some
other all-rounders' records in first-class cricket around the same
time: with Derek Pringle it was 28 with the bat and 26 with the
ball, Kevin Curran a highly impressive 36 and 27, David Capel
30 and almost 32, Chris Lewis 31 and 29, Phillip DeFreitas 22
and 28 and Craig White 30 and 30. My career first-class batting
average stands at 34.8 and 26.8 with the ball. So I don't think
that in the longer games I have been inferior to other key all-
rounders in county cricket. It's just convenient to label me a
one-day player.

When I finally started to make some impression as an all-
rounder at Edgbaston, it was inevitable that I would be built up
as a rival to Ian Botham, as a potential England all-rounder. That

was just a good line for the press, because Botham had been a great performer for England, one of the most charismatic and successful players we ever had. Anyone who stepped into his shoes in the national side would dread the comparison with such a great player and hope the media would lay off him, just judging him on his own merits. It didn't really bother me when my name was mentioned as a potential Botham in the late eighties and early nineties. I knew he was in decline after some serious injuries, but he was still a dangerous player. It brought out the competitive streak in me though, and I always relished our Midland derbies against Worcestershire, when I'd try to get one over Ian on a personal level. For a four-year period, during which Ian came back from his back operation and then played his last Test, I was quite happy with our comparative figures in championship cricket:

1989: Botham: 276 runs at 16, 51 wickets at 22.
       Reeve: 581 runs at 44, 11 wickets at 14.
1990: Botham: 576 runs at 36, 17 wickets at 32.
       Reeve: 1,265 runs at 55, 28 wickets at 27.
1991: Botham: 567 runs at 37, 38 wickets at 23.
       Reeve: 1,260 runs at 48, 45 wickets at 21.
1992: Botham: 705 runs at 33, 24 wickets at 42.
       Reeve: 833 runs at 34, 13 wickets at 48.

So in that four year period, Botham averaged 30 with the bat and 27 with the ball, compared to mine of 45 with the bat and 25, when I bowled.

I couldn't be mentioned in the same breath as Ian Botham, but he wasn't the only one troubled by injuries in that period, with three of those seasons featuring only fitful bowling from me in first-class cricket. But I was happy that my record in that time didn't lose out in comparison to the legend.

So is Dermot Reeve more valuable in one-day cricket than in the longer game? That's for others to decide. I like all forms of cricket, especially if I'm winning and the team are right behind me. I suppose the generalisation about me comes from all those Lord's Finals, most of them successful, with three Man of the

Match Awards coming my way. I've been so fortunate to play in six Finals, and three of them have involved fantastic finishes. There's no doubt I play better when the adrenalin's pumping. For some reason, I can actually see the ball better when I'm batting in one-day games than in the championship. The game is there to be won or lost in a couple of overs, and you've simply got to get cracking and pump yourself up. Sometimes when I walk out to bat in a tense one-day situation, I'm looking for something or someone to galvanise me. It may be an opponent's remark, which will force me to rap back a waspish comment, or perhaps my team-mate will get me going. Roger Twose used to be terrific at that, with comments like, 'Come on Skip, let's show them how it's done – enjoy the pressure!'

It's hard for many to change their game when batting in a Sunday League game during the middle of a championship match. You go out there on a Sunday and there's little time to scratch around. I've sometimes let the ball go through and suddenly thought to myself, 'What am I doing? This is a Sunday game.' If my adrenalin is surging, though, I seem to be pain-free, quick on my feet and see the ball well. I'll look to nudge the ball around early on, getting used to the conditions, the pace and bounce of the pitch. I'll always look for that productive shot between the wicket-keeper and slip, that would get you out in a four-day match. I don't play in a wide area like someone such as Neil Fairbrother, because I lack his expansive range of strokes, so I'll concentrate on areas that have worked for me – the sweep/slog on one knee, the paddle, and of course, the reverse sweep. I go for the slog/sweep off the faster bowlers because I don't drive all that successfully. I don't hit well through the line of the ball unless I've been able to use my feet and swing my arms. Perhaps it's my grip on the bat, but I don't usually back myself to clear mid-off or mid-on, a distance of around 35 yards. On the legside, the square leg fielder is only 20 yards away, so I can clear him easier with my dominant bottom hand. It's a percentage shot that I have practised, but bowlers have been getting wise to me. They move the fielder from deep backward square leg to forward square leg to block my slog/sweep, so I have to look elsewhere for a safe, attacking shot. Bob Woolmer helped improve my driving and I scored runs in different areas in my last couple of seasons which was both satisfying and enjoyable. You can never stand still in one-day cricket.

Things happen so quickly in one-day cricket, that you can be out of the game in a couple of overs. We have a couple of sayings in our dressing-room that we use to keep us concentrating – 'Every Ball's an Event' and 'Control the Controllables'. In other words, leave the captaincy to the guy in charge and make sure your own game is up to scratch on the day. Input is welcomed by the captain, but the frenetic nature of these games – especially on Sundays – means there is little time for extended thought and group discussion while out on the pitch. The captain has to keep his eye on the scoreboard much more than in four-day cricket. Generally you are more defensive in the field, balancing the needs of getting early wickets with the necessity to save runs. When do you put the sweepers back and take out those two slips? Your fielders must be in the exact place when the bowler is running in, you simply cannot afford doziness, when a guy strays. Every single ball is crucial. You can't afford any looseners from your bowlers. That is permissible in a four-day game, because sensible looseners from your bowlers mean they've got a better chance of avoiding injury. In a one-day game, a loosener is often a four-ball, and no gifts are encouraged.

In some ways, one-day cricket is harder than Test cricket. You're under the spotlight in one-dayers, you can't get away with a wayward spell or block it at the crease. If you're patient in a Test, you get praised for a responsible innings, but that's bad batting in the one-day context. The 'dot' ball is a godsend to the captain in one-day cricket, whereas the Test batsman easily keeps that out and just waits for the bad ball. Of course, Test cricket is mentally draining, but all that scampering around in the field and high-adrenalin drama of one dayers is also demanding. A routine Test Match day lasts just 90 overs, but a one-day game can take up 120 overs and not be finished until around eleven hours after you've arrived at the ground. Fatigue sweeps over you very quickly once you slump in the dressing-room and the adrenalin ebbs away as quickly as it appeared.

Many people seem to think I experiment all the time when I bowl in one-day games. They see my very slow, looping delivery and say, 'There he goes again, old Dermot – every ball's different, isn't it?' Not true. In my early days at Sussex, we had a lot of strike bowlers who traded wickets for runs, and my coach, Stewart Storey, told me, 'Your job's to bowl maidens.' That's what I've always tried to do. In the 1995 Nat West final I attempted to bowl every ball the same way and in the same area. It wasn't a great surface to bat on, so runs had to be chiselled out. There was no justification for much experiment, and the ball wasn't swinging, so for 60 deliveries I tried a stock ball – full up to the batsman, on a tight line, bowling to my field. That was a case of using my experience, adapting to the conditions, but there are times when you have to mix it up.

Since my shoulder operation in 1988, I've lost a yard of speed, so I had to think about varying my pace. That's when I discovered my slower ball that proved effective for a long time in one-day cricket. When I was playing grade cricket in Western Australia, I saw Simon O'Donnell and Steve Waugh bowling a slower delivery out of the back of the hand in a one-day series against New Zealand. I remember a great delivery from O'Donnell that completely foxed John Bracewell, the ball hitting the leg stump as Bracewell ducked to avoid the looping, slower ball. I decided to work on that. I had built a net in my back garden in Perth and practised bowling with the back of my hand facing the batsman. I tried it out in the nets at my club, and I had batsmen ducking into what they thought was a beamer. In our next match, I got two wickets with the slower ball, one of them an lbw when the guy ducked away and the ball plopped on his foot. When I came back to Warwickshire, I got wickets with it in one-day games straight away, including Viv Richards when he whacked it straight up in the air. All four of my wickets in a Sunday League game against Derbyshire were from deliveries out of the back of my hand and I found it was particularly effective on a loose surface that helped the spinner. I found that even if the batsman spotted it was the slower ball and allowed it to pitch, it might hold up on him if he went for the big shot and the ball would occasionally go up in the air. For a while, it had great surprise value, but after a time batsmen were waiting for it, so I had to conceal it and work on other slower ball variations. It's a constant guessing game. Adam Hollioake possesses the best slower ball I have faced and showed in two one-day internationals against Pakistan how crucial it is. To be honest, without it Adam is a pretty average seamer but its value is so great that Adam could play a vital role for England in one-day cricket for a long time. He is a fine, hard-hitting batsman, a brilliant fielder and he should have been in the England squad for the 1996 World Cup. I would have picked him before any other all-rounder for that tour.

Bowling at my speed, which has reduced every year, its vital to swing the ball.

I used to watch closely a swing bowler like Terry Alderman who was so dangerous with those little outswingers that would tempt the batsmen into the nicked off-drive. Then he would bowl straighter and quicker and skid one through for the lbw. Ian Botham was very good at that as well. You have to have some ingenuity to bowl well in cricket, because a good batsman wants to get into a rhythm, he likes batting against a medium-pacer who is the same speed every delivery. On a flat wicket against someone like Graeme Hick, my stock delivery would probably go for four, so I'll look to mix up my line and speed. Perhaps I'll bowl an over of blatantly slow deliveries, with a quicker one slipped in that might scuttle through for the lbw.

In four-day cricket the condition of the wicket is the deciding factor as to how to bowl. If it's got pace in it, I'll bowl more 'effort' balls, in shorter spells, with a third man. If it's a slow pitch, that generally suits my bowling, I can get the wicket-keeper up, looking for the legside stumping and inhibiting the batsman from skipping out of his crease. I'll bring the third man up into the ring, and bowl a full length, with a couple of slips in for the outswinger. In one-day cricket, I'd rarely have more than one slip. You're always testing the batsman's technique, because he has to hit the ball harder to get pace on to the slower deliveries to pierce the inner ring of fielders. Because I'm bowling slow-medium floaters, some batsmen feel they have to get after me, as I look so innocuous. That suits me, because there's always a chance then that they'll slog it up in the air or get lbw playing across the line. In one-day cricket, the onus is on the batsman to play shots, so I just try not to go for runs. In four-day cricket I enjoy tempting a batsman, trying to bore him out particularly when the wicket is low and slow. It's a matter of adapting to the conditions as quickly as possible. Some bowlers are very clever at concealing their intentions. They cover the ball as they run in, so it's impossible to see which way the ball will swing, or indeed if a slower ball is on the way.

One day at the Oval, Bob Woolmer's attention to detail had us in stitches at his suggestion for coping with Waqar's reverse swing. Bob thought he would sit in the stand behind the bowler, with a green and a red flag. He said that he would be able to spot which way the ball would be swinging when Waqar placed the ball in his hand before turning to run in. Green flag for the outswinger, red flag for the other way. Bob was partly serious about it, until it was pointed out that it wasn't really on!

Another hilarious moment with a slower ball came in a match against Hampshire when Michael Bell was running up to bowl. The non-striker, Adrian Aymes, spotted Keith Piper walking up to the stumps and shouted, 'Slower ball!' to his partner. We all stopped and I asked David Shepherd if Adrian was allowed to do that. A compromise was struck – no shouting from Adrian, but a loud cough when he saw Piper move in. I told Piper to walk forward then back, going for the double bluff. Adrian coughed loudly just as Michael bowled it, and it turned out to be a quick seamer, rather than a slower ball. Piper just got to it and we all saw the funny side of the incident.

Many dismiss me as a lucky cricketer, especially in one-day games, because of the way I get batsmen out. It appears a fluke as they hit me straight up in the air off what looked like a very ordinary delivery, or I bluff them out with a change of pace. They used to say the same about a far greater all-rounder, Ian Botham, without giving him the credit for the self-confidence to try something different, to unsettle the batsman. Branding you 'lucky' tends to ignore the hard work that goes into dismissals. You can't just run up and bowl a slower ball against good batsmen, you need to work at it for hours and hours in the nets. The same applies to the reverse sweep or any other shot that enables you to get the ball through the field. Style is an irrelevance in one-day cricket, especially when the gaps seem very small and the fielders are choking the run rate.

It's attitude that's more important than style in one-day cricket and it was that never-say-die spirit which won us the Nat West Trophy in 1993 against Sussex, as we chased 321 in 60 overs. David Smith and Martin Speight batted marvellously for Sussex and some of our bowlers took a real pasting, but strangely enough, we took strength from that as we sat in the dressing-room before our innings. It was a case of breaking down the run rate, and forgetting we'd make history if we got there. It was simply five runs an over. We lost our openers for 18, but they hadn't used up many overs and the reaction from one of our openers was very encouraging. Jason Ratcliffe was, of course, dis-appointed at getting out, but soon he rallied and said to us, 'That wicket is a belter, the best I've ever batted on! We'll get these, lads, come on!' That was great to hear, and typical of our team spirit. Paul Smith and Dominic Ostler carried on playing posi-tively, and we just had the feeling that it was going to be our day. We didn't subscribe to the theory that wickets in hand were vital, because bowlers have got better at bowling the death overs, they vary the pace more imaginatively. The field placings are more professional now, and the standard of fielding generally is vastly improved. So it was a case of going at the rate of five an over, and expecting to dominate the spinner, Ian Salisbury. He went for five-and-a-half an over, but when I joined Asif Din at 164/4, the rate required was now above a run a ball. Asif then played the innings of his life, the fastest hundred in a Lord's Final. He had a wonderful eye, and improvised marvellously that day – stepping back to carve over backward point. As the chase was really on, I was full of adrenalin, shouting instructions to Asif. Asif kept touching the little bag he carried round his neck that reflects his Muslim faith, and looking skywards for inspiration. We let the required rate get up to beyond eight an over, but were confident we could still win. We kept talking about having one big over, which would get us back on track – just one over that would get us around fifteen and it was ours for the taking. But we never managed to do it, and we needed 20 off the last two overs. Ed Giddins bowled a fine over for Sussex, giving away just five runs – and he also dismissed Asif. It was up to me, now; you couldn't expect Roger Twose, our new batsman, to pick up the pace just like that in the gathering gloom. In that over from Giddins, I was looking to get him away with the sweep/slog, but he bowled a very good full length. I dug out an excellent yorker fifth ball, then squeezed out another for a single off the last ball. I was dejected, while the reaction of Giddins made it clear he thought Sussex had won. So we had to get 15 off the final over, to be bowled by Franklyn Stephenson, an experienced fast bowler with a deadly slower ball and the hostility and accuracy to restrict any batsman if he got his radar right. At that moment, Roger Twose was fantastic. He marched down the wicket, shook me out of my disappointment and shouted, 'Come on Skip – we can do it!' Roger was always very vocal at the crease, and I needed his support then.

As Franklyn ran up to bowl at the start of that final over, I can clearly remember thinking, 'What am I going to do? He's got one of the best slower balls in the world. Will I see it?' He had fine leg up and long-on and long-off out, so I thought there was a good chance he'd bowl the slower one. I just told myself to look hard and I managed somehow to club a fast ball straight back over his head for four. The next I struck out to long-on and I should have been run out, but Peter Moores' throw from behind the stumps missed. The third ball was a yorker, dug out to short extra cover, and Bill Athey's misfield brought us two more to long-off. Eight off the first three balls: a good start. Roger roared at me: 'Wherever you hit it, we're coming back for two!' 'OK!' I bellowed back, amid the noise of the crowd. He was right. I was the man in, seeing the ball well considering the darkness that was closing in. Roger's vocal encouragement was proving to be an essential boost to me keeping the adrenalin flowing. The fourth ball amazed me – a sweet shot through the covers, a stroke I rarely play. Franklyn was astonished and afterwards, in the bar, he still couldn't get over it. I don't know where that shot came from to this day.

At that stage, Franklyn had bowled all quick deliveries, and no sign of the dreaded slower ball. The fifth was the slower ball and

I picked it up late, got an inside edge to fine leg and we scrambled a single. To this day, I wish I'd set myself to hit him for four, but I made the mistake of concentrating on getting a bat on it, rather than swinging my arms. That left Roger on strike for the last ball of the match. We needed one to win, provided we didn't lose a wicket, because they had lost six and we were five down at that stage. Two runs would be even better, making it a clear victory. By now it's almost dark and we're both breathing heavily. Alan Wells rearranges his field, the crowd is hoarse, the lights on the scoreboard are very bright indeed, and Roger and I are trying to make sense of it all. I told him, 'Their wicketkeeper is standing up. I think that means he'll bowl a slower ball because he won't risk a quicker one with the keeper up. If he bowls you a quicker one, get the bat on it and we'll run through. But look for the slower ball.' I've watched that final ball so many times on the video and sure enough it was the slower ball. Roger spotted it, slowed down his bat swing, waited for the ball and then hit in the air. For a moment, I thought he was going to be caught by Neil Lenham at third man, up in the ring, but it squirted away. We sprinted the first and ran the second, just to make sure the scorers hadn't made a mistake, all the while yelling our heads off. I grabbed a couple of stumps for souvenirs and raced off to the pavilion. I wanted to stand there and savour the moment, but no chance. Someone ripped the helmet off my head, Franklyn said, 'Give me your bat' and he then too raced off the field. I felt for Franklyn afterwards – 19 times out of 20, you would have expected a bowler of his class to defend an asking rate of 15 in the final over.

I was so high on adrenalin at the time, and then for a time afterwards, until the enormity of that win sunk in and I felt very tired. Those surges of adrenalin out in the middle had got me through, helping me see the ball so clearly and swing my arms freely. I was so proud for the team, for the aggressive way we had pursued that target, at the refusal to give in. I still get the shivers watching it again on the video.

Two years later, we were in another cliffhanger at Lord's and Roger and I were at the centre of the final stages. It was one of those games that ebbed and flowed, but Northants would probably have won it but for a slice of luck that came my way. Well, a large slice of luck, actually. We were struggling on a slow pitch to get 201 to win, with their Indian leg-spinner, Anil Kumble, bowling magnificently. When I joined Roger, we were 122/5 and Kumble still had plenty of overs left. Early in my innings, he did me for pace as I played a sweep and the ball hit my back leg. Dickie Bird gave me 'not out' to the inevitable lbw appeal and I could have kissed him. Kumble and his fielders couldn't believe it, and after watching the video, neither could I. It was a straight, full delivery on the line of middle stump, and just a foot or two ahead of the stump. I don't know how I got away with that one. I know Dickie is known as a 'not outer', but he must have had a mental block for that ball. I finished 37 not out, and, with a tight bowling spell, I picked up another Man of the Match award, but it could so easily have gone to Anil Kumble instead. I got all the favourable publicity – all that 'Captain Marvel' stuff – but I enjoyed the one thing that is a variable in tight one-day finishes: luck.

We weren't at our best in that Final. Injuries had robbed us of Gladstone Small and Tim Munton, and we had to trust in the inexperienced Dougie Brown and Michael Bell. Dougie came into the game with a cracked hand, and Nick Knight was carrying a broken finger and they were two early casualties against some excellent new ball bowling by Paul Taylor and Kevin Curran. A score of 28/3 with 17 overs gone already was hardly the victory platform on a slow pitch with some variable bounce. Then Kumble came on and he bowled Dominic Ostler with one that hurried on straight: a disappointing dismissal that one, because we had talked before the game about not going back to Kumble's quicker ball. He is so fast off the pitch that it's a major risk to step back and try to cut him; he had picked up so many wickets that way in county cricket that season.

I know the TV cameras picked us out on the balcony, looking cheery at the time of our batting crisis. I was next man in, and I didn't feel lucky, but we all put up the bold front when the cameras were on us. Bob Woolmer rang up at that stage from Cape Town to wish us well, and I shouted 'Hello!' to him across the dressing-room. I don't know if Bob had detected some uncharacteristic tension, but he would have been pretty dense if he hadn't. We were in trouble, and Kumble was winning the game for Northants. Eventually when I joined Twose, it wasn't just a case of seeing off the danger man, we had to get runs off Kumble as well. With Paul Smith next man in, a player more comfortable against the seamers than Kumble, I gave Roger the reassuring viewpoint: 'If you get out now, we'll struggle.'

Roger was dropped twice, I escaped thanks to Dickie Bird, and it was very hairy. I had told Roger I was going to try sweeping Kumble, but I mistimed the shots because of his pace. Roger would tell me, 'I'm going big this over, Skip' and I'd tell him: 'Fine, but don't get out.' I tried the sweep again, but only got one leg-bye off Kumble to the short boundary, and I remember thinking, 'How am I going to get a run here?' By then, Kumble just had to go for runs, otherwise we would probably lose. I noticed Allan Lamb put a man finer on the offside for the reverse sweep, but I still decided to try it off Kumble. I got down at the right time, played it correctly and it went very fine, to beat the fielder. That was a nice moment. So Lamby moved the fielder even finer and I decided not to try the shot again. If Kumble had bowled it slower and I'd got a top edge going for the reverse sweep, it would have been a routine catch to that fielder who had been placed finer. So I settled for playing Kumble square for a single or two and we ended up taking eight off his final over. I suppose that boundary was decisive, but we never got on top of him. He's a fabulous bowler, and his figures of 1/29 off 12 overs didn't do him any justice at all.

So Kumble was off at last, and we had four wickets in hand. Roger was then run out on his call to the keeper after we had put on 54 at four an over. Kevin Curran came on. He's a bowler I've enjoyed jousting with over the years, a guy I get on very well with off the field, but we strike sparks off each other when we're out there in the middle. I knew Kevin's strong competitive instinct would have him fired up for this battle against me, and with 20 needed off the last three overs, this one was going to be decisive. For the first ball, mid-on was up for the single and the wicket-keeper back, which suited me. On that slow pitch, I would have had to slog from the crease if the keeper had stood up. I would have been more vulnerable then, instead of being able to come down the crease and hit through the line of the ball. Four runs.

After that boundary, the keeper still stayed back and I was delighted. The next three balls went to extra cover, stopped by Allan Lamb and finally another boundary over mid off. With four leg-byes also coming in the over, we got 12, leaving us eight for the last two overs. We got home with seven balls to spare, but it was far closer than that. If Kumble had enjoyed more luck, and Curran had insisted on calling up the keeper to keep me in the crease, it may have been Northants' day. Again I was amazed at the way the surges of adrenalin had helped me think clearly and see the ball well, but I knew what a hard-earned victory that was. Only in our fielding were we clearly superior to Northants, as the tension got to them in the final overs. For me, the biggest pleasure in that win was that we hadn't played all that well, but still came through with grit and guts.

We had been much more impressive on our way to Lord's that year. In the quarter-final at Derby, we bounced back the day after losing that dramatic championship game against Northants by seven runs – a draining, tension-filled match spread over four days that left the players on both sides shattered. It was the best game of its type I had ever played in and our defeat meant Northants had overtaken us at the head of the championship table. A less resilient side would have faded away in the last six weeks of the season, but we put it right the very next day. We lost Neil Smith in the first over, but good batting all the way down the order brought us to 290/6. We then swept away Derbyshire, with Allan Donald blasting out the later batsmen after the stranglehold applied by superb fielding and nagging bowling by Tim Munton.

The semi-final at Cardiff was an even better team performance than at Derby. Glamorgan really fancied their chances that day, and I couldn't blame them. They had some fine stroke players, an excellent bunch of fielders and bowlers ideally suited to the home conditions. They won the toss on a slow pitch that was certain to deteriorate for batting. It would turn and bounce, and in Robert Croft and Steve Barwick, they had potential match-winners. A score of around 200 would be a tall order, and with the ground absolutely packed with noisy Welshmen, it seemed as if we were playing a country, as well as a county.

When they went out to bat, their home supporters looked forward to the day with understandable optimism. At lunch they were 80/8 and the game was effectively over. Tim Munton had bowled unchanged to take 2/18 in his 12 overs and Trevor Penney's glorious fielding had been underestimated yet again. Trevor is a marvellous athlete, so quick to the ball, so swift at releasing it – but we had felt for a time that he ought to be hitting the stumps more with his throws. Phil Neale worked hard with him before the Cardiff match, and the result was the direct hit that pinged out Matthew Maynard's middle stump as he struggled to get back. Getting the dangerous Maynard like that is as good as bowling him with an absolute beauty, and Trevor followed that up with a great piece of fielding to get David Hemp run out.

That demoralised Glamorgan, and as lunch approached, they stopped looking for runs. I crept in at silly point as they blocked it, and snaffled Colin Metson to make them eight down. Soon they were all out for 86 and we had won by eight wickets in the 25th over. It was a comprehensive thrashing, a fantastic all-round performance that contained all the ingredients we had looked for in recent years, but I was amazed at Glamorgan's passive approach as we got among their wickets. We wouldn't have played for lunch, as the wickets fell. Our attitude would have been, 'Come on boys, someone will get runs. If one of us gets 50 and the rest chip in, that gets us to 200, and they'll struggle to get them.'

You must always believe you can win a match, and that self-belief has got us out of so many tight situations in one-day cricket. That was the reason why we got through against Kent in the 1994 Nat West semi-final at Edgbaston. Kent really ought to have won that at a canter. We made 265/8 in our 60 overs, and on a good batting wicket that was about 30 short. They started well and I had to use up most of the available overs from Tim Munton and Gladstone Small as we searched for wickets. On such a good pitch, I knew that we needed to bowl them out because otherwise they'd get the runs. It didn't work for a long time, though, and at 183/2, with Neil Taylor and Carl Hooper established, they needed only 83 with 14 overs left. Nine times out of ten, that would have been a stroll for the batting side. Then Dominic Ostler took a great catch on the square-leg boundary to get Taylor and Kent began to panic. Graham Cowdrey went to a stunning catch behind the stumps by Keith Piper, leaping high to claw the edge down with one glove, and that inspired us. We kept Hooper away from the strike, he got frustrated and got himself out. We nagged away at the rest of the Kent batting and they buckled. The crowd really got behind us when we needed lifting, and we wouldn't let go. They lost by eight runs in a game that typified the crazy, unpredictable nature of one-day cricket.

If you sat down and analysed the various ways in which you can throw away a one-day game, you'd probably shrivel and underachieve. That's why I tell our guys to strip the game down to its bare essentials and don't think about how easily it can all go horribly wrong. I find the mental demands of one-day cricket fascinating, with the need to keep several overs ahead in the field uppermost in my mind. I believe your best one-day sides possess six reliable bowlers. Look how important it was for England in the second Texaco Trophy international against Pakistan to be able to call on Adam Hollioake after Ronnie Irani had started badly. You need options. All-rounders in quantity are very valuable, and we have been lucky to have the Smiths, Dougie Brown, Graeme Welch, Roger Twose and myself to call on, so that we bat a long way down and our main batters aren't compromised by the need to be cautious. They have licence to play their shots and extemporise as much as they want.

It's fascinating to see how much the one-day game is evolving, though. Every season, there seems to be a new train of thought that overturns the established conventions – like starting carefully, having wickets in hand for the last ten overs, using your fastest bowlers at the death, putting the spinner on during a quiet period. All those ideas have been challenged in recent years and I like that. You need to keep thinking ahead, coming up with new ways of turning a game in a few minutes. Every ball really must be an event.

9

Captaincy Hassles

I nearly resigned the Warwickshire captaincy during our second marvellous season during a row. It came at the end of June 1995, at a time when I felt I was not getting the full backing of some players and the management. For a time I felt very low and it needed some give-and-take on all sides to get us back on an even keel. By the time the rumours leaked out of the Warwickshire camp and found their way into the press, we were all pulling again in the same direction, but for a few weeks in the month of June, I was close to packing it in. The background to it just underlines the hassles involved in being a county captain when some players start to doubt you, and you don't get the full backing of the management. The irony at that time was that we were again near the top of the championship table, rolling over sides ruthlessly and looking good for another great year. On the face of it, we must have appeared our usual bouncy selves. However, the problems had been building up for some months.

I had been very unhappy at the lack of support given to me over Brian Lara's behaviour in the previous season. I will continue to stress that he is the greatest batsman I have ever seen, and that he did wonders for our performances – but he was a pain to captain. Dennis Amiss and Bob Woolmer just wanted to let it slide, get through that 1994 season without any undue fall-out, and take a breather. I went along with that, even though it rankled that the captain had received less than adequate support. So it was doubly galling to me when it was announced by the club the following February that Lara, not Allan Donald, would be our overseas player from 1996 onwards. To make matters worse, Lara would be on a three-year contract. I had not been consulted on the matter during any of the negotiations, I just had the *fait accompli*. Surely the club captain ought to have had some say in the decision, especially as our relationship had been rocky for most of the previous season? It was also terribly hard on Allan, a true professional, a 100 per cent Warwickshire man. Brian Lara didn't give English domestic cricket much respect, he saw it as a chore, too easy for him. Allan Donald was never like that, despite being a top Test player. A great supporter of his team-mates, he would sense when one of the younger bowlers was a bit down, and he'd suggest they had a bowl to get some confidence back. He would ask us for support in the field, shouting, 'It's gone quiet out here – get behind me!' Allan was as motivated playing for us as he ever was with South Africa.

I was still brooding about the Lara decision when we went to Cape Town on our 1995 pre-season tour. A chat with Allan Donald reassured me of his motivation for the coming season, which might have been his last for the club, with Lara signed up for the next three. So I had no worries in the short-term about our overseas player, but I was concerned about our general preparation for the new season. I knew we would be there to be shot at, after our record-breaking season, and yet I sensed a level of complacency in Cape Town. Apart from Dougie Brown, the fitness levels for every player were down. That indicated a lack of commitment during the winter, and it meant we would be wasting valuable time trying to get properly fit, rather than working on skills.

Bob Woolmer was with us for his swansong during that Cape Town fortnight. Bob had joined the South African national side as their director of coaching and I knew we would miss him, but it was time for his successor, Phil Neale, to make his presence felt. It was an uneasy period of transition and difficult for Phil, who sensibly took a back seat, watched how Bob worked with the players and monitored their response.

During that period in Cape Town, Bob didn't really handle things in his usual genial manner. He was upset at our general lack of fitness, felt we were sloppy in the field, and was very hurt when we lost badly to Western Province at Newlands. I realised that Bob desperately wanted Warwickshire to look impressive in front of the South Africans, because it would reflect well on his methods, and also because he had praised us highly. He's still a proud Englishman, despite living in Cape Town, and he wanted the locals to see a top unit in action. We let him down, but that was partly due to the fact that we were getting ready for a long season and bound to be rusty, in addition to some complacency. Perhaps Bob was comparing us with his South African national squad which was unfair as most of our guys hadn't played for months, or for that matter, weren't international cricketers.

I knew that Bob wanted to give some home truths to several of our players in those last few days, to get things off his chest that he had been storing up at Edgbaston over the years, and that led to friction. He really gave Paul Smith a rocket about his fielding and I could tell that Bob had wanted to say that for some time. Then Trevor Penney talked back to Bob in the Cape Town dressing-room after a remark about his batting. A couple of years earlier, Bob had spoken sharply to Trevor about the way he had batted against Martin McCague and clearly Trevor hadn't forgotten, so he came back with a volley, in front of all the players. I felt a little sorry for Phil Neale and our new signing, Nick Knight, that some players were wading into Bob, and vice versa. We had prided ourselves on the open environment, where everyone was encouraged to speak their mind, but now there was back-chat all over the place. The spirit just wasn't right in Cape Town and I had some negative vibes about our season as the start loomed.

In our opening first-class match, we were hammered by an innings by England 'A' and within a month we had lost our first three Sunday League games, and were out of the Benson and Hedges Cup. So two of the four trophies on offer seemed to have slipped away from us before we could blink. We weren't right in our approach and although other sides were successfully raising their game against us, that should have been an incentive to players with pride and professionalism – the qualities we normally show. As captain, I was struggling as well. I didn't feel I had the support of all the players, an impression confirmed when we played at Durham in the middle of May and a couple of players talked back to me on the field. Now I know that some things are said out there between team-mates in the heat of the moment, but this was different. Richard Davis, our left-arm spinner, was disappointed that he only bowled two overs in the Durham match, but the pitch was helping the seamers. Richard gave me some lip on the field, and Paul Smith also weighed in. Phil Neale, who was easing himself into his new job, was just observing the situation in his early weeks, and I told him that the spirit wasn't right, that we weren't all as together as usual. We had a team meeting at Durham after the game and I said that some of the team were judging me as a cricketer and I didn't feel supported. We weren't encouraging each other enough, techniques were being criticised behind players' backs – and it had to stop. I wasn't enjoying the captaincy and said we must pull together. It was difficult to tell how effective my words had been. Incidentally, we beat Durham comfortably in the four-day match.

I still believed I could cut it as a player, even though others might think otherwise. In the 1994 season, I hadn't done well in first-class cricket, although my one-day record was arguably better than any previous season. Because of a series of injuries, I only played in nine first-class matches. Tim Munton deputised ably for me as captain, winning eight of the nine championship games under his leadership. I decided to save myself for the one-day games in July and August as we chased trophies on all fronts, and the side kept going for the championship without me. It wasn't a blow to my ego at all. I'd had a bellyful of Brian Lara, so let Tim and Bob handle him in their own way. I felt it vital for the team that Tim had the same freedom to captain as I'd been given. I'd learned from when I led the side occasionally when Andy Lloyd was injured, finding it easier without the club captain at my shoulder. As we came down the home straight, I was fit again for the championshi games, but I stayed out of the side by choice. Young Graeme Welch was making a good impression as an all-rounder, and it was better for the team that he stayed in, and I continued to rest up for the one-dayers. When we won the championship at home to Hampshire, a lot was made of my gesture to Tim Munton, insisting that he should be presented with the championship trophy. It was just obvious to me that it was only right that Tim should be pushed to the front. He hadn't missed a championship game, had taken 81 wickets and led the side successfully for half the matches.

What I hadn't bargained for was a change in attitude to me as a player by Dennis Amiss, though. Our chief executive dropped a heavy hint before the start of the 1995 season. Dennis said that I should consider dropping myself in favour of Tim in championship cricket if my form wasn't good. A ball hadn't been bowled! Surely he should have been encouraging me and wishing me well as captain and player in all four competitions. I was hurt and angry. I pointed out to Dennis that 1994 had been my best season in one-day cricket, only to be told, 'That's not the real cricket, though.' Try telling that to the members who packed out Edgbaston on Sundays, and who celebrated three one-day trophies in just 12 months!

So I didn't feel I had the right support of the chief executive at the start of the next season, when I wanted to crack down on the players. After all, he hadn't consulted me when they decided to sign up Brian Lara for another spell, and he clearly thought my best days as a county cricketer were behind me. As for the players, I honestly felt some wanted me out of the side. There was a definite clique within the team – comprising Neil Smith, Andy Moles, Richard Davis and Tim Munton – who I'm sure would have preferred Tim to be club captain. There will always be personality problems within a team and that is understandable. You don't need to be everyone's best mate, but you should respect and support your team-mates in cricketing matters. On captaincy, Tim's style in 1994 was different to mine, but this was 1995, and a decision had been made by the club that I was to be captain in all four competitions. It was ironic that Tim wasn't even fit to play until we took on Sussex early in June, as he was still recovering from a back operation in the winter. To confuse matters, I missed a couple of championship games through back and rib injuries, and I could sense the clique were more bubbly and vocal with me on the sidelines. The freedom of expression these players had enjoyed in the past meant that some were speaking out, at times undermining my status as captain. The atmosphere was unhealthy, even though we had won five of our first seven championship matches.

I felt we had recovered a good deal of momentum after a complacent start, and was personally happy with my own game. I was averaging 30 with the bat and 28 with the ball by the time we came to Ilford to play Essex at the end of June. Before the match Tim Munton, Phil Neale and I looked at the pitch, and discussed what our final 11 would be. Phil and Tim wanted to play our spinner, Richard Davis, because they were sure the ball would turn and Essex would no doubt be playing their two spinners – John Childs and Peter Such. They wanted to leave out Dougie Brown, a seamer. Yet Dougie had just taken eight wickets in the previous championship match against Yorkshire and 24 wickets in only 5 championship games. As far as I was concerned, he played in front of a few players at the moment. I wasn't sure that Tim was a hundred per cent right after his serious back operation. He had played in the last two championship games and he still looked to be feeling his way into his action and proper follow-through, which is understandable when you've had a major back problem and you're a seam bowler, who thrives on hard work. There was a possibility in my mind that Tim might sit out this Essex game, but looking at the wicket, I thought it would be abrasive and help the ball reverse swing. Tim and Dougie both bowl well when the ball is in this mode. The ball was definitely going to spin, but I felt it would turn slowly, without the helpful bounce spinners love. I was happy to leave out Richard Davis because of this and play just the one spinner, Neil Smith.

It was then suggested that we play both spinners and leave out a batsman, young Wasim Khan, but I wasn't happy at weakening the batting. For me, Dougie Brown had to play, not just because he was in good form with the ball but his batting would be important. So we talked round and round the subject till Phil asked if I had thought about dropping myself. He said, 'If we were playing at Edgbaston, there'd be a strong case for you dropping yourself, but you're a good player of spinners, so on balance you ought to play here.'

I had never considered there might be a thought about me

standing down, and my brain started to race in all directions. Tim said nothing, just shrugging his shoulders, which made me feel slightly betrayed. Surely a supportive vice-captain would have insisted I played? The three of us sat out in the middle while the others practised and we were getting nowhere. Phil was adamant about two spinners, I was insistent that Brown played, while at the same time shocked that the possibility had been raised about dropping me. If I had felt it right for the team, I would have dropped out for the Ilford match, but I didn't. I felt my form and fitness were decent and that I deserved to be backed. In the end, Tim came down on my side and we made Richard Davis twelfth man. When we batted, I dropped myself down to number seven in the order and asked Phil Neale to walk around the ground with me. I was seriously thinking about resigning the captaincy and I wanted Phil's honest opinion: was he voicing what the players were saying? Was Dennis Amiss interfering? As a former county captain himself, he needed to understand why I felt let down. I told him I was gutted and needed to talk this thing through. 'Imagine, Phil, that you're back at Worcester as captain, with five wins out of five under your belt. Imagine that you're averaging in the mid-30s with the bat in the championship. How would you feel if the new coach suggested that someone like David Leatherdale came in to replace you as a player?' I hadn't lost respect for Phil as a person: he was expressing an honest opinion on the way he saw how the squad should best be utilised. However it was obvious he didn't feel it was vital who was captain. Phil's response to my question was sympathetic but cagey. I was on a real downer at Ilford, keeping myself apart from the players, sitting in my hotel room, just playing my guitar, wondering exactly where I stood. The only spontaneous support came from Allan Donald, when I told him I was thinking about jacking in the captaincy: 'I want you to stay on. I've got total respect for you as skipper and I'm right behind you. If you resign, you'll play into their hands.' That was inspirational at a bad time for me, and I shan't ever forget Allan for that. I decided to carry on.

I also felt vindicated in the team selection at Ilford, and the ball did reverse swing. Donald picked up six wickets and I took

3/37 in the first innings. Munton got three wickets in the match and Neil Smith took seven. There was turn, but it was never unplayable. Peter Such took 2/122 in the game and John Childs 2/104. Dougie Brown scored an invaluable 85 as we built a big lead, and we won impressively by ten wickets. So we prepared for the trip to Leicester. Before I left, Dennis Amiss deflated me again, when he said: 'It might turn there, perhaps you shouldn't play yourself.' I know that at that stage, Richard Davis had been in to see Dennis about not being in the side, but I did think I might have had more support from the man in charge, especially as he had played the game long enough, and knew the various interests and factions involved. Surely the captain has to be supported, especially when the side's winning every game? Yet the Warwickshire team spirit that had impressed so many in recent years wasn't 100 per cent. I was determined to get it sorted out at Leicester. I called for a meeting and said, 'Listen fellas, we talk about helping each other along when we're tired and a bit down. That's what we need now. You may have heard a few rumours about me at Ilford, but don't worry about it. I'm not jacking in the captaincy, I'm totally motivated and on the field, I'll be my normal self. So just concentrate on your own game. Let's get it back to where we were.' I didn't want to know who was for or against me. The players must have realised that I was looking for extra support. I had seen it happen to John Barclay at Sussex, when his form declined because of injuries, and the players started to question him as captain. I was going to dig in and see it through.

We beat Leicestershire inside two days by an innings, and I had match figures of 33.4-17-47-6. Surely Amiss and any other detractors would take notice? I got runs and wickets in the Sunday League match as well and started to feel more confident. Then a vital game a couple of days later, one of the turning points of the season. We beat Kent by ten runs in the second round of the Nat West after a hard struggle. We made 262, and with dangerous players like Aravinda De Silva, Trevor Ward, Graham Cowdrey, Matthew Fleming and Mark Ealham in their team that day, Kent must have been favourites to get through at just over four runs an over on a good batting surface. But we raised our game superbly, operated as a tight unit again and our big-match experience saved the day. At last I felt the whole team was pulling together again and supporting me. The atmosphere was brilliant in the dressing room afterwards.

After that Kent game, we got on a roll and played brilliantly for the next two months in all three competitions. We lost just two games – by seven runs to Northants in the championship and by two runs to Worcestershire in the Sunday League. We steamrollered opponents and the season got better and better for me as the weeks progressed. I was absolutely chuffed to take 5/30 in the final championship game at Canterbury when we clinched the title. All season, the ball felt pretty good coming out of my hand and I backed a hunch and decided to open the bowling that day.

The week leading up to Canterbury had been the longest of my career. We thought we had the title won after rolling over Derbyshire, thanks to Allan Donald's magnificent bowling. All we had to do was endure a couple of hours while Leicestershire managed to get a draw down at Uxbridge against our closest challengers, Middlesex. Rain had affected that game badly, but Leicestershire still had a chance for prize money, so they were very keen on victory as well. So when Mike Gatting declared after some friendly bowling, he knew that Leicestershire would go for the target of 251 in two sessions, a very generous rate for the batters. At 131/2, it looked as if Middlesex would lose, but I couldn't stay any longer at the ground. After agreeing that we'd all be back at Edgbaston at 5.30 for the victory celebrations if Middlesex hadn't won, I went home.

I lay on the sofa, picking at my guitar, wondering what was happening at Uxbridge. Our supporters stayed at the ground, watching in agony as the latest Uxbridge score was updated after each over on Teletext in the members' bar. A friend rang me at tea-time and said, 'They're six down.' So Gatt had manipulated it, he'd thrown the bait out to Leicestershire and they'd swallowed the hook. I went back to the dressing-room, sat in a hot bath and Keith Piper said to me, 'Parsons is out – they're eight down.' That was it, I thought, there are too many overs left, they won't hold out against Tufnell and Emburey. Adrian Pierson, our old team-mate, was now in, but there were 12 overs to go. I phoned the Uxbridge ground and a guy told me there were only seven overs to go and still eight wickets down. Come on, Adrian, do it for us mate! Then another wicket fell and Adrian had just Alan Mullally left. It seemed to take an eternity for the Teletext pages to change at the end of each over: three overs left, 12 needed, one wicket to fall. By now our physio, Stuart Nottingham, had found the commentary on the radio, on BBC Five Live. We stood in the physio's small room, listening to Henry Blofeld talking down the overs. It came down to two runs for victory and we're hanging on to each other for dear life. A draw or a tie would give us the title, so one run would be enough – not much to ask! We're starting to bounce up and down together in the room, as Blofeld said, 'Tufnell comes in to bowl, and Mullally hits it.' We had our arms up in the air, with our mouths open, just waiting to roar and then we hear, 'It's in the air, it might be caught – Emburey's caught it. Middlesex have won by one run!'

We had gone from elation to despair in one instant. We looked at each other and everyone started cursing Mullally – why couldn't he leave it to Adrian, why go for death or glory? I started to laugh hysterically, saying, 'Why couldn't they lose by 30? Why just by one?' I suddenly felt totally drained. Gladstone Small said, 'All we do now is go down to Canterbury and win it properly, without relying on anybody else', and Allan Donald said, 'We've proved people wrong all season, all we have to do is win one more time!'

Great reactions from two senior players and of course they were right, but I felt inconsolable that night. At home, I plugged in my electric guitar and hit the strings full bore: it must have been a terrible row! I didn't go to the Professional Cricketers' Association dinner that week in London, because that would have meant seeing Mullally, and Gatt's gloating face. As a joke I wrote a song about Mullally in the style of a Sex Pistols' number and the lyrics were very uncomplimentary. At least it got a laugh out of the boys on a practice day. All week I kept thinking, 'We've won 13 out of 16 and that would win the title easily in any other year. We're going to start nicking a few sometime, and dropping some in the slips, it's the law of averages. We can't keep winning, can we? I was waking up in the middle of the night, with Henry Blofeld's radio commentary ringing in my ears, convinced that Middlesex had lost by one wicket. Then I remembered.

On that first morning at Canterbury, I was more stressed out than at any time of my life. I just didn't know what to do if I won the toss, I was so worried I'd make the wrong decision. There was a bit of moisture on the surface, but it looked a decent wicket, so it would be best to bat first. The pitch would get worse, we could play two spinners and they would use the rough against the Kent batsmen. Supporting Neil Smith's off-spin was Ashley Giles, who had replaced Richard Davis in mid-July and looked a fine cricketer, totally at ease in the first team. We had won so many matches by winning the toss, putting the opposition in, bowling them out cheaply, then controlling the game. Tim Munton, Phil Neale and I agreed we'd bowl if I won the toss: it seemed the easier option. Fifteen minutes later, when I went out for the toss, I felt the wicket. It felt dryer, so I decided to go with my gut feeling. Be positive, bat first. When I came back after calling correctly, I told the guys, 'It looks a good batting wicket, there's a bit of moisture, so it may do a bit early on. Get over the new ball, fellas, and we'll see you at lunchtime!'

It was all a big act from me, I was terrified in that first half-hour. Tim gave me a sideways look and I said, 'I just hope it doesn't go all over the place off the seam.' We both laughed nervously. I sat on the balcony willing Wasim Khan and Nick Knight to a large partnership and they did us proud. Nick got a big hundred and by the end of the first day, I could relax – especially at the news that Middlesex hadn't got onto the pitch at Taunton, because of rain.

We beat Kent by an innings with a day to spare and we had a brilliant party that Saturday night in Canterbury. The wives and girlfriends came down to celebrate, we took over a restaurant and all the players had to do a party piece to keep the fun going. Wasim Khan's impersonation of Dennis Amiss was a particular hit and we chanted 'You Bears! You Bears!' as the drink flowed. Just as well we had a late start the next day for the final Sunday

League game. We had no chance of retaining our title, even if we beat Kent, as they had a far superior run rate. We had played on some poor one-day wickets on Sundays, particularly at Durham and Worcester, where scores of 132 and 152 proved beyond us. Coincidentally, we didn't face any spinners in those matches. We beat Kent by five wickets, which was very satisfying, and left us in no doubt that we were the superior side. If rain hadn't wiped out our match the previous weekend when we had Derbyshire 81/5, we would probably have retained the Sunday League title. As it was we finished level on points, runners-up.

That was a brilliant weekend at Canterbury and I felt very happy at how the season had turned out. I felt I had vindicated myself as a cricketer, finishing second in the first-class bowling averages behind Allan Donald, and ending up with an average of 36 with the bat. That was hugely satisfying after my poor figures in '94. I also felt I had the team behind me again, after a bad couple of months. All 14 championship victories came under my captaincy, including eight in a row, but I was pleased that I could still hold my own place down in the side as a cricketer, irrespective of my captaincy. No one was suggesting any more that I should stand down for the good of the team.

Captaining Warwickshire has given me great fulfilment but there have been times when I've wondered if it was worth the aggravation. I know the best aspect of my captaincy was when I was out on the field, that I wasn't the best at working behind the scenes, within a committee structure. That's partly my fault because I have a restless nature and get frustrated when I cannot win a proposal around a committee table. For example, on several occasions, I brought up in the cricket committee a recommendation to help get our players fitter and better-prepared for the county season. Players at Warwickshire aren't paid anything during October-April, yet are expected to report fit for pre-season. I suggested a financial reward if a player registered a certain level in a fitness assessment when he reported back. The players resent that they should train in the winter and practise in the nets for no financial gain. I wanted that pre-season period to be spent on fine-tuning cricket skills, rather than getting the players properly fit. Your technique suffers when you are tired and I thought that just a few hundred pounds would have been one way to motivate their attitude to fitness. Ideally, I believe players should be on eight-month contracts, reporting back on February 1, and over the next two months, they would then become fitter and more athletic under supervision. That way, they'd be more likely to meet the demands of the over-loaded fixture list. This would cost the club more than £100,000 in extra wages, so I believed my suggestion of a few hundred pounds a player was more realistic. I never got anywhere with that idea in cricket committee. In fact, one committee member suggested that, instead of an incentive, we fine the players if they reported back, unable to reach the necessary level on the fitness assessment. The committee didn't seem to realise that most players don't like training unless they have to, that it's difficult for the captain to bite his tongue when we reassemble, if three or four aren't fully fit. for a few weeks, and you're losing valuable preparation time. So the captain goes into important early matches in a season unsure about some of his players' fitness, and that's something which shouldn't be allowed in the modern game. This despite all the cash pouring into the game from the TV deal with B Sky B, and the increased revenue from marketing such a successful club.

I found my influence as club captain at committee level to be peripheral and frustrating. Yet they say the captain's input is vital. So why did no one consult me about hiring Brian Lara for another three years, after our disagreements had been well documented? I got a large say in picking the eleven for the next match, but not in terms of future development of the staff, or consultation about the next overseas player. In the end, the most important thing for the captain is to maintain your form as a player: otherwise you're really on the back foot. Mike Gatting's advice to me when I took the job about keeping up your playing standards is so true. Those doubts nearly saw my demise during a season when we won two more trophies. Is it any wonder that experienced county captains get worn down by it all?

10

Playing for England

My England career lasted almost five years – from my debut at Lord's in a one-day international in 1991, to that sad day in March 1996 when we slunk out of the World Cup, thrashed by Sri Lanka. We didn't deserve anything from that tournament: one-day cricket at that level had passed us by. Our management team of Ray Illingworth and Michael Atherton must take the bulk of the blame for that. They were way off the pace in terms of preparation, tactical flexibility and man-management. It may sound as if I have an axe to grind, having been treated dismissive in South Africa at the start of 1996, then originally missing out on the World Cup party, but that would have been a complete irrelevance to me if England had looked the part on those two trips. But we didn't. Above all, I wanted England to compete properly, to look fresh and businesslike and tactically innovative. Those few months certainly knocked on the head any arrogant ideas that, having started one-day cricket 30-odd years earlier, we still knew best how to play it. We had been left behind. The quality of management by Illingworth and Atherton was also streets behind the leadership of Graham Gooch, Mickey Stewart and Keith Fletcher when I first played for England.

The break-up of my marriage in 1990 had something to do with me becoming an England cricketer. It's sad, I know, but I turned to fitness training as a sort of therapy to get over it, and I became a fitness fanatic in the winter of 1990/91. So the 1991 season saw me raring to go, fitter than ever before, and I probably played the best all-round cricket of my career. Fortunately, I had that bit of luck you need and was selected for England. Julie and I had been married for four years when we split up, and she took my two-year-old daughter, Emily, back to Australia at the end of the 1990 season. With hindsight, I probably didn't work hard enough at my marriage, but I was still shattered when it ended. For the next year, I hated going back to an empty house. Early on, I'd sit there, unnerved by the silence, staring at the photos of my daughter, bashing the phone, trying to catch family and friends if they were at home, and then talking to them for ages. I was an emotional wreck. I had to snap out of it.

For therapy, I went to the gym. In the end, I became addicted and unless I did some vigorous exercise every day, I would feel tense and uneasy. Exercise was the one thing during that time that made me feel content and after a workout I could face the empty house and the silence. I met a sports scientist called Karen Rodkin, who was tremendously helpful to me. She taught me about the physiological side of training, how you should best prepare yourself for your sport. Karen told me that cricketers need to train anaerobically, rather than aerobically because cricket is all about bursts of energy. She said a cricketer should train like a sprinter, rather than a marathon runner, because it's all about short bursts. So on a training run, I wouldn't go for the long slog, to build up stamina: I'd do a 100-metre sprint, then walk 100 metres, then back to sprinting. In the pool, I'd swim sprints – 50 metres as fast as I could, then rest for 30 seconds, then repeat the process. Eventually I got up to 20 50-metre sprints in the pool, followed by 20 seconds' rest. I read all the books and really got into the subject. The greater your capacity to produce energy anaerobically, the less lactic acid and therefore stiffness you will get. Many cricketers are stiff before they bowl and that produces injuries. Before this fitness regime, I used to feel stiff when batting after bowling 20 overs, and I realised I wasn't properly fit for the all-rounder's responsibilities. I really pushed myself in that gym, to blot out for a few hours the pain I was feeling at the absence of my daughter. I deliberately didn't have a night in alone for a year. I would either arrange an evening out or stay at the gym until 10 o'clock. I became addicted to the endorphins produced after hard exercise. You feel as if you're floating – I'm told you feel that way after a narcotic, like opium. It got me through a very emotional period.

So I had more time to focus on my dream of playing for England. I hadn't forgotten the scepticism of Alan Wells when I voiced my ambitions in my early days at Sussex and his conservative attitude shared by some others only fired my ambition all the more. My form at the start of the 1991 season was good, and I got into the one-day squad at the expense of Ian Botham, who had torn a hamstring at Edgbaston in the first match. I was playing down at Chelmsford at the time, and I just flew up the motorway to Old Trafford. I was amazingly exhilarated, thinking that I'd surely get one game out of the two remaining ones, even though perhaps not tomorrow. That's how it turned out, although I got on the field as substitute fielder. That was great fun: a big crowd, with England doing well and the ball coming to me a lot at backward point. Gus Logie kept me busy there and I eventually caught Carl Hooper. It was great to be on the field at the finish, wearing the England gear. Mum was there to watch me and I met the Prime Minister, John Major, who popped into our dressing-room for a chat. It's a different world playing for England!

Off down to London then for the third game in the one-day series, with me desperately hoping to play at Lord's. I nearly didn't make it after a car crash on the M6 that saw me narrowly miss a concrete bridge as I slammed on the brakes and went backwards down the motorway. Despite whiplash in my neck, I slept well and waited for the result of Allan Lamb's fitness test on his bruised instep. As we warmed up, I saw our physio, Lawrie Brown, working on Lamby and he soon shook his head. The captain, Graham Gooch, came over to me and said, 'Dermot, you're playing. Congratulations – good luck and well done.' The adrenalin just shot up from my toes – I was playing for England! I didn't get a bat but I bowled 12 efficient overs, including a good shout for lbw against Brian Lara and a maiden at Viv Richards. As I sat on the balcony, waiting to go in to bat, I noticed the field that the off-spinner Carl Hooper was using.

It was a 6/3 field to the right-hander and I said to the coach, Mickey Stewart: 'If he bowls at me with this field, I'm going to reverse sweep him first ball. Is that OK?' Mickey's answer was very reassuring: 'You've got this far playing that way for Warwickshire. Don't change your approach just because you're now playing for England.' That was a great attitude and Mickey encouraged me to think that way all the time we were on England duty together.

I didn't want that day at Lord's to end. We won by seven wickets and I didn't get in for a bat, but I loved it all. Rory Bremner came in for a natter, and it was relaxing to hear him do some impersonations. When the game was over, I was still on a high and wanted to party. When Goochy said, 'That's it, boys, well done – see you at the First Test', I felt deflated. I didn't want to leave the England dressing-room, it was such a fantastic pleasure to be part of it all. I didn't get the call for the first couple of Tests, but my form held up and I kept hoping. I was called into the 13 for the Trent Bridge Test but the balance of the side, with Jack Russell keeping wicket, meant I couldn't break through once they had decided to play the spinner, Richard Illingworth. So off I went to Portsmouth to play against Hampshire, with hopes of playing at Edgbaston. I took eight wickets in the championship game and felt good about my all-round form. On the Sunday morning, Graham Gooch called me at the ground to say, 'Bad luck, Dermot. You've done nothing wrong, but we know what side we want, and we're only going in with 12 for Edgbaston.' They had actually gone back to Chris Lewis as the all-rounder. That was the worst moment of my career so far, and I was inconsolable for a while. I had gone from euphoria to despondency in a fortnight and now thought my chance might have gone for good. Bob Woolmer stood over me and said, 'Let it out, boy – I know how you feel, it happened to me as well.' That just made it worse and, covering my head, I lost it for a moment or two. Everyone had told me I had done nothing wrong, that I had impressed them, but all I had to show for it was a single appearance in a one-day game. That wasn't the same as playing in a Test Match.

With Ian Botham on his way back to full fitness, our rivalry was now being built up in the press. With England now 2/1 down in the series, it was felt the team needed to sacrifice Jack Russell, play Alec Stewart as the wicket-keeper, leaving the side with four front-line bowlers plus an all-rounder. We played Worcestershire in a championship game just before the Oval squad was announced and Ian and I both did well. He got 81 on the first day, I made 97 the day after, and Ian got the nod on the Sunday. To celebrate his recall, he took 7/54 to beat us by an innings. England won that Oval Test, and Both's presence undoubtedly helped raise the side's morale, but all I could think of was that it could have been me there. The boys tried to cheer me up by making a positive out of a negative, that I might have missed out on the tour that winter if I had failed at the Oval – but all I wanted was that sweater with the lions on it.

More disappointment came when I was left out of the senior tour to New Zealand with the consolation prize of going to the West Indies with England 'A'. That was more than I could have expected 12 months earlier, but I felt disappointed that I had come so near, and yet I hadn't made that final vital leap. Still, I was put on stand-by for the senior tour, because there were doubts about the fitness of Angus Fraser, who had a hip problem. I thought it strange that an all-rounder would be a possible swap for a seam bowler, but there you go. In the end, I got on the trip to New Zealand and to the World Cup, because Angus couldn't make it. It was a fantastic experience to play in front of 87,000 spectators in the World Cup Final, even if we did lose it, and to play in all three Tests in New Zealand was a huge thrill; but before we left England, I incurred an injury that had serious consequences for the next couple of years.

We were training at the National Sports Centre at Lilleshall before flying out to New Zealand and I was fired up to do well and impress Graham Gooch. After my fitness regime, I had never felt so strong, my all-round record for the 1991 season was good, and I wanted the captain to know how keen I was. I bowled for an hour and half on the first day and Goochie said, 'Derm, well done – you're bowling with a bit of zip,' which was a big boost to me. Next morning, I could barely move. Every joint in my body ached and all I did at the gym was have a massage, sauna and light swim. I was in agony. The next day was more nets and I could barely carry my bag to the dressing-room. Phillip DeFreitas and David Lawrence were already changed and I told them how I felt. They said they felt exactly the same after Tuesday's bowling session. Chris Lewis listened to that and said, 'I bowled here last year and ended up with a stress fracture of the back. There's no way I'm doing the same thing. I'm coming in off four paces.' The pain didn't go away. We mentioned it to Mickey Stewart and he arranged for us to have a different set of training shoes to absorb the impact of the hard surface. We eventually found out what caused the pain; it seems the shock pads where the bowlers land had been taken out because it affected the bias when indoor bowls was played. So the surface was similar to concrete and England bowlers were damaging their bodies, just so that a game of bowls could be played properly! We just couldn't absorb the pressure satisfactorily when we landed. Chris Lewis had the right idea, although I think our management felt he was just coasting. Poor David Lawrence, who only knew how to bowl flat out, was in agony as he charged in on that hard, unyielding surface. I've often wondered whether Lilleshall contributed to the terrible injury that ended his career, when he broke his left kneecap soon afterwards in New Zealand. It was, after all, his left knee that caused him a lot of pain during those training sessions.

By this stage, with three weeks before we left for New Zealand, I had a pain in my buttock. It was there when I did the sprints and a deep rub from the physio and anti-inflammatory tablets didn't really help. When we got to New Zealand the pain got worse and I struggled to bowl with any pace. I was just trotting in, concentrating on moving the ball sideways. I was lucky that the pitches out there were so slow, that my lack of pace wasn't exposed. In the World Cup, I wasn't able to bowl the odd quicker ball, so I lacked variety. I collapsed in pain in the match against South Africa and got through by popping pills and on the adrenalin from playing in such a fabulous atmosphere. I bowled three overs in the World Cup Final and, basically, I was in varying degrees of pain for most of the time.

When I got back to England in the spring of '92, the injury

was finally diagnosed: a stress fracture of the pelvis. No wonder it had been so sore. Rest was the only cure and I didn't really bowl with consistent conviction for the next three years. It was funny that Ian Botham was fit at the start of the '92 season and I wasn't, yet I had attended the pre tour Lilleshall sessions whilst he did his pantomime. Late in '92, when I was picked to go on the England tour to India and Sri Lanka, I trained at Lilleshall in the way recommended by Chris Lewis, taking it easy off a few paces when bowling. By then, a large foam sponge area had been laid down to absorb the pressure on landing, but that was a little late for me – and for poor old David Lawrence.

Apart from that injury, though, those three months at the start of 1992 were a wonderful experience for me. I shall never forget the moment I was told I was going to play for England at last in a Test Match. We were at Christchurch and Graham Gooch called my room, asking me to go and see him. I knocked on Goochy's door, walked in and he was in the bath. He stuck out a hand through the foam and said, 'You're playing tomorrow, we haven't told anyone else yet, so keep it quiet. I know you'll do well.' I raced back to my room, beaming from ear to ear, and my room-mate, Chris Lewis, said, 'Well?' I just jumped up and down on my bed, nodding. Chris put his hand out and said 'Congrats.' I shook it fiercely then said, 'But you can't say anything, Lewie.' I couldn't keep it all to myself and that night I saw Mum and whispered the good news to her. She'd taken the first available plane out when there was a chance of me playing after a good performance in the first of the one-day internationals and I was really happy for her when I broke the good news. I saw her eyes start to water and I felt the same.

We batted first and by the time I came in at number seven we had a lot of runs in the book. I got off the mark first ball, blocking a good-length delivery from Danny Morrison to square leg, shouting 'Yes!' and racing in. I kept thinking, 'I've got a run for England!' and then started to look for more as the declaration came near. Chris Lewis played a top knock and I started to club a few blows on the slow pitch. I got to 50 by smacking one from Dipak Patel to the mid-wicket boundary and I immediately pointed my bat to Mum in the area where I knew she was sitting.

That was a fabulous moment, making all the waiting a few months earlier that much sweeter.

We won that Test and I celebrated with the boys after climbing out of my sick bed. I had gone down with food poisoning after a pasta marinara caught me out, but when it looked as if we would win, I caught a cab and presented my green face to the dressing-room. I wasn't going to miss that on my Test debut! I was struck by the level of intensity in the dressing-room during a Test, compared to a county game. Robin Smith got out for 90-odd and he was really annoyed at missing out on his hundred. Over the years it's seemed to me that guys play more for themselves than in county cricket, which I guess is understandable, but can be a problem when you need everyone to give it their all in a tight situation. That was never the case on this tour. In this series, we were clearly the better side as New Zealand struggled to come to terms with the retirement of Sir Richard Hadlee and John Bracewell.

There was an air of confidence in our team, and I was in the thick of it at short leg or silly point, shouting encouragement to our bowlers. I even gave Phil Tufnell a volley in the dressing-room when it appeared to me that he was worried about Chris Cairns' bowling. It was the second Test at Auckland, and we had been sent in on a damp pitch of uneven bounce. Something around 200 would have been a handy score in such conditions, and as we clawed our way past 150, Tuffers said to me, 'How fast is Cairns, Derm?' I said, 'Tuffers, you're going out there to bat for your country and we need runs. It's a slow wicket. Get behind every ball.' When he went out to join Derek Pringle, I was thinking, 'Don't back away!' as Cairns ran in to bowl. There was a slight movement to leg as he played the first one, but then he played a short delivery quite well and you could see his confidence rise. He and Pringle added over 30 and Tuffers came in at the end of the innings full of himself: 'Yeh, it wasn't that bad, Derm!' Tuffers and I got on straight away on that tour. He's a fun guy, with a fast bowler's temperament, who really wants to do well for the side. We had a lot of laughs together on that tour and he took my verbal attack on him that day very well.

We won the first two Tests and drew the third, and that was

the end of my Test career. My last Test innings was a first-baller: bowled around my legs by Murphy Su'a. So my Test career began with 59 and ended with a first-ball duck. Cricket is a great leveller. As far as I was concerned, anything in Test cricket after that first appearance in Christchurch was a bonus for me. My lifetime's ambition had been achieved and I hadn't felt out of my depth as we won the series convincingly.

A week or so later, and we were deep into the World Cup. It was a marvellous experience, playing in so many high-pressure games all over Australia. To see my daughter again was a major plus and the atmosphere in the day/night games was wonderful. If you couldn't motivate yourself for those matches, you were in the wrong profession. It was fantastic to beat Australia at Sydney and at one stage, as I sat watching us bat, I thought, 'Great, we're going to hammer the Aussies!' I felt like a spectator at that point and our confidence was sky-high. I enjoyed smashing Allan Donald for 17 in the last over of our innings in the semi-final, but I was never fully fit as a bowler because of my pelvic injury. I was fortunate to be bowled at some good times, and not relied on to always bowl a full quota of ten overs. With far better bowlers than me in the competition it was an injustice to finish top of the World Cup bowling averages. I played in all but one of the games, took some good slip catches and did enough with bat and ball, but I wasn't at my best. It didn't matter so much, though, because we had a lot of all-rounders and the spirit was terrific.

It was a major blow to lose the Final to Pakistan, but they were the better side on the day. It's been said we ran out of steam, but I think it was more a case of brilliant bowling by Wasim Akram. The two deliveries that bowled Allan Lamb and Chris Lewis were beauties, and before I went into bat, one or two of our guys said, 'Derm, when you go in, ask the umpires to have a look at the ball.' I faced an over from Aqib Javed that featured deliveries which swung very late and I carried out the instructions, but Brian Aldridge could see nothing wrong with the condition of the ball. I wasn't convinced the ball had been tampered with. I think we ought to give them credit for some brilliant bowling, and don't forget they were without the injured Waqar Younis.

And give credit also to their leg-spinner Mushtaq Ahmed, who bowled superbly. I couldn't get after him and he got me finally caught at mid-off.

It was the last chance to win the World Cup for a lot of our players like Ian Botham, Graham Gooch and Allan Lamb, but it was only when we walked around the boundary afterwards to thank our supporters that I realised the enormity of the occasion. A massive wave of people greeted us in the South Stand, which has a greater capacity than the whole of Lord's. I suppose it was like the World Cup Final at Wembley in 1966 – except that, sadly, we didn't have our version of Geoff Hurst.

A year later, I toured India and Sri Lanka, with hopes of playing in Tests as well as one-dayers, but it was not to be. It was more memorable for my Mum, who came out for the tour, staying in backpackers' accommodation, travelling everywhere second class, but loving the experience. When she ended up as England's official scorer for the last three Tests of the tour after Clem Driver's illness, she was in her element. Although Mum was happy to experience all aspects of life in India, I was glad that she was upgraded into the air-conditioned, five-star hotels that are one of the plusses of a cricket tour to that country. Unfortunately, she didn't get much chance to record great deeds by her son. I played in all eight of the one-day internationals, but missed out on all four Tests. It might have been different if Alec Stewart had kept wicket in all of the Tests, because that might have made room for me, but he wasn't that keen on the job on that tour, so I ended up doing a lot of net bowling and drinks carrying. There was always the chance of getting a late call-up for a Test, though, because of the usual stomach upsets you associate with touring those parts, but it was not to be.

It's certainly different touring India, and I mean no disrespect when I say that. The crowds are unbelievably keen on their cricket, and I was more recognised in a Madras street than in Birmingham. Some of the crowds were very hostile and excitable, preferring to throw rocks than garlands of flowers. If you fielded at third man in some of the one-dayers, you couldn't hear your captain's instructions because of the noise from firecrackers. Transport difficulties were huge on the tour. Indian Airlines were on strike and some of the pilots flying our planes had been bought out of retirement. One flight into Delhi was particularly hair-raising, as we came to a juddering stop just 40 yards from a fence and the co-pilot gasped over the intercom, 'Oh, it's only through the grace of God that we have landed safely, we've had total hydraulic failure!' It all added to the fun of the proceedings! I took a video camera on the tour, taking shots of the odd rat and Phil Tufnell throwing a wobbler about the umpires.

Yes, the umpires: their interpretation of the lbw law did us no favours. The Indians would just put their bat behind their front pad and literally kick the ball away. It was so obvious there was no attempt to play a shot but countless appeals were always turned down. They didn't play the sweep shot and when I was given out lbw on the sweep and asked why, I was told, 'Bad cricket – sweep shot not good. Play straight, good cricket.' So the laws of the game didn't seem to apply. Eventually the likes of Alec Stewart and Neil Fairbrother would just stick their pads down the wicket and play no stroke, a style that was foreign to them. The Indians didn't even appeal, it was bizarre! If you missed a sweep shot and the ball struck your pad a foot outside the line of off stump everyone appealed. It was a nightmare. Kumble in particular troubled us with his extra bounce, but that tour convinced me of the need to have neutral umpires. We were outplayed, though.

That tour wasn't frustrating just for me. Several of our guys didn't get the breaks and it told against them in the future. Paul Jarvis bowled his heart out, and he came back with a lot of credit, but he never played another Test for England. He got in for the first two one-day internationals against the Australians, but didn't make the First Test and faded away. I thought he was very unlucky. Chris Lewis bowled the quickest spell of the tour at Colombo in the Sri Lanka Test, taking the new ball ahead of Devon Malcolm, and yet England haven't used him properly in his time in the side. He shouldn't be viewed as a stock bowler in the medium-fast mould of Angus Fraser; he should be thrown the new ball, told he's going to operate in six-over bursts and bowl quick. Bowling is hard work and I don't think Chris has seen himself as a fast bowler: he is too attuned to 20 overs a day, so he paces himself. In doing that, he has let the management believe he isn't really giving it his all, and I don't believe that's fair to him. He needed his ego to be boosted, to be told he's a top player. I think Chris felt a bit of an outcast and that he wasn't with a group of mates when he played for England around that period, but he's such a talented cricketer that we were in danger of wasting his talents. Phil Tufnell is another misunderstood cricketer. Because he cares so much about doing well for England, he gets carried away, but that aggression, if it is channelled in the right way, is good for him and the team. I think he has been the most talented slow left-arm bowler in the country for some years now: he has the variations, the loop, the flight and he turns it just enough. Perhaps it's been a combination of poor man-management and Tuffers' own defects that has contributed to his spell in the wilderness, but he should have played more times for England.

I suppose David Gower's non-selection for that 1993 tour summed up the English attitude to individuals. There was a huge fuss from his supporters, and Graham Gooch was pilloried for picking Mike Gatting ahead of David. Well I thought Gooch was right to go for Gatting, even though he had a disappointing tour. To me the basis on which a batsman gets picked for England is that he performs in county cricket. A top batter ought to be churning out the runs if he's committed and focused and there was a question mark there against Gower. Gatting was still the best batsman in county cricket, a record far superior to that of Gower. David hadn't done that much in the last few seasons in county cricket, even though he had performed against the Pakistanis in 1992 in the Tests, but you can't keep other batsmen out who have staked a claim with consistent runs. It's different for a fast bowler, because of the heavy workload, and in that case you go for the guy you believe will get the best players out and will keep running in for you in the Tests.

I didn't buy all this garbage about Graham Gooch being the Roundhead to David Gower's Cavalier. As a batsman myself, I've seen Gooch play with so much flair for so many years, dancing down the pitch to smash the spinners through extra cover, getting after them with the slog/sweep over mid-wicket. When I watched him bat in the one-day international against Pakistan at Old Trafford in 1992, I was amazed when he was bowled by Aamir Sohail, giving himself room to play on the off-side. This was after he had swept Aamir for a couple of twos and he was really motoring. I couldn't believe Goochy changed his game plan after milking the bowler with the sweep. I bided my time till he was relaxed after his dismissal and then asked him why he didn't just carry on sweeping Sohail. He said: 'I could only get two for that, I wanted to hit him for four!' More Cavalier than Roundhead, I think. Goochy was a deceptive bloke with a great, dry sense of humour, despite that solemn demeanour. I had total respect for him as player and captain and for the way he treated me. I agreed with his attitude to full commitment and intensive training and I relished the way he encouraged me to play my own way. Mickey Stewart's successor as coach, Keith Fletcher, was just as supportive. He told me that he liked the fact that I could adapt my game to the state of the match, that I should always follow my instincts and treat playing for England in the same way as with Warwickshire. I appreciate some England players of my period had some problems with the England hierarchy in terms of man-management and attitude to their responsibilities, but I can't speak highly enough of the way I was treated by Gooch, Stewart and Fletcher.

I'm sure I would have had a fairer crack of the whip if Mike Atherton and Ray Illingworth hadn't been in charge of England for the South Africa tour and the World Cup of 1996. During that depressing period, I found myself comparing the support and encouragement I'd had in those two World Cups, and the Atherton/Illingworth combination didn't come out of it very well. Now that's just on a personal level and my gripes would have been a complete irrelevance if we had done ourselves justice in South Africa, then in the World Cup – but we didn't and the hierarchy have to take a fair degree of blame for that. Atherton gave no real indication of having a feel for captaining a side in one-day cricket. He had made no secret in the past that he prefers Test cricket, that the one-dayers aren't as important. As a result, his captaincy lacked drive, purpose and flair. Add to that his passive body language and you're struggling when the team is up against it, when the ball is flying all over the place. I felt he was quite physically and mentally drained by the end of that South African tour, and there was a case for having a different captain for the World Cup.

I was very flattered to be mentioned as the possible captain for the World Cup, but that was never on, because it had been made clear to me that my face didn't fit with the management, but there were other contenders – Alec Stewart, for instance, who has always struck me as a very positive leader, full of ideas and receptive to others thoughts. English cricket is so orthodox in its thinking that no one would take the brave step of suggesting to Atherton that he should stand down for the World Cup, and re-charge his batteries for the cricket in which he excels – Test Matches. It's not as if he would have been picked on merit for the World Cup games after tailing away badly in South Africa. Apart from runs in the one-dayer at Bloemfontein, he had failed in the other internationals and his form hardly picked up in the World Cup. He scored one half-century in six innings in the tournament, and that would have justified him being dropped unless he was captain. So did Mike Atherton waste a place? On his recent one-day record, was he one of our best five batters? Did he not gum up the run flow when he opened the innings, when more progressive sides were flourishing with the new con-cept of the pinch-hitter?

It was Illingworth who proved the biggest problem, though. He was too negative, far too dogmatic and he lacked any aware-ness of how much the game had changed. I kept hearing that he'd watched all of England's home games for the last decade in his capacity as a TV commentator, and had a brilliant cricket brain, but I saw no evidence of this. I had approached Ray the winter before in Australia whilst I was working as a commenta-tor, to see if he was interested in watching a video I had made on Warwickshire's success and premeditating against spin. That might sound arrogant but I had done my homework and England weren't performing as well as their opposition against spin in one day cricket. I had researched the figures and at the time of showing the video to Ray, they stood like this: Englands last 21 one day Internationals going back as far as the India tour of 1993.

England Run Rate against spin – 4.1
Opposition Run Rate against England's Spinners – 4.6

England Spin bowlers average – 42 runs per wicket
Opposition Spin bowlers average – 30 runs per wicket

Those differences are quite substantial and, with a World Cup in the subcontinent a year away, they needed to change it if England were to have success. I eventually managed to show Ray the video, and all he could say was, "I could tell when a player was going to sweep, because I could see him grip the bat tighter. So then I bowled the ball faster". Now any decent player of the reverse sweep or paddle would tell you that it helps when a bowler puts more pace on the ball, because you just have to deflect the ball, using the pace, thus giving you more chance of a boundary.

What could I say! Ray then changed the subject and talked about England selection, justifying to me the omission of Angus Fraser from the original tour party, and the video of spin was discussed no further.

As we slunk out early from the World Cup, we were all aware of the various inquests flying around back home in the media, but I knew the real problem. The management hadn't got the best out of the players they had selected. The players couldn't speak out because their tour contracts wouldn't allow it. There was an urgent need to be cheery and upbeat on that tour, but from the moment he got on the team bus every morning, our Raymond was moaning – about the traffic, the weather, the hotel, the breakfast – it was all so negative. Our team meetings, on both tours, were in general a joke. Neil Smith and I couldn't believe how little we talked about the opposition in our team meetings. We had come from the Edgbaston environment, where things would be thrashed out in detail, where every player had his own personal video to examine specifics in his technique.

Usually, England's meetings on the eve of the game were superficial, prefaced by the captain saying, 'Right, shan't keep you very long, lads.' But we ought to have been kept there longer, talking in detail, discussing gameplans, and oppositions' strengths and weaknesses. Not because we were losing, but because it should be a prerequisite at this level. It was exasperating that we talked so little cricket. As Neil Smith said to me, 'The lads won't believe it when we tell them we are far more professional than the England set up.' My mind went back to the first team meeting I had attended under the Atherton/Illingworth colours. When we played a one-dayer against New Zealand in 1994, we never talked about Chris Pringle's slower ball, where Martin Crowe likes to hit the ball, or that Bryan Young likes to play a forcing shot off the back foot on the offside that goes in the air. When I was out in the field, I remember thinking that Darren Gough needed a deep gully and backward point rather than two slips – and sure enough, Young played the ball at catchable height through the backward point area. We lacked attention to detail. Every side should have detailed videos of the opposition. We got one on Anil Kumble before we played him in the Nat West Final and it was invaluable for those who hadn't faced him before. England didn't seem to think such matters important, almost as if it was a confession of weakness to talk about the opposition.

Of course, it could be concluded that I have an axe to grind. I was only picked for two of the seven one-day internationals in South Africa, but I honestly wouldn't have minded missing out, or being in a losing side, if I felt we had prepared properly. I was so frustrated at the lack of intensity given to gameplans and the laid-back attitude. Not being originally selected for the World Cup was the biggest blow of my career. I was only chosen for the World Cup once the competition had started, to replace Craig White who had picked up a rib injury, and although I only played in the last two games, it was still terrific to be out there, representing my country. I had no thoughts at all about making myself unavailable, not just because of the honour, but also because I so desperately wanted us to go one better than the 1992 World Cup Final. In retrospect, we didn't stand a chance, because other countries had passed us by in their tactics and approach.

I feared the worst for my own prospects before I got out to South Africa just after Christmas. Having returned from Australia to England, I read that Craig White had been summoned from the 'A' tour of Pakistan – where he hadn't fared all that well – to join up with the squad in South Africa. Now Craig and I are good friends, we roomed happily together on that tour and I rate him highly as a cricketer – but I was the one picked in September as stand-by for the South African tour, and to fly out for the one-dayers in January. So here was Craig being slipped in by two selectors – Atherton and Illingworth – after four – those two plus David Graveney and Brian Bolus – had chosen the squad in September. It's well known that Illy rates Craig very highly, but I was baffled to know what had happened in the intervening three months to push me down the pecking order. When I later heard that Phillip DeFreitas had been asked by Illingworth at the end of November if he fancied going to the World Cup, the outlook for me got even bleaker. Daffy was playing out in South Africa for Boland and after a lively game against us, Illy popped the question. Good for Daffy, another cricketer I rate highly, especially in one-day cricket, but our squad seemed to be picking up all sorts of players in December purely on the whim of the manager. I wondered what Bolus and Graveney subsequently thought about the validity of their opinions at the September tour selection meeting.

In my first net, at Port Elizabeth, I had another hint that perhaps I wasn't an automatic choice for the World Cup. Illingworth watched me ease myself gently into my bowling, making sure that I wasn't going to tweak anything after just getting off a long flight from London. He said to me, 'At that pace, you must bowl with the keeper up.' I resisted the temptation to answer, 'Well, actually I'm just getting loose, but it normally depends on the pace of the wicket, and Keith Piper actually stood back in last year's Nat West final. Did you watch that game?'

After drawing the Port Elizabeth Test, we moved on to Cape Town for what we all thought would be the decisive game in the five-match series. Everybody was weighing in with their opinions about the pitch, what side we should play and how we should approach the game. Experts like Ian Botham and Geoffrey Boycott were saying we had to play the wild card, Devon Malcolm, and risk dropping a batsman, to go for broke. I felt at the time that our batting would be a bit thin if we dropped one in favour of another bowler and I looked at the South African line-up, noticing that they were going in with only four front-line bowlers. Criag Matthews was dropped for a batsman – Jacques Kallis – who bowled a bit. They were backing the main bowlers to bowl us out twice and I thought that significant.

We lost the Cape Town Test badly, and Devon Malcolm took the brunt of the management's anger, which I thought was out of order: when you get bowled out for 150 on the first day, you are in trouble, whatever your erratic fast bowler does. Devon got the blame for failing to clean up young Paul Adams when he joined Dave Richardson for a vital last-wicket stand when they weren't all that far ahead. Fair enough, Devon's radar wasn't at its best, but he was rusty after playing hardly any cricket the previous month, and wasn't there a bowler at the other end? As we sat dejectedly in the dressing-room after we lost, Illingworth flipped and told Dev that he had lost us the Test. That was very hard but Atherton made it worse by pointing the finger at Dev in his press conference. Such thoughts should be kept in-house, and in any event, the batters should have shared the responsibility, having been bowled out cheaply twice. Illingworth also had a go at Graham Thorpe after he got himself out in the first innings. Thorpey was undone by a ball that went late across him, and was caught behind. As he sat on the physio's couch, brooding about it, Illy came in and said, 'It was a bit wide, wasn't it, you should have let it go.' Thorpey had only been out five minutes earlier and I could tell he was put out by Illy's comment, so I tried to smooth it over. 'It looked like a good ball to me, I thought it went late off the wicket,' I said. I was trying to be constructive and avoid Illingworth belittling a disappointed player at the wrong time; perhaps Illy put the black spot on me for disagreeing with him?

So we started the one-day internationals after losing the Test series. There were seven games to be played in a hectic period of

12 days and then the World Cup party of 14 would be picked. We started off with a day/night friendly at Newlands against Western Province, which we lost. It wasn't looking good. John Barclay, the assistant tour manager, had said, 'Dermot, we don't talk enough cricket. It would be wrong if you didn't speak up at team meetings, you're a successful county captain and you're entitled to have your say.' I respected John Barclay's honesty and when Illingworth asked to have a chat with myself, the captain and vice-captain before the first one-dayer at Cape Town I was delighted. We fixed the meeting for three o'clock the next afternoon and I wrote a lot of thoughts down, ready for a detailed discussion. I got to Illingworth's room five minutes early. He told me the side for tomorrow and I was in it. He asked if Allan Donald was likely to open the bowling against us; I told him he didn't like the white ball when it was new and preferred operating with it first change. He asked if I thought Richard Snell would open the batting for them as the pinch-hitter; I said I wasn't sure because Dave Richardson had opened in recent one-dayers. The four of us then talked generally for a few minutes but time was slipping by: the coach was due to leave at 3.30 for practice under the lights. I was looking for an intensive discussion about bowling options, where we should have our best fielders, my feeling that Alec Stewart ought to keep wicket and that Phil DeFreitas or Neil Smith should be the pinch-hitters rather than waste them at numbers 9 or 10. Illy then said, 'Right, let's get on the bus' and that was it.

It was the only time I was invited into a closed meeting with the management on that tour. Perhaps Illy was just being political by suggesting it that day, so he could turn round and say, 'We did ask Reeve for his thoughts', but he hadn't really. He and the captain had just skated over the subject. After our practice session under the lights, Atherton said a few words, then launched into DeFreitas, saying, 'That was a dreadful shot you played against Meyrick Pringle the other night. You've played a lot of one-day cricket, you should know better.' I couldn't believe he would be so tactless and insensitive as to single out a player like that in front of the others. DeFreitas is at his best as a batsman by being positive, but we all knew there was a personality conflict between the two of them, dating back to their days together at Lancashire. Daffy said afterwards 'It's started already'.

We lost the Cape Town one-dayer narrowly and if Shaun Pollock hadn't been so inspirational, we would have won it easily. There was no cause for alarm and I said so at the next meeting when we were asked for our views. I pointed out that Dave Richardson likes to drive straight, so we needed mid-on to be straighter, while Jonty Rhodes likes to clip it through mid-wicket, closing the face and scampering quick singles, so we needed to block that shot. I said that we were the better side for 80 per cent of the game and that we were a little rusty. Graham Thorpe had played splendidly in that game, but got out at a bad time when we needed him to nail down the win. I made a point of saying what a top knock he had played and then suggested that he used his feet more to the medium pacers, Kallis and Cronje when the wicket keeper is standing back. When I bowled that was Bob Woolmer's idea to get after me in the last game, because he knew it disconcerted me. I told the squad that if a batsman skips down to my bowling when the wicket keeper is standing back it's very unsettling. You have to make the decision of whether or not to bring the wicket keeper up to the stumps. If you do it puts pressure on the keeper and usually results in more extras. If you don't bring him up to the stumps it's always in your mind that the batsman might advance down the track, and turn a length ball into a half volley.

I continued that with mid off and mid on up, if the ball's in the right spot you can play it over the top and probably get mid off or mid on back. If the ball's not in the right spot, you can just defend it and you'd be surprised at how many captains will still immediately put a fielder on the boundary, giving you more gaps for singles. I also pointed out that Kallis and Cronje bowled lots of slower deliveries to Thorpey and Neil Fairbrother. Thorpey took the advice well, and I felt I expressed my views articulately and constructively enough. I hadn't blundered in, I'd waited till we were all asked if we had any thoughts. Robin Smith came over to me after the meeting, saying it was good to hear my thoughts. And he was impressed with how quickly I picked things up. Atherton and Illingworth appeared to be happy with my contribution, but I couldn't believe how Illingworth ended the meeting. He said, 'Oh yes, you tailenders, you didn't look like you could hit a one, never mind a four. I want you to have some batting practice, work at your batting.' So the meeting had ended on a big negative! Neil Smith was one of those tailenders who didn't have a bat in the nets the day before, because we ran out of time and bowlers. The wicket was excellent on the side of the Newlands square, but I had to ask if I could have a bat and by that time, the enthusiasm had waned. I faced Neil Smith, Graeme Hick, Darren Gough (off a short run, and he was wearing rubbers), and the physio Wayne Morton. After about ten minutes, Hicky shouted, 'Last round!' as he had bowled enough and the wives were waiting back at the hotel. I had to hold in my anger. I really felt for Neil Smith and the others who weren't offered a bat yet criticised by Illingworth in the meeting the next day. We won the next game at Bloemfontein to square the series.

Off to Johannesburg for the third and fourth games over the same weekend and Atherton began the team meeting with, 'I don't want to keep you long. Good win at Bloemfontein, we're back on the winning track. Anyone got anything to say – Dermot?' It was the way that Atherton said 'Dermot?' that stung me a little. He hadn't teed me up beforehand that he was going to call on me, and I thought he sounded a little sarcastic, as if I had said rather too much after the Cape Town defeat. I felt he was having a dig at me, but I recovered to say: 'You've caught me out a bit, Skip, but now you ask me – yes, I think we can learn from the South Africans' mistake at Bloemfontein. They were too expansive in the second half of their innings because of their good start. Too many batsmen went for big shots early in their innings and they ended up getting only 60 in their last ten overs, rather than 80 or 90. They should have milked us more, and gone really big, with wickets in hand in the last five overs.' I still felt we ought to be having precise discussions about our game and the opposition, but clearly Atherton, at that stage of the tour, didn't.

I played the next day at Johannesburg, a game that we lost. I suffered a slight tweak in the groin while chasing a ball in the field, and was worried I might not be fit for selection for the match at Centurion Park the following day. I thought I should inform the chairman that I might be a doubtful starter. When we arrived back at the hotel I asked Ray Illingworth if I could have five minutes with him. He said 'I'm going for a shower and then I'm playing bridge. We'll talk tomorrow'.

I was gobsmacked! I iced the groin and hoped it would be just a twinge that would not prevent me from playing. I informed Michael Atherton the next morning at breakfast that the groin felt sore and I would need a fitness test when we got to the ground. I went through a detailed fitness test and satisfied myself that I was fit enough to get through the day, the groin was no worse than a little pre-season twinge, something you could play with. I told Atherton I was fit and available, and he replied, 'We're playing Craig White today.' That was another big hint that I was going to miss out on the World Cup. I felt I was being marginalised; time was running out for me to impress Atherton and Illingworth, but I was bound to play at Durban, where the ball swings. In the nets at Durban, I bowled well at the captain, beating him several times, with Illingworth looking on. I told them I was fit, but they didn't pick me. I couldn't believe it, I was the only one of the fast bowlers to miss out, in conditions that were absolutely right for swing bowling.

When we were in the field at Durban, I had first-hand experience of Illingworth's knocking attitude to the players. We weren't fielding well, and the last straw came when Phillip DeFreitas dropped a difficult catch, but one that this excellent fielder would usually take. Illingworth stood up in the dressing-room and shouted, 'You f****** stupid w******!' in front of the lads who weren't playing. I'm not saying Illy was the only person to ever swear in the dressing room, of course he wasn't and he's entitled to let off steam and have a blast at a player if he wants to. I just believe it's not the way of getting the best out of your team, in fact it's detrimental. Players in the dressing room who heard the outburst may play the next game or field as substitute if there was an injury. If that player then mis-fielded you could be sure his mind would flash back to the dressing room and he would wonder how much stick he was getting from the chairman. He probably wouldn't want the ball to come to him in the field. The old 'Fear of Failure Syndrome'. Illingworth's outburst was bound to get around the whole team. When we lost at Durban, Atherton stormed into our dressing-room, threw his hat into a corner and shouted, 'Bloody fielding!' So again the finger was being pointed at certain individuals, rather than a cool appraisal of how the fielding could be improved. Later that night, in a bar in Durban, I told Atherton to his face that he needed to talk to his players about their own game, to lift their spirits. I said that communication with the players was poor and that Illingworth was now a laughing stock, that not many in the squad took any notice of him, and laughed behind his back. Atherton seemed to take it well enough, but maybe that was the final nail in my coffin.

So we were 4–1 down in the series, with two to go, and I realised clearly that I must play in the last couple of games; otherwise I was out of the World Cup. I felt that the pitches at both East London and Port Elizabeth were slow enough to suit my type of bowling, so that I might get picked. Dominic Cork and Darren Gough were particularly supportive at that stage, and so was Alec Stewart, who has been a good mate for years. It was nice to have the support of the vice-captain

Clearly Alec's support for me wasn't relevant because when Illingworth read out the 13 players for the East London game, my name wasn't amongst them. I was shattered, and when Atherton started talking about our running between the wickets, I had to bite my tongue. I had felt all along we were terrible in this department, with us not backing up far enough, but I was so choked I couldn't speak. I wanted to, but I would have cracked up if I'd tried. After that team meeting, Alec Stewart was very sympathetic to me, saying that we were going round in circles in team meetings. Neil Fairbrother agreed, saying that we had got the balance of the side wrong all along, that we should have tried to win the series at the start with our best one-day side, then experimented. In short, we were a shambles, lacking in direction and leadership. No wonder the South Africans thrashed us.

Deep down, I knew my fate but I wanted to force it out into the open, to make Atherton face me and tell me what was going on. During our innings at East London, he was on his own in the dressing-room and I asked him what were my chances for a game at Port Elizabeth and for the World Cup. He said, 'I don't think it looks hopeful.' He asked me where I thought I could fit in. I said that one of Peter Martin, Phil DeFreitas, Neil Smith and myself would probably miss out, if they were going to take Jack Russell. I asked if England were likely to play Richard Illingworth and Neil Smith together or would they use Hick as the second spinner. I was clutching at straws. Atherton said he was concerned about my fielding and overall fitness. I pointed out that I had missed just a couple of games last season, that when I arrived in South Africa I had won the fitness test organised by our physio, Wayne Morton, that featured Neil Smith, Neil Fairbrother, Devon Malcolm, Darren Gough and myself. I agreed that I had slightly strained my groin at Johannesburg, but it was only a niggle that had now cleared up. As for my fielding, I said that he was putting me out of position. I hadn't been mid-on or mid-off consistently for almost ten years, that at Warwickshire I did short extra cover or short mid-wicket, and when necessary, slip. I believed I had good hands and added the information that in the 1992 World Cup, I had caught very well at slip. As for batting, I should ideally be the last of the batters, at number seven, and one of six bowlers in the side. He listened patiently to all that, and I left thinking that although I had little, if any, chance, it was good to get a few things off my chest.

When we got to Port Elizabeth, Atherton came to my room and asked my room-mate, Craig White, for some privacy. The conversation was short. I wasn't going to the World Cup, because of my fielding and fitness. I shook his hand, saying, 'Good luck, Mike'. I sat on my bed fuming, then stood in the shower for half an hour, to cool down. Craig White returned and was very understanding. He's a great guy and I wished him well. He knew that Illingworth's regular public support for him was a bit of a millstone around his neck and he had his own fitness problems. Craig had been carrying a hamstring strain for a few games and he nearly pulled out of the Durban game. I overheard our physio tell him, 'If you don't play here, you might miss out on the World Cup.' So Craig played.

Actually, I never saw it as a straight fight between me and

Craig for one place. I would have taken us both, because you can't have too many all-rounders, as we proved in the 1992 World Cup. If one of them fails as a bowler there are always options. I wouldn't have taken Jack Russell, because I think he lacks the power of stroke to do well in one-dayers, on slow wickets. Jack is a brilliant keeper and you couldn't ask for a better team man but for balance in one-dayers I would keep with Alec Stewart. Illingworth kept going on about the left-hander doing well against leg-spinners like Shane Warne and Mushtaq Ahmed, but Jack's forte is in the longer games. His steadfast effort to help Mike Atherton save the Johannesburg Test was a wonderful effort, full of courage and character – but that was an innings to save a match, not win it. Yet I believe Jack was told soon after that he was going to the World Cup, as a reward. Alec Stewart ought to have kept wicket and opened the batting, because if he has a weakness, it is going in and having to face spin immediately. If he's opened the innings and has runs on the board, he's more likely to collect runs in his orthodox manner when a spinner is introduced into the attack.

That night in Port Elizabeth, I went out for a few drinks with Mike Watkinson, Darren Gough and Wayne Morton and ended up on my own, talking with some Afrikaaners, which nearly got me into trouble. I woke up next morning, with all my clothes still on, with a furious hangover. I got more and more annoyed as the day wore on, because I felt I hadn't been given a fair crack of the whip. I'd heard some TV commentators saying, 'Is Dermot Reeve past it?', but they hadn't said that three months earlier when I was playing well for Warwickshire. I was simply a bit rusty in that first one-dayer at Cape Town and I had been given hardly any chance to shake off that rustiness in the next ten days. How do you find form when you don't play? Perhaps I was never going to be picked for the World Cup, and it took too long for it to dawn on me.

At Port Elizabeth, I bumped into Illingworth in the lift and he had to speak to me. 'Bad luck, kid, someone had to miss out,' was all he managed. I thought of giving him a mouthful, but there was no point. From early on, he and Atherton had pushed me sideways. My emotions were blurred, of course, but I remember thinking at the end of that series that it would have been a travesty of justice if we had beaten South Africa. We would only have beaten them because of the talent of our players, rather than any planning, or attention to detail. I felt for Atherton because Illingworth kept chiming in with negative comments in our team meetings. Perhaps that's why Mike tried to keep the discussions short. Mike probably felt there was very little he could do about it. John Barclay and Wayne Morton did their best to be upbeat and positive, and I know John Barclay was desperate for us to talk in more detail on gameplans and tactics.

On the day the South African tour ended, I gave an interview to BBC Radio, admitting my disappointment and saying that I was upset and angry. I thought I spoke reasonably, pointing out the facts, that I had hardly played, that I still felt rusty and that it was difficult for me to stake a claim to the World Cup when I'm not being picked. I agreed it was the lowest point of my career but made a particular point of wishing the lads well, sincerely wishing them to come back with the World Cup. I believe it was a dignified interview in the circumstances, and I could have said a lot more that would have really made people sit up. The tabloids picked up the interview off the radio, turned the quotes around, and the banner headlines were there for us all to read when we flew into Heathrow. The headlines didn't do justice to the tone of the interview but never mind – some England boys were delighted. Over breakfast, some said, 'Well done, Dermot, give Illy more of that, he deserves it.' They wanted him out, and were fed up with his carping.

His back-up coaches weren't that popular either. John Edrich, the batting coach and Peter Lever, who looked after the bowlers, had been with England for the first part of the tour. Most of the lads were upset at the way that Devon Malcolm had been singled out by Lever, who described him as 'a cricketing nonentity'. That was out of order, guaranteed to demoralise a guy like Devon. It was certainly an opinion not shared by the South African batsmen who were very wary of Devon after his sensational bowling at the Oval in '94. I didn't blame Devon for getting back at Illingworth and Lever when he went back home, early in January. He gave a long interview to the *Daily Express*, which was printed over three days and it was faxed to us in the hotel at Durban, making interesting reading. I thought he was right to hit back.

As for Devon's suggestion that there might have been a racial element behind his treatment, I'm not sure. All I can say is that Illy referred to Devon as a 'Nig-nog' in the nets at Port Elizabeth at Christmas. It came after Devon had bowled out of turn. It wasn't directed at Devon, but I heard Illingworth utter the word in exasperation. That may appear a racist comment when set down on paper, but possibly Illingworth didn't realise the significance of what he was saying. He is not a subtle man. A month earlier, at East London, John Edrich was helping to supervise some practice, and there was no sign of Devon. Edrich was heard to say, 'Where's the black boy?' Again, that may well have been Edrich's style of address, without thinking of the deeper ramifications. If so, it was still insensitive. We are all products of our environment and the era in which we played cricket, and when Edrich was an England regular, black players didn't feature in the England set-up. In blurting out the words 'black boy' he may have meant no harm, but it was heard by a couple of the England squad, it did nothing for team morale. That remark confirmed to some players that Illingworth and his lieutenants didn't understand the psyche of modern England cricketers. The game, and the society in which it was played, had moved on from their day.

A few days after we got back from South Africa, Illingworth went on television to defend himself and had a go at me over my mildly critical radio interview. He showed a strange grasp of the facts in the process. He said that I hadn't been fit for a couple of one-day matches, so I rang him up and challenged him about that. I reminded him that I had told him to his face that I was fit for Durban, and that, after a vigorous fitness test at Centurion Park, I was available for that as well. In other words I was fit for all seven of the games, even though I was only picked twice. I suggested he should talk to the press to clear the air about that issue, but he said he was fed up with the press, though he conceded my point.

He must have thought he had got shot of me, but then Craig

White injured his rib and I was flown out to join the World Cup squad. When I first saw Illingworth, I told him I was absolutely delighted to be there, that our difference of opinion was water under the bridge, and that I'd be doing my utmost to help the team. Illy said he didn't like me using the word 'angry', but I felt he would have expected a player with any pride to be angry at missing out on the World Cup. If you don't feel any passion about playing for your country, should you be considered in the first place? Anyway, we patched it up. He didn't say another word to me for the next ten days, even after I got 80-odd in as many balls in a warm-up match. Then, at the last moment, as I walked on the pitch for the game against Pakistan, he patted me on the back and said, 'Good luck, kid.' I mentioned this to Robin Smith who said, 'That's nothing, Dermot. He barely said two words to me on the whole South African tour.'

Robin felt Illy had been unfair to go on the record to the press, saying that he and Alec Stewart had to prove themselves all over again after the South African trip. He believed that batting with the tail in South Africa meant that it was hard to get big scores when you have to play shots as others are getting out at the other end. That's the problem when you're at number six – you need someone to stay there with you, but the lads kept getting rolled over in the lower middle order. It was hard to see how Robin could get hundreds in those circumstances. He had also suggested to Illingworth that a sports psychologist would help some of the England players, let them talk out their tensions and relate to a sympathetic person, but Illingworth was having none of that. It didn't matter that the South Africans used such innovative methods, Illy felt if you were good enough to play for England, you had to sort it out for yourself.

In Robin's opinion, Illingworth had instilled a fear of failure. In the World Cup he felt the batters were all determined to get a score, no matter how long it took, because it was down there in the scorebook and they would be picked again. It didn't seem to matter that those runs weren't coming at a run a ball. Illingworth's negative vibes were making the guys play for themselves, not the team interest. Just because Mike Atherton averages over 40 in one-day internationals doesn't mean he's the ideal opener, because his ratio of runs per ball in his career is slow for this type of cricket. We would talk briefly about getting off to a quick start and making use of the field restrictions in the first 15 overs but I bet our openers let more balls go through to the keeper than any other team. The Sri Lankans were successful in the 1996 World Cup because they were positive throughout. They lost two wickets in their first over against India, but that didn't faze them. They still got to 251 in their 50 overs, playing with great style and courage. This in the semi-final of the World Cup, against the home side, in Calcutta. How would England have approached such early setbacks? In the quarter-final against Sri Lanka, with only two fielders outside the inner ring for the first 15 overs, we managed 35 in the first ten overs.

Our team meeting before that quarter-final match against Sri Lanka showed we hadn't advanced our thinking all that much since South Africa. Sanath Jayasuriya, their opener, was an obvious danger man to us. The left-handed opener had smashed a few attacks early in the tournament and I was looking forward to hearing how our think-tank was going to combat him. Atherton said he wanted Peter Martin to bowl to Jayasuriya with a 6/3 field. Pete looked shocked at the news, and I don't blame him. The six fielders were to be on the offside, with just three patrolling an area where Jayasuriya is so strong – he loves to flick the ball over mid-wicket or mid-on and there was to be no-one on the leg-side boundary. Atherton told Pete he had to bowl straight, because Jayasuriya loved width but this ignored Jayasuriya's knack of hitting straight balls over mid-wicket. Now Pete's a swing bowler, with the ability to bring the ball back into the left-hander for the lbw or to be bowled through the gate: surely he needed his legside to be strengthened?

I spoke up at the meeting: 'Can I just clarify this? You want Pete to have no one back on the legside at all? You want him to give Jayasuriya no room at all? Personally I'd find it hard to bowl with that field.' Pete said, 'I'm worried about that, I thought I'd have a split field.' What disturbed me was Peter Martin was told this on the eve of the quarter-final, when we had been netting at Karachi for days, and no one had spoken about such a ploy. Pete could have had time to work on the idea at left-handers in the nets, but instead it was sprung on him the night before. He would be going to bed worrying about where he'd been told to bowl and what the field was. I really felt for Pete. The captain also said we would be swapping the bowling around in the first 15 or so overs. He clearly believed that was tactically flexible, but it wasn't. I got the impression he feared there would be a lot of stick flying around in those early overs, and that the burden would need to be shared around – but what if someone is bowling well? Do you take him off after a couple of overs because it had been discussed the night before? Wasn't there just a chance that England's bowlers might do well the next day? That suggestion hardly built up the confidence of the bowlers.

Next day it all went predictably wrong. We were too slow at the start of our innings and we finished at least 40 short, with 235. Jayasuriya plundered us for 82 off 44 balls, until I had him stumped during my marathon stint of four overs. We lost with ten overs to spare and we slunk deservedly out of the competition. It was our tenth defeat in succession by a Test-playing country in one-day matches. There were no excuses, we had been caught up and overtaken in this type of cricket by so many other countries. We had been complacent and unimaginative, thinking we could just turn on good performances like a tap.

Raymond Illingworth's contribution in the team meetings had been a little more muted than in South Africa, possibly because it had dawned on him that he wasn't getting through to the players. He did provide us with one comic gem, though. After South Africa had beaten us comfortably at Rawalpindi, Illy made the relevant point at a team meeting that we mustn't let bowlers tie us down with line and length. If the wicket-keeper is back, we have to use our feet and get down to the pitch of the ball, even against the quicker bowlers. He was right to point out that the South Africans had mid-on and mid-off straight, and so they were difficult to beat. All we were getting was scrambled singles to them, there was no chance of getting twos. So we had to use our feet and clear their heads. That was good advice, but surely better off before the match or during the innings. Anyhow he suggested we practice this method the next day at nets.

So we're in the nets at Karachi and Neil Fairbrother is twinkling down the pitch and depositing the ball for six as if it had been a match. It's going well, this new strategy, isn't it? Well no, actually – Illingworth is tearing his hair out, saying, 'What's he doing, the bloody idiot? He'll lose the balls if he hits straight!' In the end, Fairbrother got fed up of Illy's nagging and said, 'That's it, I'm not batting', and walked out of the net. Illy had discovered that we were down to our last batch of balls, and we couldn't afford to lose any of them. So there we were, practising a desirable discipline in our attempts to progress in the World Cup – and we had to stop it because we had run short of cricket balls! And we're supposed to be a professional outfit. We were in hysterics as the manager back-tracked on his suggestion of the night before.

On the flight home, the players agreed among themselves that we were still none the wiser about what was our best one-day side. We had been too complacent. Before the Sri Lanka game, our physio Wayne Morton gave a good, upbeat pep-talk to us. The gist of it was, 'We're better than this lot, lads', but I sat there thinking, 'No we're not. It all depends on the day.' Wayne is an excellent physio and a good motivator, but it was odd that the captain wasn't giving that upbeat message. The Sri Lankans were obviously a top side. When I was in Australia, I'd seen them at first hand. They had limited success there, but you could see how useful they would be on the sub-continent. Batsmen like De Silva and Jayasuriya would be doubly useful because their bowling would be effective on slow wickets. That meant they would have two all-rounders in the first four of the batting order and a keeper opening the batting. I always think there is less pressure on all-rounders or keepers in one-day cricket when they bat, because of the extra chance with their other speciality and so this gives them more freedom when they are at the crease. The Sri Lankans also looked good in the field. Their batsmen would struggle when the wicket had bounce in it, but they were unlikely to come across this surface in the World Cup. They played all their group matches at home and odds of 20/1 before the tournament didn't do them justice. I told my brother to stick some pounds on them and he celebrated the night Ranatunga lifted the trophy. Our think-tank hadn't seemed to have grasped what was needed from us in the World Cup. We ought to have looked at our record against spinners. It's not good in recent years. The opposition spinners turn the ball more than ours, and on those slow pitches in Pakistan, we may face around 30 of the allotted 50 overs against spin. Yet no one seemed to have talked through a strategy of playing the spinners with flair and boldness.

I didn't think that Atherton saw any of this as his area of responsibility. He concentrates very much on his own game and expects others to have their techniques in good shape. He is a terrific Test batsman and as courageous as they come. He is very hard on himself and expects a certain level of intensity from the players. At times I felt Mike's 'hard man' image and visual commitment would go over the top. At fielding practice, he would get very aggressive, snarling and shouting if he, or anyone else, fumbled a pick-up. I felt if he lightened up a little, he might find that the guys would field better, because they too would relax. There were times I was afraid to say, 'Bad luck, well tried!' in the dressing-room in an attempt to keep up morale. It was as though you had to show severe disappointment for a time and Mike certainly did – but at times I wished he had been consoling his team and lifting their spirits for the next day.

His ability to motivate is suspect. He finds it hard to avoid showing disappointment when a catch is dropped. The captain should be the first to shout out, 'Bad luck, never mind!', because the other players take the lead from their skipper at such times. If you show negative body language, you are then motivating by intimidation, there's a fear of failure. To get the best out of a team, you need to be bubbly and chirpy and make them feel it's their efforts that are important.

I had to bite my lip so many times under Atherton and Illingworth. Significantly, after the World Cup, Mike Gatting said on television that Atherton would learn the ropes of captaincy more if he did the Lancashire job. He said, 'It would be good practice.' I believe Gatt is right. I mean no disrespect to Mike Watkinson, who does a fine job at Lancashire, but Atherton needs to learn more about man-management, and how to react quickly out on the field. He is by no means a bad tactician on the field, and it wasn't any captaincy weaknesses on the park that resulted in England's poor performances in South Africa and the World Cup – more the planning behind the scenes and handling of players.

On a personal note, I've no idea how I stand with Mike now! Perhaps I got his back up by speaking too openly at team meetings in South Africa, but I had been asked to do so by the assistant manager, John Barclay and I always tried to sound constructive. I believe Mike and I have got on OK socially, and we seem to have enjoyed a good laugh from time to time.

One thing about Ray Illingworth: he contributed some amusing moments. After we had crashed out of the World Cup, we were driving through Lahore in a team bus and Robin Smith asked Illy if he had ever previously toured Pakistan. Illy didn't realise Robin knew the answer, and launched into a monologue. 'No, I was picked, but made myself unavailable. It wasn't like it is now, no nice hotels. We would have had to stay in places like that' – pointing out of the bus at some shacks on the roadside. 'Anyhow, I had started up a business selling Christmas cards and I could make more money in a week in Scotland than I would playing for England. I mean, you can get someone else to work for you, but they never work as hard as you, do they?' I couldn't believe my ears and couldn't resist saying, 'Actually, I had to cancel a dozen dinners to come out here, and it's cost me money, but I never gave it a second thought. you don't when it's for your country.' Graham Thorpe had to choke back the laughter and we had a big chuckle about it later.

I wouldn't have recounted this anecdote if it wasn't for what I read when I returned to England. Illy had sounded off in the *News of the World* about how money-conscious modern English players were. The gist of his whinge was that current players didn't seem to love the game as much as he did. He had come back and played for Yorkshire at the age of 51 and would have chopped off his little finger to play county cricket! Strange this from a bloke who would rather sell Christmas cards in Scotland than play for his country!

11

Is Cricket Dying?

At the end of England's tour to South Africa, the boss of their cricket, Dr Ali Bacher, said to me: 'You know, we're not just representing our country, Dermot – we're selling the game worldwide.' I thought that was a great attitude, very much in tune with the modern demands of the entertainment industry. Dr Bacher realised that cricket is now in a fiercely competitive market place, that it must adapt to new ideas and reach out to a base that hasn't really been tapped yet. The same is so true of cricket in England.

We must ensure the game appeals to youngsters in England and break the hold that football has on their affections. County membership in general caters for a clientele that's getting older, that likes the game just as it is, with a few reservations. That's all very well, and I do respect some traditions of English cricket, but not a great deal is being done to sell it to the generation that's coming through. Unless you have dedicated parents, or a club that caters for youngsters, the Bothams of tomorrow will lack positive encouragement. You can't look to their schools to provide that inspiration, unless they're lucky enough to go to fee-paying schools with excellent facilities or get coached by unselfish teachers prepared to give up their spare time.

In Australia, the future for cricket is much brighter because they have worked out the market. Kerry Packer was tremendously important to Australian cricket, even though many diehards didn't think so at the time. He glamorised it with top-class camerawork and extra razzamatazz, so that the punters thought they'd be missing something if they didn't go to the games or watch them at home. Night cricket was a fantastic innovation, it's so exciting to watch or play. The slow motion replays conveyed the drama of the occasion, to see the passion that goes into playing the game at such a high level of intensity. It's not about strawberries and cream when you're playing for your country, it's about a bowler desperate to get you out and the resulting triumph for batsman or bowler makes for great theatre if it can be conveyed to the public. That's what Packer achieved. For me, there'll always be room for the sedate, village green atmosphere of cream teas and genteel behaviour, but that doesn't inspire youngsters to play above themselves. You need passion, a rock 'n' roll atmosphere to get the kids into the ground. Cricket has to compete these days with more sports encroaching on the season. Football seems to start earlier than ever, in mid-August, and the World Cup and European Championships come along every two years. Rugby league is now a summer game and major athletics tournaments – like the Olympics and the World Championships – are staged during an English summer. I can't imagine that many youngsters turning on the television in 1996 were turned on by England's cricketers. We need colour, noise and excitement to grab their attention and get them hooked on this great game. Hopefully, they'll then become as addicted to cricket as I was when I started at school, and graduate to loving the longer game – Test cricket.

In English professional cricket, the crowds sit there for six or seven hours and go quietly off in the early evening, without being entertained all that much. That is often the fault of the players or the regulations by which we have to play, so why not have a competition whose sole aim is to entertain? We could have a 20 or 25 overs a side competition in midsummer, when the light is still good in mid-evening, and the game wouldn't need to start until around five o'clock. The bowlers would be limited to four or five overs and the object of the exercise would be entertainment. Risks would be taken, the fielding would be sharp and, because the overs are few, you would surely get a lot of close finishes. There is nothing as tedious as a one-day game over 60 overs that is cut and dried fairly early or goes into a second day.

With these shorter games, admission would be very cheap and you could get a live band in to jazz it up. Every time a wicket falls, let's have some loud music celebrating the fact, youngsters love all that. You could turn up at the ground after work or school and it would all be over by about eight o'clock. The atmosphere often takes a long time to warm up in one-day games – I prefer to watch it on TV for that reason – so let's warm it up right away. So many people think that cricket is boring, so if we take steps to broaden its appeal, we are halfway to getting kids interested. For too many, cricket is a very long game and football and rugby attract them for their brevity. If we shorten the game and make it a spectacle, with live counter-attractions, you've got a chance with the next generation.

To stage that midsummer competition, the amount of championship cricket would have to be reduced. A total of 17 county matches, plus three other one-day competitions, means you have tired players, unable to perform consistently with the type of verve and commitment you need to sell the game. The championship should consist of only 14 four-day games per county, which would mean you would miss out on playing three counties per year but that's less important than the rest players need.

In a championship match, we are supposed to bowl just a handful of overs less than in a five-day Test, with the rate in a county game set at 18½ an hour, compared to 15 an hour in Tests. At times I'm bored stiff watching Test cricket, when nothing seems to be happening and the players get away with 12 overs an hour. If I'm bored, and I'm in the profession, what about the uncommitted? They should be made to bowl the same amount in Tests as in championship cricket, but the county quota should be reduced to 17 an hour. Before this season you had county players having to rush around in championship games, in order to bowl the required 18½ overs per hour are unable to perform to their full potential as a result. I know that counties want their members to be happy, but I'm sure that the members would rather see top quality cricket. It makes professional sense to bowl the seamers on a pitch that favours them, rather than the spinner, and that means you're out on the field till after 7, because the seamers take longer to bowl their overs. Yet you see people leave the ground at six o'clock because they've got better things to do. So we end up performing for a public that's not even there any more.

A friend of mine attended the 1993 Nat West Final that we won in breathless fashion in semi-darkness, and was amazed to hear a chap say to his wife with four overs to go, 'Come on, dear, it's time we left.' He had the MCC tie on, clearly a lover of cricket, and he and his wife had sat there all day with their hamper and wine – but the game had gone on too late for them because the over rate had been understandably slow. One of the great finishes in one-day history and they walk out! That's the kind of traditionalist thinking that we are up against in English cricket. It's time the game was marketed more vigorously to give alternative forms of cricketing entertainment to those who would see it in a different way to that couple.

I know it's a constant gripe among English professionals, but we do play too much. We need a more balanced programme that allows more time for rest, with more qualified people to treat us. It's ridiculous that each county has just one physiotherapist who ends up having to treat too many players within half an hour of the game starting. You tend to go to the physio when you're injured, but what about getting advice on how to avoid injuries? In American football, the players have to come in on a rest day to get rub-downs to stop potential injuries from occurring, and it's the same in Australian rules football – but we're years behind. Every county should have a rubber, as well as physio – someone whose job is to work on the vulnerable areas, to massage deeply to get rid of general stiffness and potential injuries. I spend around £1,000 a summer getting that kind of specialised treatment at health centres away from Edgbaston, because the club's physio just doesn't have the time to give me the sort of attention I need. It's like giving your car a general service. The public don't realise the level of fitness that's needed, and bowlers will tell you that batsmen don't either. They'll say, 'Come and have a bowl at me in the nets' without realising how stiff and tired you are. Some players give up the game simply because they can't run up and bowl any more, nothing to do with age.

Experience does help get you through the physical demands. You tend to rely on adrenalin. I'll hobble in to the ground in the morning, convinced I won't be able to bowl, put my boots on and just hope for the best. But once you get the blood going, it feels like a different body, and if someone hits you for four, that really pumps you up. But it isn't a great idea just to rely on adrenalin to get you through as a bowler. I believe that there are too many county clubs who are over-keen to push cortisone into you, to disguise the injury. Over the years, such injections take their toll: why not find out why there's an inflammation in the first place?

There isn't a professional cricketer who doesn't worry about injuries and their effect on his career. Batsmen don't realise what a bowler has to go through in a season. One year, I couldn't bowl much because of injury and played as a batsman. It was like a holiday compared to being an all-rounder, and that experience only increased my admiration for the sheer will and strength of Ian Botham, who had to bowl so many overs for so many years. The strain on a fast bowler is incredible. I was out in Australia for the 1994/5 Ashes series and I marvelled at the way Craig McDermott kept running in. It was calculated that during the Adelaide Test, McDermott had run more than a half-marathon over five days, in terms of approaching the wicket, following through and returning to his bowling mark – and that ignores the physical strain of actually bowling the thing. McDermott had two days off after Adelaide and then it was off to Perth for the next Test. He injured his back there in the nets, as he hunched over in his stance having a bat. I'm not surprised, that was surely the after effects of Adelaide. He still bowled at Perth, taking six wickets in the second innings. In effect, he was being asked to run a second half-marathon within a couple of days. Just how advisable was that?

The science of getting fit for cricket and then maintaining that fitness is in its infancy in England. That's why I was so disappointed that Warwickshire wouldn't go with my suggestion to pay our players a couple of hundred pounds if they excelled in a fitness assessment at the start of pre-season. Ideally they could come in around mid-January for training and lectures on nutrition, the science of the body, the prevention of injuries – as well as practice in the indoor nets – they would be better cricketers because they'd be fitter. Then in April they could work hard on their technique, rather than playing catch-up on their fitness. The players need an incentive to get fit during the winter, because if they're not getting paid for it, they'll concentrate on their job, to pay the mortgage. I was happy for them to be fined if they weren't fit enough, provided the club gave them a financial carrot, but they wouldn't agree. The club seemed to feel that it was the players' own responsibility, but they just didn't understand the thinking of the players. Those still in England in the winter are expected to be on call to do the public relations tasks, going around local cricket clubs, handing over cheques, etc etc – all for nothing, for the honour of representing Warwickshire. But those appearances don't pay the bills. In 1994, the Warwickshire players created history by winning three domestic trophies, and being second in the fourth – yet an Aston Villa footballer earns more in a week than we picked up for our bonus that season.

The club's attitude, in common with other counties, is 'If you don't like it, someone else will take your place.' They have you over a barrel because of the benefit system. It's semi-feudal and archaic and it allows the county club to dictate a good deal of your career. It was because I was hoping eventually for a benefit that I bit the bullet over Brian Lara in 1994. The best batsman in the world was not setting the right example to the rest of the team, the captain who wished to have him disciplined was not getting enough support from the management – and I knew I was the expendable one, not Lara. I thought of my daughter out in Perth, aware that a successful benefit would allow me to see her more often, and then I picked up the phone and offered the olive branch to Lara. If it hadn't been for the prospect of a benefit – which was later confirmed for 1996 – I would have refused and gone public. The promise of a benefit ties you to a club, and they don't have to pay you your market value. Some shrewd cricketers are realising that now, and are leaving for more money and banking on a benefit eventually with their second county. I don't blame them. If a player backs his own ability, he should just sign a one-year contract because he's then in a stronger bargaining position when he's a free agent. The clubs prefer a two-year deal, wait till there's a year to go, then add on another year. They don't like long-term contracts, because they then doubt a player's commitment. It's becoming a game within itself. There's more talk now among players about salaries than I can remember. The grapevine tells you how much can be made elsewhere, so that when a player kicks up a fuss about money, the club that doesn't want to lose him usually finds some extra cash from somewhere, unless of course he's waiting for a benefit – in which case nine times out of ten he will stay put and not kick up a fuss.

I honestly feel players should be allowed to move freely between counties without ever being contested. At the moment, if a player's existing club offers him a contract when his previous one has ended, that player would be put on list one and considered a contested player if he moved. A county can only sign two List One players in five years. I can only deduce that the reason is that it prevents a wealthy county from buying all the best players. If they could, then these players would be earning their market value and probably wouldn't need a benefit year.

You can have a situation at the moment where a talented youngster cannot get into his county first team and plays all year in the second eleven. If he could move to a new county and play first-class cricket immediately he may wish to, but if his present county don't want him to leave, he becomes a List One player. It could be that the county willing to offer the youngster terms has already used up two List One signings or that they may not wish to use one up on a second eleven player. So the player would remain at his present county to play second eleven cricket and perhaps be frustrated by the system. If that isn't restraint of trade, what is?

The whole category of Lists One and Two should be abolished immediately and counties made to work harder to keep players happy and loyal. We must also attempt to get talented young sportsmen aspiring to play cricket, rather than football, and if wages weren't so far apart that would help.

Good luck to the younger players who are now flexing their muscles and manage to move on. I think of David Smith, who was sacked by Warwickshire after nine years as a capped player and didn't get a benefit. The club holds all the aces in those circumstances. They know that young players won't go out on strike over money because they'll just get dumped by the clubs, so it's up to the star players to flex their muscles and ensure all the English players are treated with more respect. I also believe that overseas stars earn too much from the English game. Some get touted around for as much as £100,000 a season by their agents and I know that certain counties have been willing to accommodate such demands. I think that's extortionate, when you consider how little some do for the club, apart from on the field, and that's only if they are fully committed. They're not all like Allan Donald. I'm all for having one overseas player on a county's books, but even the best of them shouldn't be paid more than £50,000 a season. That's more than enough for about five months' work – they are rarely there for the pre-season work in the cold of early April.

English cricket is stuck in an administrative time warp. How many innovations have come from England, rather than Australia and South Africa? I can think of one-day cricket, back in 1963, but it was Australia who staged the first one-day international back in 1971. That was because a Test match in the Ashes series had been washed out and the Aussie administrators were quick to see that a one-day game would bring in some money and entertain the public who had been frustrated at missing out on the Test match. Would our administrators have reacted so swiftly, or would they have set up a committee to investigate the feasibility of such a game in the future? Innovations like night cricket, the white ball, names on shirts, coloured clothing, logos on the outfield, electronic scoreboards and TV replays have all come out of Australia and South Africa. We ought to play more one-day internationals in England, and in coloured clothing because that would attract youngsters and bring more money into the game for the players, but the traditionalists at Lord's mutter about the sanctity of Test cricket. Of course, it's the best form of cricket, but many people can't afford to give much time and attention to such a long form of cricket. It's fine for senior citizens or those with a lot of leisure time and patience, but we have to look at ways of spreading interest in cricket. The Test and County Cricket Board need to understand that the customer base for Test cricket and the four-day game is getting older, and the vacuum needs to be acknowledged and filled.

Coaching is also still very traditional in English professional cricket. The MCC Coaching Book is too venerated, in my opinion. In Australia, they talk about getting a good technical base, but they concentrate on scoring runs, not just staying in. Rod Marsh, who runs their Academy, tells the players that they simply must look to score at four an over minimum, whereas we coach lads to hit the bad ball and defend the good ones. Sometimes you just have to take risks, though. The MCC manual says that if the ball is pitched outside the off-stump, you hit it through the offside – but what if all the fielders are on the off-side? Why not take a middle and off guard and smack it through the deserted legside area? Is there anything wrong with premeditating a shot against the spinner, or is the object of the exercise to be technically correct, not to get out and hope for some loose deliveries? Coaching in England isn't innovative enough: there's a feeling that you've got to look the part. Yet Steve Waugh doesn't care what he looks like and he has a fantastic record at the highest level. Allan Border stands out more in my mind than any other player for effectiveness rather than elegance. Everyone would like to bat like Mark Waugh, but it's just not possible. Strength of mind is vital. That's why Ian Botham was so great, he tried everything with the ball, he wanted to entertain and always approached the task with boldness, despite the conformists huffing and puffing.

Now that I've finished playing, I would love to make a video about how to play the modern game. It would be an alternative to the MCC manual and I'll hammer home the need for enjoyment, for effectiveness, working out your plus points, going for results not style. And the reverse sweep would be in the video. I'm glad to say that a short video I compiled on playing spinners has been shown around some Birmingham schools by Andy

Moles, when he spent a winter spreading the gospel of cricket. Andy told me that the reverse sweep seemed very popular. Gordon Lord, one of the regional coaches for the National Cricket Association, also asked to see that video, so perhaps at last the old conservative notions are being challenged. Not before time.

It seems to me that English cricketers need to be more positive in their attitude. Perhaps we are short of heroes at the moment. In Australia and South Africa, the youngsters look up to the likes of Warne, Slater, Rhodes and Donald because they project themselves impressively and the game is marketed so well. In England, we are crying out for new heroes to replace people such as Botham and Gower. In Australia, their best young players are taught how to deal with the media early on, and that can help open commercial avenues for the players, as well as selling the game. I remember hearing a radio interview with Justin Langer about his pleasure at being picked to go to the West Indies with the senior Australian squad. Langer was just a young player, who would probably have been earmarked as a reserve batsman unless something went wrong with injuries or form with the established choices, but he wasn't bothered about that. He said, 'I'm really looking forward to it, I'm sure I'll do well.' He wasn't being bombastic, it was said in a pleasant, matter-of-fact tone that underlined his quiet confidence. In similar circumstances, a young English player would mutter a platitude like, 'They're a very good side, but we'll go out there to do our best and hopefully we'll do well.'

Our players are too worried about how they are perceived by fellow professionals, that they might be accused of being too full of themselves if they spoke positively and said what was really on their mind. I'm sure that's one of the many reasons why some in the English game have never taken to me, because I'm a positive guy who makes no apologies for it. Warwickshire as a side have become unpopular on the circuit because we are confident and successful, as well as being led by a captain who doesn't care about being popular, so there's been a backlash against us. That doesn't bother me or the players, as long as we keep annoying people by winning trophies. If Dominic Cork was in our side we would be hated even more, because many see Dominic as obnoxiously full of himself and irritating. I hope he takes that as a compliment: it means people take notice of him, because he is a success. He feels good about his game, he has that spark of self-confidence that helps your game when you're up against tough opponents. I'm not a great believer in this false modesty that seems so typically English. I know that my job is fairly irrelevant, chasing a small red ball around the field. I don't help save lives, but I do help bring pleasure to some people by leading ten other guys to success. So if I'm asked what I do by others who don't know me, I'll tell them that I played cricket, and captained Warwickshire. Why be shy about it?

Professional cricket has always been hard, I'm sure, but I believe the attitudes out in the middle are tougher now than when I started in 1983, and that's not a bad thing. At least that is closer to the kind of atmosphere you get in a Test Match, so that a young player is less likely to freeze when he plays for his country. I'm quite happy to look for a verbal confrontation on the field if my mind isn't sharp enough that day. I find that igniting my adrenalin gets my legs moving more freely and helps me see the ball better. Paul Allott used to hand out some major verbals when he was bowling for Lancashire because that helped him get through any pain. I have seen him get a wicket through abusing my team-mate Alan Green, who stood there for 15 seconds before he walked. Afterwards he said that he hadn't hit the ball, but that Allott went on about it so much that he thought the bowler had to be right. That wasn't cheating by the bowler just competitiveness to the extreme, and it happens a fair amount. Bowlers appeal when the ball has gone down the leg-side and they know the batter hasn't touched it. They hope the umpire has heard a sound, that's all. I don't blame the batsman for thinking, 'I've hit that, but they've been trying to cheat me, so I'll do them'; but if I know he's nicked it, and he knows I know, he'll get some verbals. Then again, if I get verbals for not walking, I'll turn around and say, 'Oh you walk do you?' or 'I'm so very sorry' in a sarcastic tone.

There are times when you nick it and no one appeals and other times when you've hit the ground or your pad and been given out. I've stood beside Keith Piper at slip and been convinced there was a nick, but he's said, 'He got nowhere near it.' There are swings and roundabouts and a fine line between supporting the bowler and cheating. It's cheating when the ball hasn't carried and you appeal for the catch, but if you're not sure that's simply giving your bowler the support he deserves. You're out when the umpire says so, not the opposition. I've seen guys in Australia who have stood their ground after hitting the ball to cover, hoping to get away with a bump'ball decision. That's cheating.

Mind you, players are getting more sophisticated about bluffing the umpire. Roger Twose gave me a masterclass one day after he had made a fuss about being given out caught behind in a 2nd XI match. He didn't look at the umpire, stood hand on hip, disgusted at the wicket-keeper's appeal, marked out his guard again at the crease, finally looked up at the umpire's raised finger, and looked astonished that he was given out. He shook his head as he stalked back to the pavilion and we all sympathised when he stomped into the dressing-room. 'Bad luck, Roger – you didn't hit that then,' I said and he answered, 'Oh yes I did – I used to do acting at school. I did a good Julius Caesar.' He then went through the whole performance for us, after I told him I could never get away with that because I always look guilty. He went on and on for ages, about looking scathingly at the slips and the keeper, ignoring the umpire, and all that rigmarole. Eventually, I had to tell him we were pulling his leg, that I'd done the same thing – but it was an interesting insight into the way that some young players are now approaching the game. Doing the umpire no favours is the norm these days.

It's not easy for modern umpires. There's more pressure on them, but I do think the standard has improved since I started. All I look for in a good umpire is consistency. Dickie Bird is not the kind of umpire you want at your end when you're bowling, because his natural reaction seems to be 'not out', but at least he's the same when you're batting, as I happily discovered when Anul Kumble had me plumb lbw and Dickie let me off in the 1995 Nat West final. Good umpires like John Holder, David Shepherd and the Palmer brothers don't chop and change their views on what constitutes a dismissal, and that gives confidence to the players. There are some daft rules, though. The one about one bouncer per over protects batsmen unduly. If he has a weakness against the short ball, he ought to be peppered with it, it's part of the fast bowler's tactical armoury. If the umpire is strong enough, and understands the nature of the individual contest, he will judge it accordingly and the captains wouldn't complain if he told the fast bowler to ease up. Just because a number eleven batsman is grafting away, that doesn't mean we have to be nice to him and pitch the ball up. The bowler has to get him out before too many runs are scored, but this rule protects the tail-ender. You're trying to get him out, rather than hit him, but the sentimentalists say, 'Oh, it looks awful to see a tail-ender getting bouncers' – but the professionals have to get results. We are the ones who have to contend with the huge gap between aesthetics and reality.

Another rule that does bowlers no favours is the one-day rule about wides and no-balls. Now I think it's right that a beamer above waist height is called a no-ball, but what if it's a slow full toss? That's not intimidatory, and as Franklyn Stephenson used to prove with his slower ball, it is a subtle ploy that surprised batsmen. Calling that a no-ball is robbing a bowler of a skilful tactic and just making life easier for the umpires. The readiness to call wides in one-day games is a problem, too; there seems little margin for error, and interpretation seems to vary from umpire to umpire. So you end up bowling more overs because of this inclination to call wides, yet the game's rulers keep banging on about the slow over rates. It seems to me that there are too many former batsmen on the committees at Lord's who formulate the laws. Not many favours seem to be done for bowlers.

I think cricket in England from a supporter's point of view is different from other countries because they don't mind all that much if the national side loses. Of course, ignominious performances like that in the '96 World Cup lead to knee-jerk reactions in the media and the usual rash of phone-ins calling for the resignation of everybody, but that only happens when the England team has played particularly poorly. Admittedly, such events aren't as rare as they used to be! I believe that the typical

English cricket fan isn't desperate for us to win at all costs and is happy if there has been attractive cricket to watch, from whatever side. That's fine if you are a genuine cricket lover, who admires individual skill and doesn't expect your national side to win most of its games. It's not an attitude that's all that common in other countries. Effigies of unsuccessful captains get burned in India and Pakistan, their personal lives are made a misery, and politicians get involved, demanding public debates. In South Africa and Australia, you get sacked from the job, because their culture is all about winning. The quality of the opposition is not a matter to dwell on, you are expected to beat them. That's why they have an enlightened attitude to their top players. They don't believe in over-working them, by making them play in low-key games for their State side. Their national boards of control have the power to pull a player out of any game to ensure he is fresh for the time when he represents his country.

That's not the case in England, and it should be. Raymond Illingworth was quite right to lobby for this, and it was short-sighted to deny him the wisdom of his argument. Look at the experience of Robin Smith in the 1995 season. His heroic batting in the Edgbaston Test, when he was battered around the body by the West Indian fast bowlers, was a terrific display of guts. His reward? He had to drive down to Southampton to play for Hampshire in a Sunday League game because the Test had ended on the Saturday and his county said he had to play. Robin was exhausted by that working-over at Edgbaston and the delayed reaction hit him over the next few days as he answered his county's call. Then his cheekbone was fractured in the next Test at Old Trafford and that's his season over and he becomes a borderline case for the tour to South Africa. Robin finally made that trip, but he would have probably been in a better shape to face the West Indian fast bowlers at Old Trafford if he hadn't had to play straight away for Hampshire. He needed rest, and time for the psychological scars to heal. If he had been contracted to England, rather than Hampshire, Ray Illingworth would have ensured he was in a proper frame of mind and his body refreshed before he next played for England.

So England supporters must realise that our national side will only succeed despite the system rather than because of it. I don't think the professional game is dying in England. Greater media exposure and more money for the players have helped, but the interests of the counties and the need to cater for the memberships at those counties mean the progress of professional cricket as a major spectator sport is being checked. The game needs to be more vibrant, the competitions should be streamlined, and the players must be faced with a programme that galvanises them sufficiently to make the paying customer want to see the entertainment in the flesh. Traditions in cricket are all very well, but that doesn't mean some of our administrators have to live in the past.

12

A Sad Farewell

I played my last game for Warwickshire on Monday, June 17 at Headingley, where we lost to Yorkshire by ten wickets. Of course, I didn't know that at the time, but the hip injury which had bothered me for some time was to prove more serious than I realised. I had been limping around like an old man for a week or two and I was embarrassed when I saw my discomfort in the field whenever I watched us on television. In the end, the decision was made for me a month later, that I had to retire on medical grounds: there was a lot of arthritis in the hip joint. The hip would never be normal and if I tried to play any more continuous cricket, the quality of my life in the future would be a problem. I was quite philosophical after my initial feelings of shock and disappointment. I was aware that many professional cricketers have their careers ended prematurely on the say-so of someone else – the captain or members of the cricket committee – and that they often feel frustrated and unfairly treated. For me, there could be no complaints, the matter was out of anyone's hands. I had exceeded my expectations as a professional cricketer and had a great deal of fun along the way. The captaincy of Warwickshire had helped me stretch myself as a person as well as a leader, but now I had to think positively about other matters. It was more important to ensure that I could be fit enough to walk around a golf course without much pain for the next 20 years, and to be able to kick a football with my future offspring. My life now had to take another course.

So there was no fairy tale ending to my final season.

Warwickshire didn't consolidate on its success of recent years and the captain didn't go out in a blaze of glory. Yet we had no divine right to keep winning trophies, even though we were very confident at the start of the 1996 season. We'd enjoyed an excellent pre-season tour in South Africa and I was particularly pleased with my batting. I was hitting the ball better than at any stage in my career and my good form with the bat carried through to the start of the season, when I scored a big hundred against Sussex and we won that championship match easily. It all looked set up for us, with Shaun Pollock settling in very well as the replacement for Allan Donald. Yet it all slid away. It was galling to myself and Phil Neale, because we were determined to avoid a repeat of the complacency at the start of the '95 season, which took some time to eradicate and cost us the Sunday League. I can't put my finger on the main reason why we didn't repeat our triumphs in the '96 season. Although I just had the occasional feeling that some of the players weren't giving me their total concentration in team talks. Now it's understandable that players are tempted to switch off when they hear the same old things from the captain in team meetings and I think it became a bit of a yawn at times to some of the players as I continued to drum home the familiar points that had helped us to our high status. I do believe that true motivation must come from within that player, but it's also up to the captain to ignite that spark. So perhaps I wasn't as inspirational in motivation as I should have been.

You only need to be a little off-centre in your preparation and approach to start missing out and that's what happened to Warwickshire. Forget all the injuries – we had surmounted those handsomely in the '95 season. We began to lose out in close finishes, when we would normally get through with a combination of determination, boldness and high morale. It was a blow to lose the Benson and Hedges Cup semi-final at Northampton, when we had gone a long way to winning the game.

Northants won through in the manner of Warwickshire, pulling their innings round after a bad start, then fielding brilliantly and bowling to a plan. Opposition sides were more switched on to our strengths and many had caught us up in terms of attention to detail. No longer were there gaps for the paddle and reverse sweep when we faced spinners and we had to work harder for runs. I was impressed by the overall standard of fielding and most counties were approaching their cricket in a positive manner. Warwickshire didn't have the copyright on success and it was up to us to keep trying innovations. We were there to be shot at and we were victims of the Manchester United syndrome: opposition teams were raising their game when we played them. That's the way it should be, and if we had won the 1996 championship, that would have been a great achievement, because of the fresh challenges to us from many revived sides. But it wasn't to be and there's no point in moaning about it.

I suppose my preoccupation with my injured hip didn't help my captaincy on the field. It's hard to be upbeat when you're carrying your right leg and can't follow through on delivering the ball. I'm sure my body language on the field during that last month of my career wasn't very dynamic. I had been mulling over extending my career when my contract ran out at the end of the '96 season and I had been optimistic about having perhaps another two years left. But the hip had bothered me since a warm-up game at Karachi during the World Cup. I thought it was just a strain in the groin or lower back and put it down to stiffness in the morning: anyway, you bite the bullet when you're hoping to play for your country in the World Cup. When I came home, I had an X-ray, and although there was some abnormality in the hip, I was advised to keep playing and hope it would go away. It didn't, though. I would wake up with an ache on my right hip, as if someone had put an ice pack on it. In my final game, against Yorkshire, I set off to walk from slip to the other end and I had a curious sensation in my hip. It was locking as I walked, and I had to drag it along. I was worried now. I had a scan, then saw a doctor in Cambridge who had treated Angus Fraser and Dean Headley for hip problems. I had an injection into the hip joint in the hope of getting me through the season, but still was unable to bowl or sprint. Finally, we accepted an arthroscopy would be the next step, but that would put me out for the season. After the operation, Dr Villas informed me there had been a lot of soft tissue damage in the joint, which he had hopefully cleared up, but the arthritis was a major worry. He recommended I give up for good.

The following day I dealt with the media enquiries about my retirement and met up with Dennis Amiss and Mike Smith at Edgbaston to talk through the implications. They told me that I was still club captain, and therefore would still have a say in team selection. They wanted me to stay close to the side, which was nice of them. I made it clear that my replacement as captain, Tim Munton, should now be the one that led team meetings and ran the show. I would offer my thoughts if pressed, but Tim was now in control and the transition had to be handled smoothly and quickly. It was good of Dennis and Mike to insist I could still make a contribution when my morale was rather low, but there were still conflicting emotions as I cleaned out my locker that day in the dressing-room and put everything into a black bin-bag. Things I had accumulated over nine seasons at Edgbaston were shoved into that bag, but it would be some time before I'd be able to sit down and wade through it all.

But it wasn't all anti-climax and personal trauma in my final season. There were still plenty of laughs to be had – sometimes at the expense of other players. When we played Leicestershire at Edgbaston, I enjoyed jousting with their players out in the middle as we blocked it out for the draw. Leicestershire had made a good start to the season and they were full of themselves when they played us. They are one of the most vocal sides – a match for Warwickshire in that department, and we're not exactly a sullen lot – and as they scented victory, they were doing a lot of yapping. Alan Mullally bowled superbly, putting in one spell that was as good as anything I had come across in all my years of county cricket – and didn't he know it. As I tried to bat out for a draw, he kept chipping away at me and my partner Keith Piper, so I answered back: 'You've been getting a few wickets then, Alan – the mouth's coming along with it.' Then their wicket-keeper, Paul Nixon started to shout, 'Come on Larashire! Come on Donaldshire! Let's get them out, they've only ever had one player!' Mullally got more and more frustrated and said to me, 'You're hopeless, you blokes – you won't win anything this year.' Now I hadn't forgotten how Mullally had given away that game to Middlesex at Uxbridge last September, so I said, 'If that's the case, Al, we'll have to re-name ourselves Leicestershire.' That brought a high-five from my delighted batting partner, Keith Piper and extra satisfaction when we held out for a draw. Those words have come back to haunt me, but I am sincerely happy for James Whittaker and Leicester for their success this year. It was particularly nice to hear James say that they had learnt a lot from Warwickshire.

So, despite struggling physically out on the field, I hadn't lost my ability to get under the skin of some opposition players. I was still getting the blame for certain flashpoints, though, which were none of my doing. Take the game at Northampton in June. On the first day of that championship match, the press box was full of most of the luminaries in the cricket press. Ours was the most attractive championship game on offer, and with England places there for the taking between the first and second Tests, there were a few players keen to make an impression. The first day's play was great value, with Northants batting well early on, then we hit back after tea and bowled them out. I managed to pick up five wickets, but that all seemed an irrelevance judging by the following morning's papers. Once again, I had been allegedly involved in an ugly spat on the field with David Capel, as I stuck up for Keith Piper. We had the sight of players squaring up to each other, the umpires having to mediate and Reeve right in the middle of it all, stirring up trouble. The press dusted off the game six years earlier, when Curtley Ambrose beamed me, they revived the old cliché about there being friction between the two sides in recent years, and just blew the whole thing up, just to make a few cheap headlines. The implication was that it was my fault. The truth was easy to discover if the reporters had been bothered to look for it.

This time, I was actually the mediator, trying to calm things down. Gladstone Small bowled one at David Capel, and although I heard no noise there appeared to be a deflection as Keith Piper dived in front of me to take the ball. I shouted, 'Howzat?', umpire Tony Clarkson said, 'Not out' and that was the end of it as far as I was concerned. But Capes turned round, glared at me, and abused me for daring to appeal. Calmly, but sarcastically, I said, 'David – you bat, I'll field and we'll let the umpires do the umpiring. OK?' Piper, as is his wont, joined in and shouted, 'Yeh! Shut up Capes!' At the end of the over, as Keith and I walked past David, I said to the other umpire, Trevor Jesty, 'Trev, I'm allowed to appeal, you know,' and as Keith chipped in again, Trevor told him to stay out of it. As Keith passed Capes, he gave our wicket-keeper a pointed stare. Keith said to him, 'I'm not allowed to say anything,' and Capel shouted back aggressively, 'What did you say?' Keith replied, 'I can't say anything, I'll tell you later.' Capel shot back: 'You want to fight me later?' It was a total misunderstanding but Piper then changed his direction, walking towards Capel, as he raised his bat at him. I was walking towards slip and I heard Keith say, 'You're ugly'. Capes replied, 'I'm not as ugly as you' and by now it was all getting very silly. The pair of them were like a couple of rutting stags and I was finding it hard not to laugh at the puerile level of abuse they were hurling at each other. Capes shouted to me, 'You're always having a go at me, you're past masters at this. Just leave me alone,' Trevor Jesty had to tell Capel to calm down and get on with the game. When it had calmed down, I reminded Trevor, 'Just to confirm one point with you Trevor. This wouldn't have happened if Capes hadn't complained about me appealing for that catch. It's not always Warwickshire who start it, you know.' That night, I told the press my side of the story, but they still fingered me the next morning. They chose to ignore my version and beat up the line about Warwickshire and Northants having another go at each other, and my provocative part in past spats, as well as this latest one. It was a classic case of reporters deciding on their line and refusing to budge from it, in the face of contrary evidence. As for supposed hostility between both sides – David Capel phoned me up in sympathy when I announced my retirement and Kevin Curran suggested that he and I should stage a mock fight on the field during the Sunday League game, because he knew it was being covered by television. Kevin thought it would be a great laugh to have us wrestling on the ground, then get pulled apart by the umpires and fielders. After all, didn't many reporters and commentators state as a fact that Kevin and I didn't get on? Therefore it must be true! I thought that was a very funny idea, but in the end, we agreed it might not look very pleasant, even though it would only be a leg-pull.

There's never been any problem with my relationship with Kevin Curran, but sadly Michael Atherton made it clear in my final season that he had little time for me. He had agreed to turn out in a major benefit match -Warwickshire v. The Rest of the World, alongside top players like Aravinda DeSilva, Merv Hughes, Richie Richardson and Gary Kirsten. A fortnight before the game, Atherton told me he was pulling out because he disapproved of remarks I had made about him on television a few weeks earlier. I had been a guest on *Sport in Question*, hosted by Ian St John and Jimmy Greaves, and I responded honestly to a question about Atherton's quality as a player to be in England's best one-day side. I made some mild criticisms about his batting in one-day matches, coming to the conclusion that I would have a different strategy and balance for the side and not pick Michael for one-dayers. I said that guys like Alastair Brown and Adam Holioake ought to get preference, but I went on to say what a top Test batsman Atherton was, praising his courage and his stickability. In the end, though, I maintained that one-day cricket required a different format and players: I also felt that a lot of players in the county game felt the same way about Atherton. I didn't feel I had been unfair to Atherton, but when we met up at Edgbaston, he said he didn't like to be criticised by England team-mates and that he wouldn't be playing for me on the third of August. I said, 'Would you rather I'd lied about you?' but he clearly felt that I ought to have been aware I'd be asked a question like that and ought to have been ready with some vague answer. But I didn't feel I had been pushed into a corner on the programme: I thought he was being over-sensitive and told him so. After all, I had still invited him to play in the game, even though he had earlier dropped me from the original World Cup Squad and criticised my fielding. Atherton then said that days off in the English season are precious and he wasn't now going to give up this one on the third of August – but when he agreed to play, he presumably had thought days off were precious. He then paused for a moment and said he'd made up his mind and was sticking to his decision. Some may feel that's a noble attitude, while others would just say that Mike was being stubborn. It was clear to me he thought less of me after my public comments, but I wasn't bothered. I'd answer the question just as honestly and comprehensively if it's put to me again.

So I'd got under the skin of the England captain and I also upset the game's most traditional body, the M.C.C. in my final season. Here again I plead innocent. During our championship game in May against Hampshire, we were battling to get a draw on the last afternoon. The left-arm spinner, Rajesh Maru was trying to get me out by pitching the ball outside of the leg stump into the rough, looking for sharp turn. Now I had seen John Emburey combat this tactic before, by throwing his bat away and thrusting his left leg down the pitch. This had the double advantage of nullifying an appeal for lbw and avoiding a catch because the law states that a batsman can only be caught off the glove provided the appropriate hand is still on the bat. Embers had got away with it, and I thought that was a good method to eliminate getting bowled, lbw or caught. It was then up to Maru to try a different tactic. I threw my bat away in the direction of silly point fifteen times and eventually Maru had to change his line of attack to me. But I was in the clear under Law 32. If Maru had brought in a couple more close fielders on the offside, he could have appealed under law 37 – obstructing the field – or the umpires could have told me to stop throwing my bat away, because I was endangering the fielders. But he didn't do that, so I was within my rights under the laws of cricket.

That wasn't the end of the matter, though. The M.C.C. rumbled into majestic action and advised the Test and County Cricket Board that I could have been reported by the umpires for unfair play, or given out on appeal for obstructing the field, or even for the 'wilful' act of handling the ball if it had struck the glove. The T.C.C.B. then ruled that any repeat of my actions would be deemed 'unacceptable' and that umpires and players had been informed that the M.C.C. was now expecting them to abide more stringently to the interpretation of such laws. I had found a grey area, and the administrators felt it wasn't in the spirit of the game. It seemed to me that they were ruling against an innovative tactic, one that might have forced left-arm spinners to attack more, rather than relying on attritional bowling outside the leg-stump. I was then invited to attend an M.C.C. cricket committee meeting by Sir Colin Cowdrey to explain my actions. I wasn't sure whether I was going to get my wrist slapped or if the M.C.C. were genuinely interested in debating the matter. I am happy to say the meeting was stimulating and illuminating. It seemed Sir Colin and others were fed up with the negative tactic of pitching the ball outside leg stump, to stop batsmen scoring. Rajesh Maru was however bowling in a semi-attacking mode and I pointed out if the words 'holding the bat' were removed from Law 32, then a player wouldn't drop his bat in future. I admitted it doesn't look too good to drop the bat, but I had to ask the question why the words 'holding the bat' were there in the first place.

I then suggested that, to combat captains instructing spinners to bowl negatively outside the line of the leg stump, a law should be introduced, allowing a maximum of five fielders on the leg-side. At present in first-class cricket, you can have as many fielders as you want on either side of the wicket, but a captain only puts six on the legside when he is being defensive and negative. It wouldn't totally stop the tactic of bowling outside leg into the rough, but at least there would be a gap somewhere for the batsman to exploit and you would get far less kicking off of the ball. It was a pleasure to give my views to the M.C.C. cricket committee, and hopefully some good will come out of the whole bat-throwing saga.

There was another amusing sideshow during the 1996 season in England and it lasted for two and a half weeks in the High Court. That libel action involving Imran Khan, Ian Botham and Allan Lamb was followed closely on the county circuit but not taken too seriously. Much was said in court about ball-tampering, with fingers being pointed in various directions and certain former players making righteous denials about ever tampering with the ball. Well I agreed with Geoffrey Boycott who took the witness stand to confirm that it's all a matter of degree. Most bowlers I know in the game have helped themselves by tampering with the ball or its seam. Of course, that is cheating, but what's the difference between that and the batsman refusing to walk when he has nicked the ball, and he gets away with it? Either both are right or both are wrong. It's such a grey area that much is open to interpretation. Most spinners walking back to their mark grip some dust from the turf to enable them to hold the ball better: is all that dust finally removed from the ball when he spins it? Isn't that a case of bending the letter of the law, because outside elements are allowing the spinner to be better at his job? When Asif Din played for Warwickshire, he was acknowledged to be our best shiner of the ball. Was that because he worked harder with the ball on his trousers or was it because he sucked Extra Strong Mints? Some of our lads believed that the sugar from the mint when mixed with saliva was a better polishing agent than pure saliva. I've heard that chewing gum is equally useful in that direction. Now you'll find a few of the Warwickshire boys climbing into the Extra Strong Mints on the field as they polish the ball. Is that paying attention to detail, so that the ball will shine up strongly, or is it cheating? I recall a New Zealand swing bowler telling me that he took out a bottle top when bowling in a Test and he turned in wonderful figures. The umpire knew something was going on and told him, 'Oh, the game is fair now – both sides are cheating.' That remark underlines the fact that professional cricketers will try to get away with a lot if they can. It's a fact of life, and we ought to be aware that sharp practice goes on in all areas of society. Why should modern cricket be immune from it? The bowler tries to maximise his qualities to get results because of a fear of failure. He must retain his place in the side – and therefore his job – on the basis of results, just like a salesman. His employers usually assess him on figures, and so the pressure is put on the bowler to produce results, rather than just go out there to enjoy it. It's no wonder that a bowler will try to get any advantage because he's playing for his livelihood. Geoffrey Boycott was right when he said in the High Court that few motorists stick to the speed limit, that they'll only abide by it if they suspect there's a police car in the vicinity. It's the same with modern professional cricket: what can you get away with? Is there a grey area to exploit?

So what now for Dermot Reeve and Warwickshire, the most successful county side in recent years? I think the club has to think long and hard about my successor as captain for the 1997 season. Tim Munton took over from me for the rest of the '96 season, and he did a good job in '94 when he took us to the championship. But that was before Tim had his serious back operation and I'm not sure he's still the bowler he was. I believe Tim has lost a bit of nip which is so important to a bowler of his type. If Tim's back can stand up to the further rigours, and he is confident that it won't affect his captaincy, then he would have my vote – but he has to be an automatic selection, with no injury worries long-term. There are other candidates. Nick Knight will make a very good captain, but I think for now he ought to concentrate on his own game, and cement his place in the England side. He'd make an excellent vice-captain over the next year or so. Andy Moles will be inevitably distracted by his benefit year in 1997, and he too has had injury problems over the last couple of seasons. I think Allan Donald would be an excellent choice as captain if Munton wasn't certain of his prolonged fitness. Allan certainly has the respect of all the players, he would be highly motivated by the honour and I don't believe it would affect his bowling. He is so impressive in his pride of performance, his attitude to the team effort and his personal maturity that he would thrive under the responsibility. Allan Donald has never been one to duck out of responsibility and Courtney Walsh at Gloucestershire has shown there is no reason why an overseas fast bowler can't captain a county side, as long as the commitment is there.

As for me, I'm at a personal and professional crossroads. I'm getting married next year, to Donna Nelmes, a sports lover who I met at the start of the '96 season. Although my first marriage failed, I'm still enough of a romantic to think it can work again for me, and I'd love to be a father again. As for work, I'm now looking for fresh challenges. Three days after my retirement was announced, I sat in front of the television and it suddenly dawned on me that I wasn't going to be able to play cricket for a living again. I started to ask myself questions: what am I going to do for the rest of my life? I would love to throw my knowledge of the game into coaching and it was nice to have the phones ringing and counties asking my plans for the future. But I don't want to just coach a county exclusively. I'd like to put my ideas into practice with youngsters and perhaps hold seminars for current club coaches. I'd also like to work in the cricket media, because I find that very enjoyable. As I sat at home, mulling over my future, I realised that my own self-esteem is fuelled by giving a hundred per cent to challenges. It won't be enough for me to coast, to speak at a few dinners and play a lot of golf. I must set myself new goals, giving all my effort to things that will tax me. Although I am sad my playing days are over, I genuinely feel excited about the future.

13

Career Statistics

Dermot Alexander Reeve
Born Kowloon, Hong Kong 2nd April 1963.
Educ. King George V School, Kowloon.
Inventive middle order right handed Batsman
Right arm fast medium swing bowler. Lively fielder.
Inspirational captain of Warwickshire since 1993.
Played for Hong Kong in the 1982 ICC Trophy.
Three test matches for England 1991-92.
Test record 124 runs in 5 innings, av. 24.80
HS 59 v New Zealand, Christchurch on Test debut 1991-92.
2 wickets for 60 runs. 1 catch.
29 Limited overs Internationals for England. 291 runs in 21 innings. 9 not outs, av. 24.25. HS 35
20 wickets in 191.1 overs, for 820 runs, av. 41.00. BB 3-20. Econ rate – 4.29.
First-class career record 241 matches, 322 innings, 77 not out, 8541 runs, average 34.86. 7 centuries, Highest score 202* Warks v Northants., Northampton 1990. 1000 runs or more in season twice – 1412 in 1990 best. 200 catches; 456 wickets for 12232 runs, av. 26.82. BB 7-37 Sussex v Lancs., Lytham 1986. Played Sussex 1983-87; Warwickshire 1988-96. Captain of Warwickshire 1993-96

Dermot Reeve for Warwickshire in First-Class Cricket
Against each Team

Cty	Mch	Inn	no	Runs	H.S.	Av'ge	C	F	Ct	Overs	mdns	Runs	Wts	Av'ge
Dby	6	9	0	327	67	36.33	–	4	7	105	33	205	9	22.77
Dur	3	3	1	95	47	47.50	–	–	3	64	27	125	7	18.85
Ess	7	11	4	335	97*	47.85	–	2	6	102.4	27	272	5	54.40
Glm	11	14	3	519	79	47.18	–	4	14	145.1	48	314	14	22.42
Glo	7	11	3	311	86*	38.87	–	2	10	129.5	35	316	15	21.06
Hts	7	10	2	226	77*	28.25	–	1	7	178	60	359	18	19.94
Knt	8	12	3	378	72*	42.00	–	4	10	159	50	380	20	19.00
Lan	6	8	4	411	121*	102.75	1	2	–	51	16	101	1	—
Lei	8	13	0	279	67	21.46	–	2	8	156.2	57	317	17	18.64
Msx	7	12	2	155	41	15.50	–	–	10	109	28	273	6	45.50
Nth	13	21	4	831	202*	48.88	2	4	12	256.3	77	560	29	19.31
Nts	7	8	1	180	70*	25.71	–	1	6	79.3	24	172	5	34.40
Som	9	13	5	461	82	57.62	–	5	7	132.2	33	338	7	48.28
Sur	6	12	1	172	53	15.63	–	1	3	100.2	33	242	10	24.20
Sus	5	8	3	414	168*	82.80	1	2	8	76.4	24	165	7	23.57
Wor	11	18	1	502	97	29.52	–	1	11	150	52	358	10	35.80
Yks	12	16	4	551	99*	45.91	–	4	13	178.5	64	374	14	26.71
CTY	133	199	41	6147	202*	38.90	4	39	135	2174.2	688	4871	194	25.10
OU	1	1	0	7	7	—	–	–	–	6	4	9	2	4.50
CU	1	1	1	102	102*	—	1	–	3	25	10	43	3	14.33
Aus	1	1	0	23	23	—	–	–	–	23	5	55	2	27.50
SL	1	2	0	6	5	3.00	–	–	–	20	4	75	2	37.50
EnA	1	2	1	77	77*	—	–	1	1	18.2	5	41	2	20.50
Bor	2	2	0	120	107	60.00	1	–	6	27	10	56	2	28.00
Mad	1	1	0	2	2	—	–	–	1	9	2	27	2	13.50
T	141	209	43	6484	202*	39.06	6	40	146	2302.4	728	5177	209	24.77

Key; CTY = County Championship; T = Total, all first-class Warwicks matches; Aus = Australian XI; SL = Sri Lankan XI; EnA = England "A"; Bor = Border; Mad = Mashonaland.

Season-by-Season Record for Warwickshire – First-Class

1988	16	23	3	431	103	21.55	1	–	11	292	71	750	24	31.25
1989	14	17	4	581	97*	44.69	–	4	13	97.4	35	163	11	14.81
1990	24	37	12	1373	202*	54.92	3	5	26	364.4	108	900	33	27.27
1991	20	33	7	1260	99*	48.46	–	14	10	402.1	117	957	45	21.26
1992	17	28	4	833	79	34.70	–	7	15	267	80	632	13	48.61
92/3	1	1	0	13	13	—	–	–	2	21	9	34	2	17.00
1993	17	28	7	765	87*	36.42	–	5	22	284.1	108	528	22	24.00
93/4	1	1	0	2	2	—	–	–	1	9	2	27	2	13.50
1994	9	10	1	116	33	12.88	–	–	18	144	48	308	10	30.80
94/5	1	1	0	107	107	—	1	–	4	6	1	22	0	—
1995	16	22	4	652	77*	36.22	–	5	17	312	117	661	38	17.39
1996	5	8	1	351	168*	50.14	1	–	7	103	32	195	9	21.66
T	141	209	43	6484	202*	39.06	6	40	146	2302.4	728	5177	209	24.77

Dermot Reeve for Sussex in First-Class Cricket
Against each team

Cty	Mch	Inn	no	Runs	h.s.	Av'ge	C	F	Ct	Overs	Mns	Runs	Wts	Av'ge
Dby	6	7	3	59	26	14.75	–	–	5	192.2	43	581	18	32.27
Ess	5	9	0	110	51	12.22	–	1	5	104.3	27	270	12	22.50
Glm	6	5	3	68	52	34.00	–	1	1	138	44	316	14	22.57
Glo	4	4	1	91	32*	30.33	–	–	2	70.2	11	213	6	35.50
Hts	7	10	3	206	65	29.42	–	1	3	187.4	48	599	12	49.91
Knt	8	9	4	148	87*	29.60	–	1	10	215.5	63	498	17	29.29
Lan	4	7	2	145	64	29.00	–	1	1	136.3	38	315	13	24.23
Lei	6	9	1	80	25	10.00	–	–	6	165	39	418	16	26.12
Mdx	7	8	3	228	57*	45.60	–	3	4	202	48	597	22	27.13
Nth	5	5	2	92	56*	30.66	–	1	3	142.1	40	421	14	30.07
Nts	3	5	1	29	12*	7.25	–	–	2	91.1	19	250	9	27.77
Som	3	3	2	43	16*	—	–	–	–	101.3	24	265	10	26.50
Sur	9	7	1	285	119	47.50	1	2	4	240.2	59	698	27	25.85
Wks	5	4	2	60	30	30.00	–	–	1	148	44	411	14	29.35
Wor	4	5	2	41	28*	13.66	–	–	–	119.2	26	330	13	25.38
Yks	4	3	1	46	35*	23.00	–	–	2	121	39	280	11	25.45
CTY	86	100	31	1731	119	25.08	1	11	48	2375.4	612	6462	228	28.34
CU	2	–	–	–	–	—	–	–	1	59.5	23	92	8	11.50
SL	1	–	–	–	–	—	–	–	1	21	8	36	1	—
NZ	1	–	–	–	–	—	–	–	1	17	0	43	1	—
Pak	1	1	0	30	30	—	–	–	–	23	5	95	1	—
T	91	101	31	1761	119	25.15	1	11	51	2496.3	648	6728	239	28.15

Season-by-Season Record for Sussex – First-Class

1983	17	20	5	192	42*	12.80	–	–	7	472.1	131	1233	42	29.35
1984	21	22	4	486	119	27.00	1	3	14	572.4	175	1420	55	25.81
1985	17	15	5	170	56	17.00	–	1	6	475.5	107	1424	48	29.66
1986	19	21	9	307	51	25.58	–	1	10	525.5	127	1411	52	27.13
1987	17	23	8	606	87*	40.40	–	6	14	450	108	1240	42	29.52
T	91	101	31	1761	119	25.15	1	11	51	2496.3	648	6728	239	28.15

Total First-Class County Career Record 1983-96

232	310	74	8245	202*	34.93	7	51	197	4799.1	1376	11905	448	26.57

Dermot Reeve in Limited Overs Cricket
Nat West Trophy

For	Mch	In	no	Runs	H.S.	Av'ge	C	F	Ct	Overs	Runs	wts	Av'ge	5	B/B
Wks	31	26	7	721	81*	37.94	–	4	12	284.5	892	33	27.03	–	4/54
Sus	12	7	5	63	26*	31.50	–	–	4	123.5	355	16	22.18	–	4/20
T	43	33	12	784	81*	37.33	–	4	15	408.4	1247	49	25.44	–	4/20

Benson & Hedges Cup

Wks	29	25	9	464	80	29.00	–	1	15	254.1	979	39	25.10	–	4/23
Sus	15	10	4	103	30*	17.16	–	–	1	127.4	569	16	35.56	–	4/42
T	44	35	13	567	80	25.77	–	1	16	381.5	1448	55	26.32	–	4/23

The Sunday League

Wks	112	99	23	2172	100*	28.57	1	9	32	617.5	2667	95	28.07	1	5/23
Sus	55	24	9	170	21	11.33	–	–	17	393	1855	69	26.88	–	4/22
T	167	123	32	2342	100*	25.73	1	9	49	1010.5	4522	164	27.57	1	5/23

Dermot Reeve in Test Cricket

Mtch	Inn	n.o.	Runs	h.s.	Av'ge	50s.	ct	Overs	Mdns	Runs	Wts	Av'ge	B/B
3	5	0	124	59	24.80	1	1	24.5	8	60	2	30.00	1/4

Reeve's three Test matches were all against New Zealand in 1991. His best score came on his debut, 59 on the second day (Jan 19) in the 1st Test at Christchurch. The innings occupied 160 minutes, lasted 125 balls, and included 5 fours. Batting no. 7, Reeve added 76 for the 6th wicket with AJ Lamb, and 78 for the 7th with CC Lewis. Reeve's Test wickets were those of CL Cairns, with the 8th ball of his first Test, and AH Jones in the 2nd innings of his third Test when he finished with figures of 4.5

overs, 2 maidens, 1 wicket for 4 runs.

Dermot Reeve in Limited Overs Cricket

Mch	Inn	n.o.	Runs h.s.	Av'ge 50s	ct	Overs	Runs	Wkts	Av'ge	B/B
29	21	9	291 35	24.25 –	12	191.1	820	20	41.00	3/20

Reeve's first Limited overs International for England was against West Indies at Lord's in 1991. His best bowling performance was 3-20 against New Zealand at Auckland in 1991/92 and he won the man-of-the-match award. His best score of 35 came in 34 balls against Sri Lanka at Faisalabad in England's final and unsuccessful match of the 1996 World Cup. Batting No.8, Reeve added 62 in 57 balls for the 8th wicket with D Gough.

Dermot Reeve as Warwickshire Captain

Reeve first led Warwickshire in a first-class match against Cambridge University on Fenner's ground 26-28 April 1990. Reeve scored 102 not out before Lunch on the second day, but rain destroyed hopes of a result. Before being officially appointed for the 1993 season Reeve had led the county in nine first-class matches, winning 1, losing 3. As official captain Reeve won 24 out of 50 first-class matches, with 11 defeats. 17 of Warwickshire's final 22 first-class games under his leadership were won.

With Reeve as official captain, 1993-95 and the first part of 1996 Warwickshire twice won the County Championship, won the Nat West Trophy twice, and were beaten finalists once. The Benson & Hedges was won once and the Sunday League saw one top spot and one runners-up placing in 1995. When Reeve resigned through injury in 1996 Warwickshire were well placed in the County Championship and Sunday League. The winning of 5 Trophies in 2 seasons (1994–95) by one county is unprecedented in County Cricket history. No captain has equalled Reeve's 14 victories in the 15 Nat West Trophy games in which he led the side.

Robert Brooke.